IMAGES
of America

AROUND COLD SPRING

I0807097

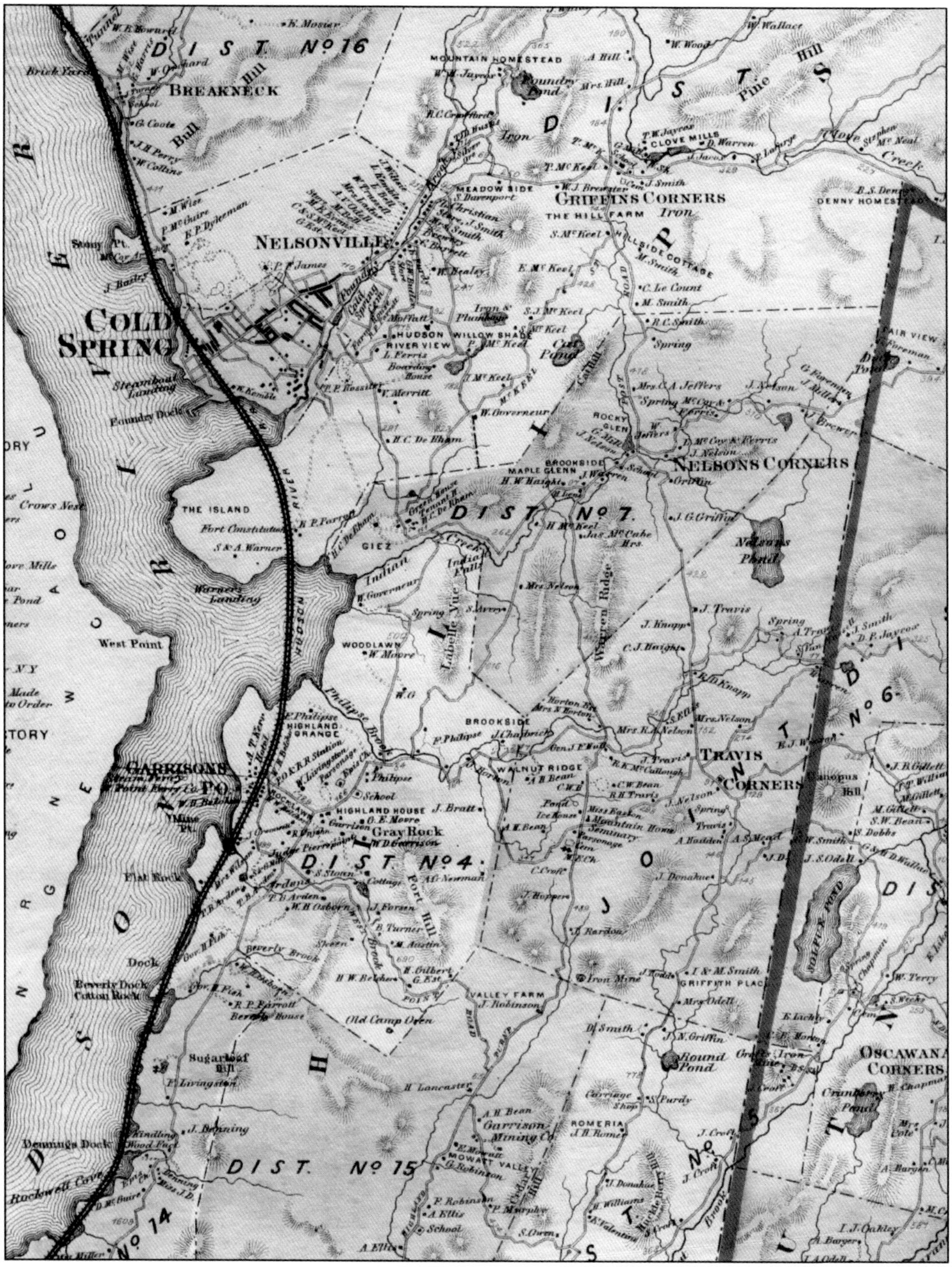

A detail of a page from the 1867 *Atlas of New York and Vicinity, from Actual Surveys, by and under the Direction of F.W. Beers, Assisted by Geo. E. Warner & Others*, this engraving by Worley & Bracher shows the greater part of Philipstown, which lies on the east bank of the Hudson River. (Courtesy of Putnam County Historical Society & Foundry School Museum [PCHS].)

ON THE COVER: In 1892, part of a gypsy caravan stands at a crossroads north of the business sections of Cold Spring and Nelsonville. A gypsy woman does washing in a wooden tub while some of the townspeople gathered here appear to be distracted by the photographer. Between 1880 and 1914, many gypsies immigrated to North America from southern and eastern Europe. (Photograph by Albert Terwilliger, courtesy of PCHS.)

IMAGES
of America

AROUND COLD SPRING

Trudie A. Grace

ARCADIA
PUBLISHING

ISBN 978-0-7385-7597-1

Published by Arcadia Publishing
Charleston, South Carolina

Printed in the United States of America

Library of Congress Control Number: 2011923112

For all general information, please contact Arcadia Publishing:
Telephone 843-853-2070
Fax 843-853-0044
E-mail sales@arcadiapublishing.com
For customer service and orders:
Toll-Free 1-888-313-2665

Visit us on the Internet at www.arcadiapublishing.com

To my friends who appreciate the history and beauty of the Hudson Highlands

Contents

ACKNOWLEDGMENTS

I am deeply grateful to the many people who have assisted in the making of this book by providing images, information, and assistance. Of special note is the Putnam County Historical Society & Foundry School Museum (PCHS), where I have been curator for 10 years, for allowing me to use many images from its collection. Local residents have also provided images and were founts of information. They include Janet Selleck Rust, who easily answers questions about Cold Spring and has a large postcard collection; Mark Forlow, whose collection of photographs and postcards is also significant; Josephine Doherty, the Nelsonville village clerk for many years, a knowledgeable source for that village's history, and a collector. Other residents who contributed images and information include John Benjamin, Francis J. Lahey, Nathaniel S. Prentice and Anita R. Prentice, the Nice family, the Polhemus family, and Victoria A. Rasche.

Local dealers in historic materials and other businessmen have been generous in making available images for this project and in sharing their broad knowledge of the area. Richard Saunders, Hudson Rogue Co., of Nelsonville, and Cathy and David Lilburne, Antipodean Books, Prints & Maps, of Garrison, are, in this writer's opinion, the most important sources for now rare and important 19th-century imagery of the Hudson Highlands. In Cold Spring, Joe Diebboll, the Highland Studio Inc.; Howard Broad, Country Clocks; and David S. Cooke, Cold Spring Antiques Center, have been helpful. St. Mary-in-the-Highlands in Cold Spring and St. Basil Academy in Garrison also provided images.

Historians, researchers, and others have given or helped to locate important information and often provided invaluable support. They include architectural historian Lisa Weilbacker; fashion historian Dr. Lourdes Font; Donald MacDonald, longtime writer of articles on historic subjects for the local newspaper; Dr. Sallie Sypher, Putnam County deputy historian; former Cold Spring mayor Anthony Phillips; editor Anne Saunders; journalist and historian Liz Schevtchuk Armstrong; Dr. Patrick Martin, Michigan Technological University; historian Thom Johnson; PCHS librarians Lillian McGuinness and Corinne Giunta; Charlotte Eaton, former PCHS curator and volunteer since 1982, and Minette Gunther, another longtime volunteer; my unflappable curatorial assistant, Beth Ann Dowler; art historians Kara Shier and Nina Sangimino; and Laura Rarick, a historian of public history. Researcher and editor Linda Faulhaber provided valuable assistance throughout. Jan Thacher, an indispensable source of information on many subjects, was especially helpful with the photographs derived from glass plate negatives in the PCHS collection.

INTRODUCTION

The village of Cold Spring, New York, and its neighbors within the town of Philipstown comprise the subject of *Around Cold Spring*. The town lies along the eastern bank of the Hudson River about 40 miles north of New York City in Putnam County, in an area known as the Hudson Highlands. Long famous for its scenic beauty, the Highlands extends for approximately 15 miles between Peekskill and Newburgh bays. The Hudson River narrows as it cuts through the Appalachians here, flowing past mountains and high bluffs in a twisting course. Cold Spring, which is north of the US Military Academy at West Point and across the river from it, sits about halfway along this course.

Philipstown, which became a town in 1788, covers nearly 50 square miles. Cold Spring, at six-tenths of a square mile, is the area's commercial center and was incorporated as a village in 1846. Nelsonville, a village one square mile in size adjoining Cold Spring to the east, was incorporated in 1855. The 2010 census counted 2,013 people in Cold Spring, 628 in Nelsonville, and 9,662 overall in Philipstown. Neighboring areas discussed in this book include Constitution Island, which projects from a marshy area of the riverbank south of Cold Spring and is owned by West Point. Garrison, also south of Cold Spring, is primarily a residential hamlet partly on the river and has undefined borders. Its small business area, Garrison's Landing, is immediately opposite West Point. Manitou is an area in southern Philipstown, not far from the Bear Mountain Bridge. Two other areas mentioned in *Around Cold Spring* are North Highlands in northern Philipstown and Continental Village in southern Philipstown.

The history of what is now Philipstown begins well before the images shown in this book were made. Native Americans, among them the Wappingers, inhabited the area. As the result of a British royal patent, Adolph Philipse acquired extensive land holdings in 1697 that included most of what became Putnam County and extended from the Hudson River to Connecticut. During the American Revolution, Continental Army and British troops skirmished in the area. Troops under George Washington's command camped above the riverbank north of Cold Spring and in other parts of the Highlands. Redoubts were built, and the first of two chains to deter British ships was stretched across the Hudson River from Constitution Island to one of the bluffs of West Point.

Cold Spring developed and grew prosperous after the West Point Foundry, organized by a small group of entrepreneurs, opened there in 1818. Pres. James Madison selected the site as one of four in the country where military weaponry would be forged. Cold Spring was a logical choice for the production of iron products. The West Point military academy across the Hudson River was easily accessible by boat. The river could be used for transport, the forests for charcoal production, and the streams for waterpower. Iron ore could be mined in the Highlands. A road to the Connecticut border, the Philipstown Turnpike, allowed the movement of goods east and west. Sloops and schooners also contributed to the commercial growth of the area. As early as 1821, ferries ran back and forth to West Point from a dock established at Garrison's Landing. The Hudson River Railroad arrived in Cold Spring in 1849 and provided excellent transportation for people and goods, especially when the Hudson River was icebound.

Cold Spring's and Nelsonville's prosperity increased further during the Civil War, when the foundry operated around the clock. Cold Spring, already an immigrant workingman's town, saw its population expand with the arrival of additional immigrants, both skilled and unskilled workers, mostly from Ireland. Later in the 19th century, they were joined by Italian workers. In 1865, the population of Philipstown reached 5,436, its highest point before 1920. On a trip to West Point in 1862, Pres. Abraham Lincoln visited the foundry, then manufacturing its most famous product, a rifled cannon known as the Parrott gun. Designed by the foundry's superintendent, Robert P. Parrott, the gun is often credited with helping the Union win the war.

The Highlands held a special place in the American imagination of the 19th century, and the memory of it resonates today, thanks to the work of that era's writers, artists, and tireless promoters. Seeing a spiritual value in nature and inspired by Romantic notions of the beautiful, the sublime, and the picturesque, Hudson River School artists, such as Thomas Cole, Robert Weir, and others, dramatized the region's beauty. Their work often sharpened the contours and exaggerated the heights of Crow's Nest (1,407 feet), Storm King (1,348 feet), Bull Hill, also known as Mount Taurus (1,420 feet), and Breakneck Ridge (1,260 feet). These mountains are seen more realistically in the photographs in chapter one.

The work of the Hudson River School brought the region to the attention both of Americans and Europeans, who flocked to see "America's Rhineland," a comparison made by many, including the writer and publisher George Pope Morris, who commuted by steamboat to New York City for a time, boarding the boat mid-river near his Cold Spring estate. Morris published the influential *New-York Mirror* between 1823 and 1842. It educated Americans on cultural matters, including the beauty of the Highlands. That subject was further developed in the *Home Journal*, Morris's joint venture, as of 1846, with the writer Nathaniel P. Willis. Morris's collaborator and cofounder of other periodicals, Willis also published *American Scenery: Or, Land, Lake, and River Illustrations of Transatlantic Nature* (1840) and included 12 engravings of the Hudson Highlands, among them a view of Morris's estate.

Since this new Rhineland had no history or mythology, the Knickerbocker writers—most famously Washington Irving, but many others as well—set about creating a body of legend, poetry, and lore about it. Joseph Rodman Drake's long poem, "The Culprit Fay" (1821), described a fairy gathering on Crow's Nest. Willis wrote a story (1837) about Henry Hudson being lured ashore where Morris's mansion later stood; and, in another story (1836), John Holt Ingraham described a visitor ascending Bull Hill and having a conversation with "the presiding spirit" of the river, none other than Henry Hudson. Willis gave the name Storm King Hill to the mountain the Dutch called Butter Hill. He also wrote extensively about the therapeutic value of the Highlands, a lure for visitors who feared the tuberculosis that plagued New York City in the 19th century and flocked to the hotels and boardinghouses that sprang up throughout the area and brought increased prosperity to the area's businesses, which are shown in chapter two.

After the Civil War, the West Point Foundry experienced financial setbacks interspersed with revivals. The Cornell Company, which took over the facility in 1897, ceased work in 1909. The population of Cold Spring had fallen to 2,340 by 1906, and by 1920 the population for all of Philipstown was only 3,272. By that time, not only the foundry but also the chemical works in Manitou had closed. During the first half of the 20th century, Cold Spring and its environs languished. The foundry's buildings and land were used by other establishments—among them was the Marathon Battery plant, which dumped toxic cadmium into the adjacent river cove, necessitating a massive Environmental Protection Agency (EPA) Superfund cleanup in the 1990s. The cove and surrounding tidal marsh were dredged to remove 189,000 tons of polluted sediment. The marsh was sealed, refilled with clean soil, and planted with native flora.

Other industries besides the foundry left their marks in the 19th and early 20th centuries, and are depicted in chapter three. Work was done installing a municipal water system in Cold Spring and building the Catskill Aqueduct in parts of Philipstown. Quarrying was a major industry on both Bull Hill and Breakneck. The Hudson River Stone Company is said to have saved many from a life of struggle during the Depression years, although it permanently changed Bull Hill and Little Stony Point. Mining and coal companies also operated in Philipstown.

How people socialized and celebrated and the clubs and associations they joined—especially between 1890 and 1920—are shown in chapter four, along with important community events that occurred in 1909, 1910, 1918, and 1946. The 1909 Hudson-Fulton Tercentennial, a huge celebration organized in New York City and in communities along the Hudson River and throughout New York State, commemorated Henry Hudson's exploration of the river and Robert Fulton's successful commercial use of a steamboat on it. Cold Spring sponsored a parade and other events. Patriotic themes dominated, appropriate to a time when America's outlook was optimistic and expansive. Memories of the Civil War remained strong, and the community warmly welcomed veterans at a 1910 reunion. In 1918, it sponsored a Liberty Day parade, one of many that took place across the country to raise money for World War I. Images of the parade are from of a set of postcards. Cold Spring's April 1946 centennial also celebrated the end of World War II the previous August.

Among residences pictured in chapter five are a number that predate the Revolutionary War. From the mid-19th century, increasing numbers of railroad barons, statesmen, and wealthy businessmen, drawn by the scenic beauty of the area, the healthfulness of the surroundings, and access to river and train transportation, purchased estates often having hundreds of acres. The homes of the Butterfields, Sloans, Osborns, Fishes, and Pierreponts are among those shown in this chapter. Architects built mansions for them in a wide array of architectural styles. Richard Upjohn, a Garrison resident who designed Trinity Church in New York City, helped to popularize the Gothic Revival style. The less wealthy generally built wooden homes, often in the popular Carpenter Gothic style. Village homes and residents also appear in chapter five.

After their homes were built, the wealthy often set about beautifying their properties, following the thinking of Andrew Jackson Downing. In 1841, this gifted landscape artist published *A Treatise on the Theory and Practice of Landscape Gardening*, a book that was to transform the American landscape and fundamentally alter thinking about the relationship of people to it. It was Downing who insisted on the primacy of natural landscape, who took the Romantic ideas of the sublime, of the spiritual value of natural beauty, and of the picturesque and showed Americans how to bring these qualities into their lives through the designs of their homes and the landscapes around them. Downing stressed the value of ornamentation in architecture and the usefulness of porches. His work drew international acclaim. The Highlands was a nursery of his ideas and decorative homes there a testament to his vision. Examples can be seen especially in the buildings pictured in chapter five.

For early residents, Philipstown's most important civic structures were schools and churches, many shown in chapter six. By the 1830s, one-room schoolhouses were scattered throughout the area. Each served families within walking distance and constituted an independent school district. Churches also opened schools, as did the West Point Foundry, and philanthropists funded them. In 1853, the state authorized the creation of "union free" districts, formed from the merger of small districts. Neighboring districts merged, and the one-room schools vanished.

While schools were merely functional, churches reflected the status and aspirations of their parishioners, from simple buildings like Mekeel's Corners Chapel to granite Gothic Revival structures like Richard Upjohn's St. Philip's Church in Garrison. It was a churchgoing era. Visitors to Glenclyffe, the Hamilton Fish estate, were not asked if they wished to go to church but whether they would walk or ride. Everyone built churches; the immigrant population that worked at the foundry and the summer-estate people both fueled the enterprise. Catholics, Baptists, Presbyterians, Methodist Episcopals, the Dutch Reformed, and Episcopalians funded and constructed houses of worship. Occasionally, estates were sold to or purchased for churches and religious orders, such as the Capuchin Franciscan Province of Joseph and the Greek Orthodox Church, which created schools, monasteries, and convents on them.

Rural scenes and activities are depicted in chapter seven. In the farms around Cold Spring, daily activities unfolded in scenic settings with the contours of mountains in the distance. People moved about the land in buggies, wagons, and buckboards, on sleighs, on horseback, and on foot. Walking the hills remains popular today. Streams, waterfalls, dirt roads, and mountains continue to be attractions. Areas once denuded of trees that fed the foundry and provided ship timber or cordwood are again forested. Respect for the environment can be seen everywhere. The opening line from George Pope Morris's most popular song, "Woodman, Spare That Tree!," resonates with many, and as the early environmentalist John Muir wrote when visiting the Highlands, "Coming to the mountains is like coming home."

Attempts to preserve the scenic character of the Highlands began as early as 1903, when estate owner Frank Healy created Femre Park to preserve more than 100 acres near Cold Spring. In 1936, prominent citizens were appalled by the destruction of the mountains wrought by quarrying and organized the Hudson River Conservation Society. Scenic Hudson was founded in 1963 to save Storm King Mountain from the construction of a massive hydroelectric plant. That organization's successful 17-year battle is considered the birth of America's modern grassroots environmental movement. Scenic Hudson has since safeguarded 25,000 acres and created 40 parks and preserves, including the West Point Foundry Preserve, which it took over during the Superfund cleanup. It helped support excavations and research at the site by Michigan Technological University and continues to develop the property for public use. The Open Space Institute has also bought and preserved many acres of the Highlands.

By the 1970s, efforts to preserve the historic character of Cold Spring's buildings had also begun. These endeavors accelerated after 1982, when Cold Spring was named a national historic district and community members decided that tourism could revitalize the village. Nineteen of the buildings and sites pictured in *Around Cold Spring* are now in the National Register of Historic Places. Strict building and maintenance codes exist, and potential decisions about the direction of development cause spirited public debate.

Most of the images in this book are photographs taken between 1880 and 1930 and chiefly between 1890 and 1920. Many are little known or have never been published. Some derive from glass plate negatives. Albert Terwilliger, an ordnance inspector at the West Point Foundry, was often the photographer. Also included are photographic images from the 1860s and 1870s made with two separate lenses and printed side by side so that, when viewed through a stereoscope, they appear to be a single three-dimensional image. These were popular from the 1880s to the early 1920s.

With the exception of several prints and a map, the remaining images are from postcards, many dating in the early years of the 20th century. These postcards can generally be recognized by their dimensions and sometimes by printed words indicating the subject. Some were published by local businessmen, including Frank Dalzell, a pharmacist in Cold Spring, and John and James Forson, owners of a store at Garrison's Landing.

More than half the images in this book are from the collection of the Putnam County Historical Society & Foundry School Museum. The other images come from 19 private collections. Historical documents, newspaper articles, and genealogical files in the museum's library contributed to the research. Its archives on the West Point Foundry are among the country's most extensive. Founded in 1906 by a group of prominent residents, the society acquired objects over the years before establishing a museum. In 1960, it bought a residence at 63 Chestnut Street in Cold Spring for that purpose. The 1830 building was originally a schoolhouse for apprentices of the foundry. A major renovation in 2005 restored part of the configuration of three 1867 schoolrooms. A permanent installation on the foundry and temporary exhibitions on aspects of the history of Philipstown now occupy these spaces.

One

Down by the Riverside
Hudson River Views and Activities

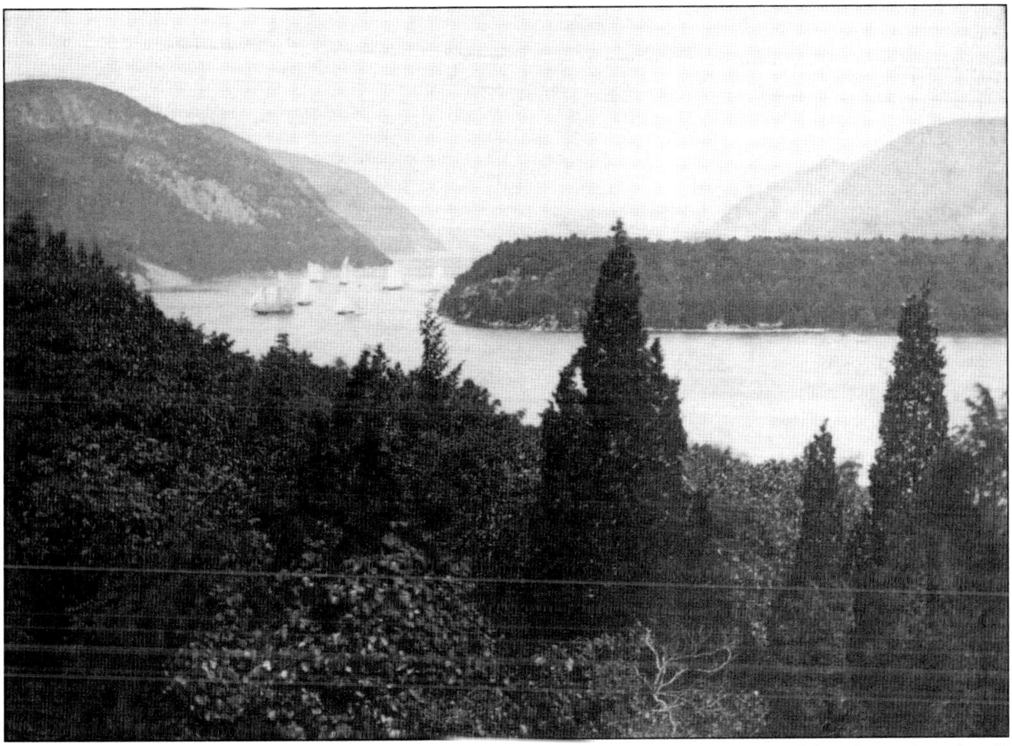

Viewed from a bluff of the US Military Academy at West Point, Constitution Island, or Martelear's Rack (Martyr's Reach) as Dutch sailors called it, extends into the river with the mountains of the northern Highlands rising beyond. The sloops have navigated World's End, the deepest and most dangerous part of the river, and are in view of Cold Spring, set behind Constitution Island. (Courtesy of Mark Forlow.)

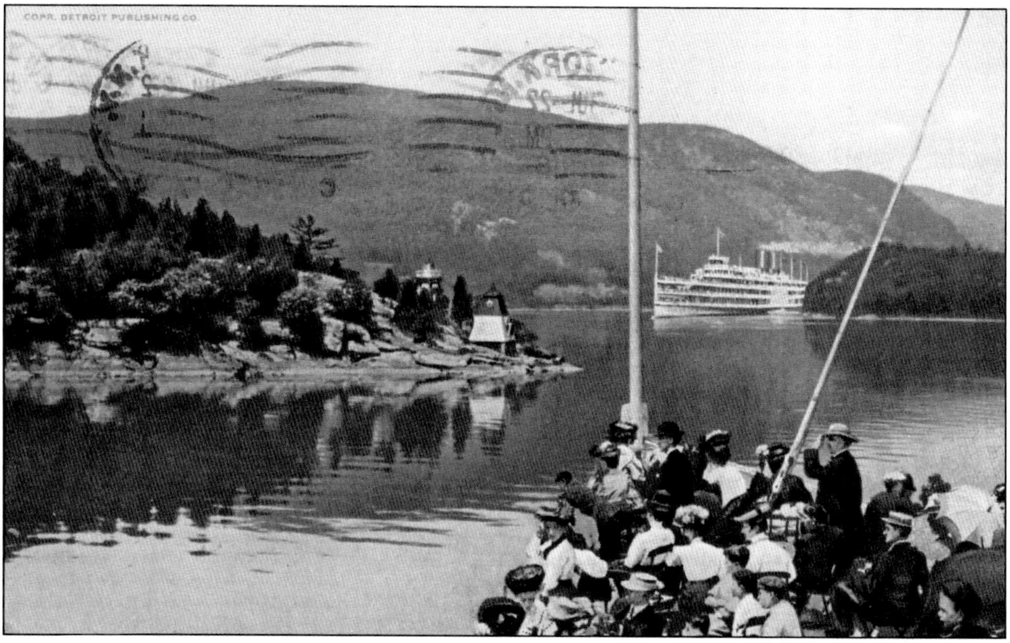

Passengers on a turn-of-the-century steamboat enjoy the sights as they pass Gee's Point, part of West Point, and approach a steamboat entering the passage around Constitution Island. Almost the full breadth of Crow's Nest can be seen in the distance, with Storm King beyond it. (Courtesy of Janet Selleck Rust.)

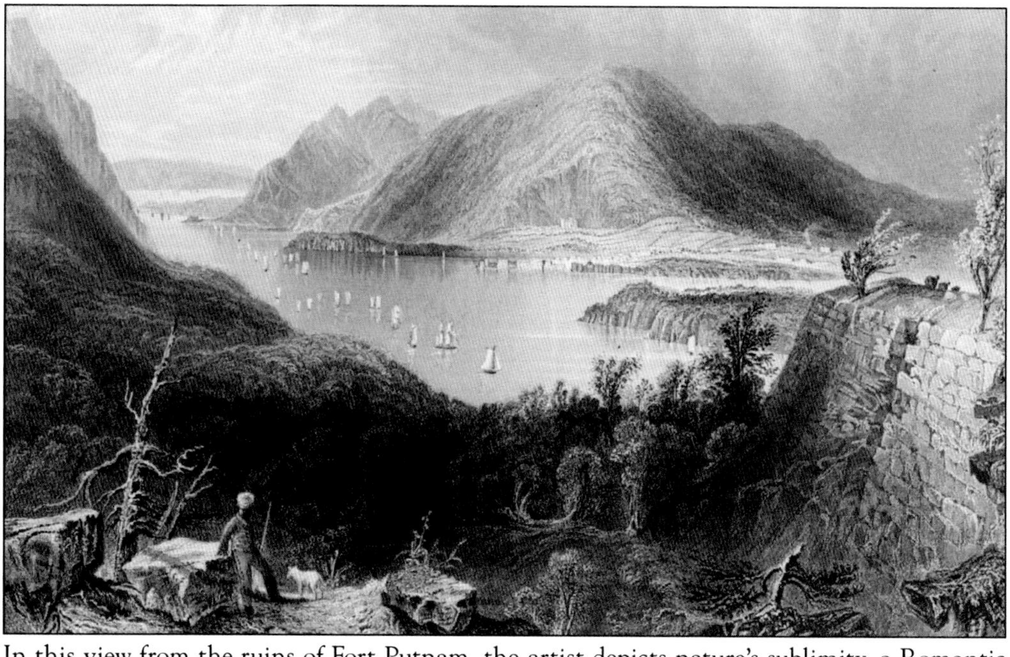

In this view from the ruins of Fort Putnam, the artist depicts nature's sublimity, a Romantic idea. Visitors made pilgrimages to the site; the actress Fanny Kemble declared, "I felt as though I had been carried into the immediate presence of God." This 1837 engraving from Nathaniel P. Willis's *American Scenery* (1840) is based on a watercolor by William H. Bartlett, a source for many painters. (Courtesy of Hudson Rogue Co.)

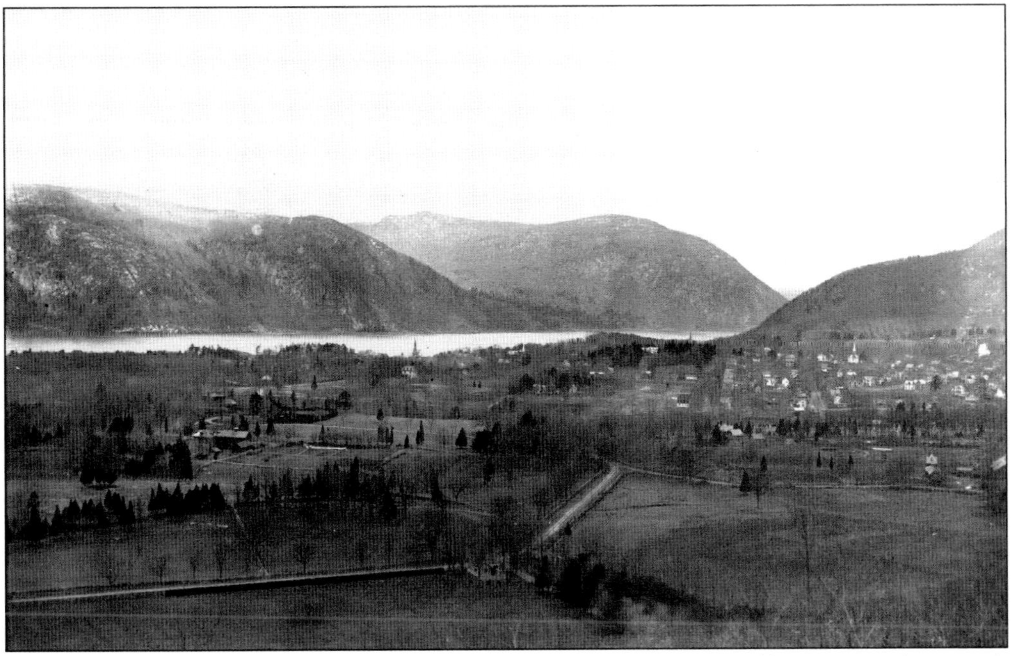

Taken from Dale's Hill, south of Cold Spring in Garrison, Albert Terwilliger's 1902 photograph looks northwest over the village and across the river to the sharp contours of Crow's Nest and Storm King mountains. Terwilliger also photographed the scene in a different season, showing leafy trees and smoke rising from the West Point Foundry along the far middle right. (Courtesy of PCHS.)

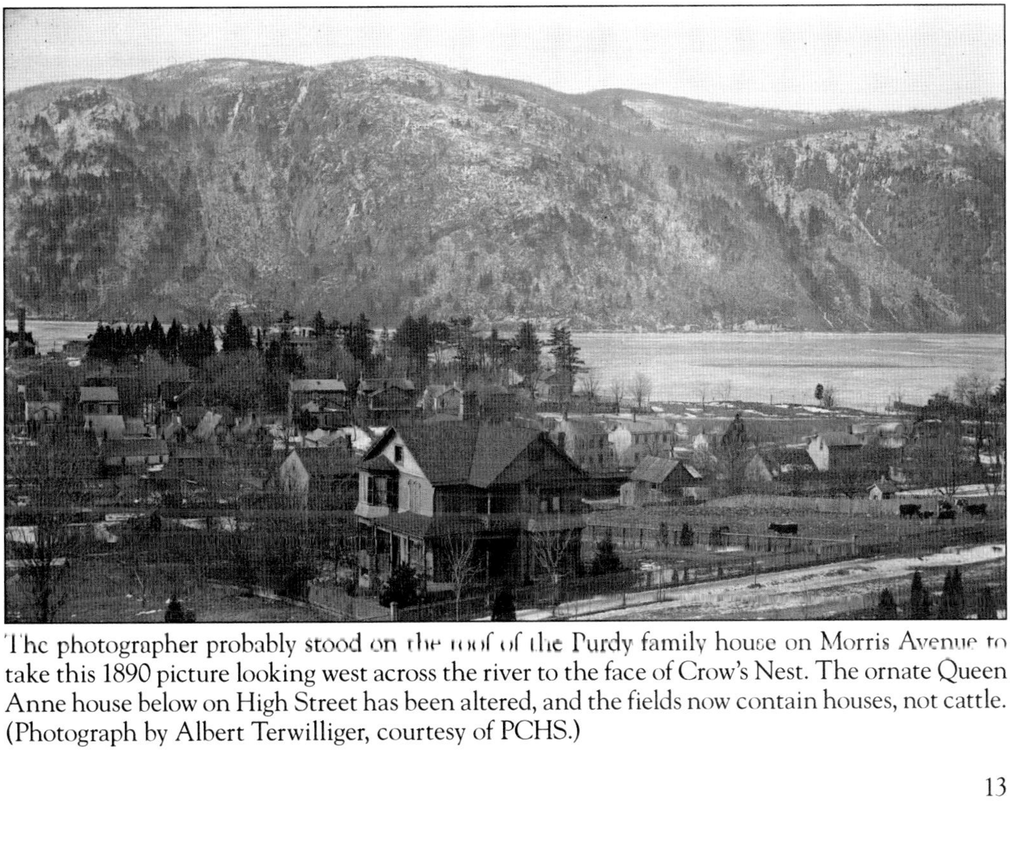

The photographer probably stood on the roof of the Purdy family house on Morris Avenue to take this 1890 picture looking west across the river to the face of Crow's Nest. The ornate Queen Anne house below on High Street has been altered, and the fields now contain houses, not cattle. (Photograph by Albert Terwilliger, courtesy of PCHS.)

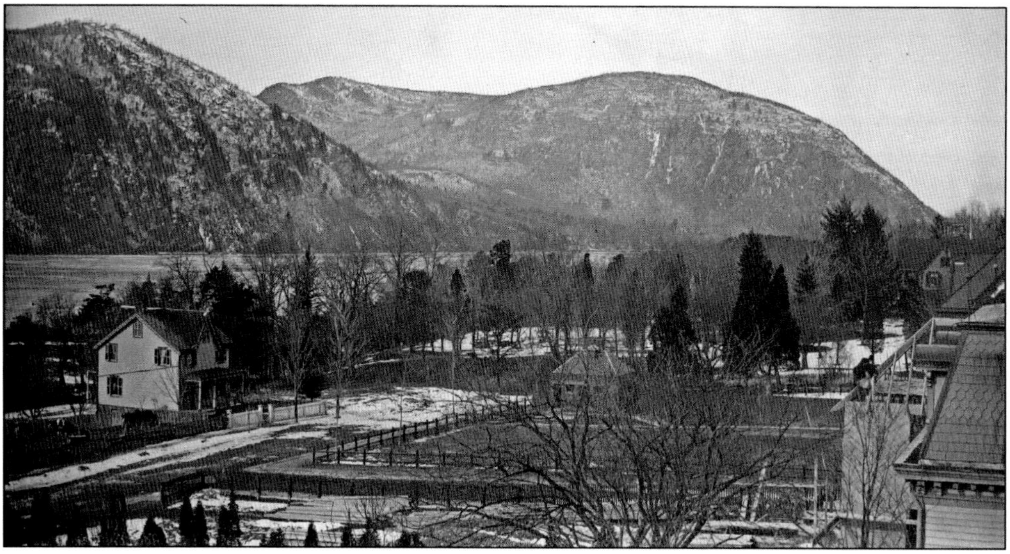

From a vantage not far from that of the previous photograph, Terwilliger aimed his camera north toward the contours of Crow's Nest and Storm King, called Butter Hill by the Dutch. In 1963, many local residents began a successful 17-year effort to prevent the Consolidated Edison Company from building a massive hydroelectric plant on the mountainside that would have destroyed its scenic beauty. (Courtesy of PCHS.)

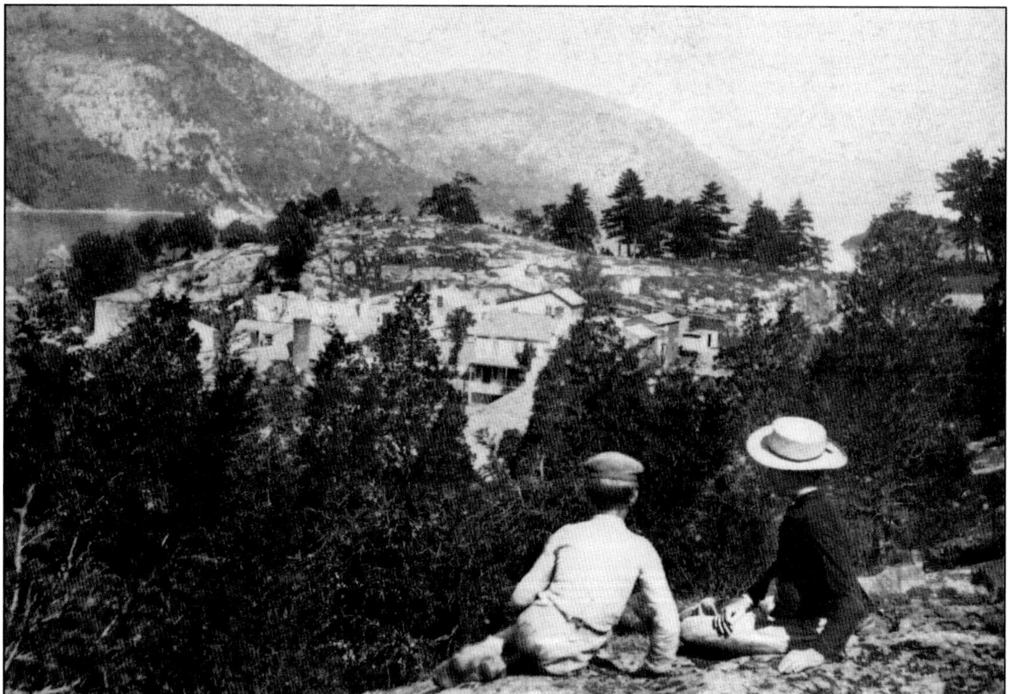

Two boys on a rocky rise near the Main Street railroad crossing take in a northern view similar to the one above. The village lies below them. A 1972 Don McLean album cover gives a view from the same location looking due west. A residence now has this vantage point. (Courtesy of Mark Forlow.)

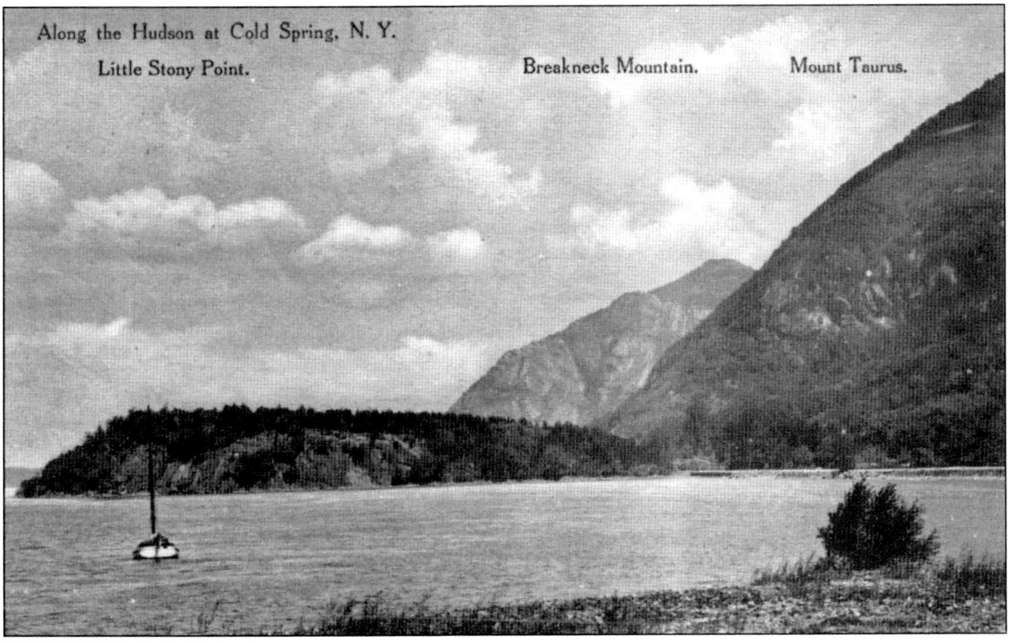

The contours of Little Stony Point, Bull Hill (also known as Mount Taurus), and Breakneck fill this view looking north from Cold Spring. The point is seven-tenths of a mile from Main Street. During the American Revolution, the Continental Army camped on the riverbank nearby. The railroad causeway can be seen at the extreme right of the photograph. (Courtesy of Mark Forlow.)

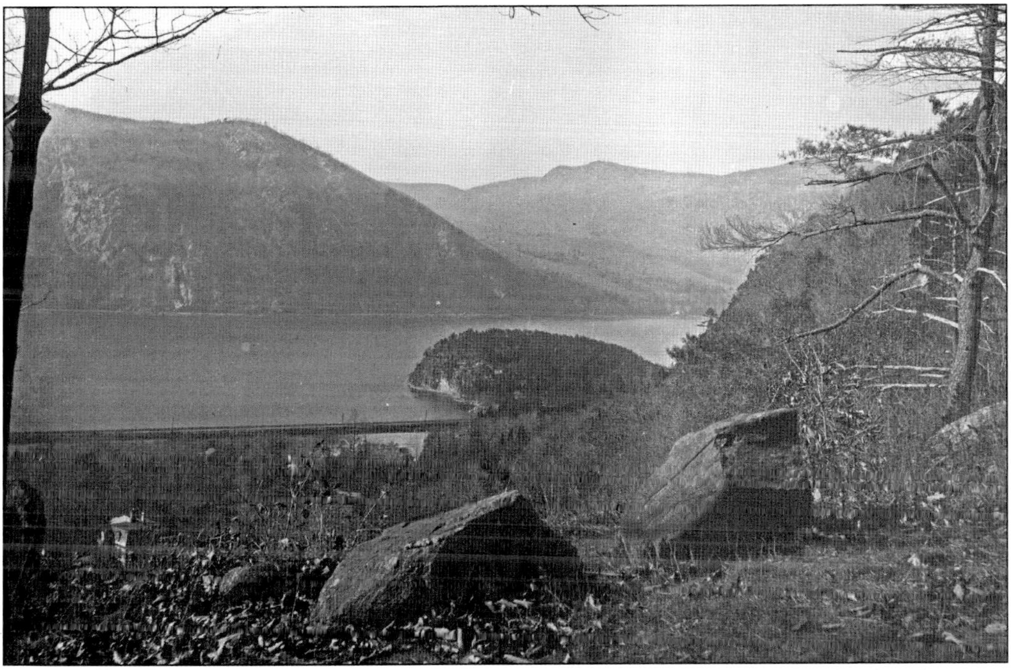

From Bull Hill, the photographer looks down onto the railroad causeway south of Little Stony Point and across to Crow's Neck and Storm King mountains. Houses are nestled in the trees at the lower left. Later, quarrying transformed Little Stony Point, creating a strip of rubble around its perimeter. (Photograph by Albert Terwilliger, courtesy of PCHS.)

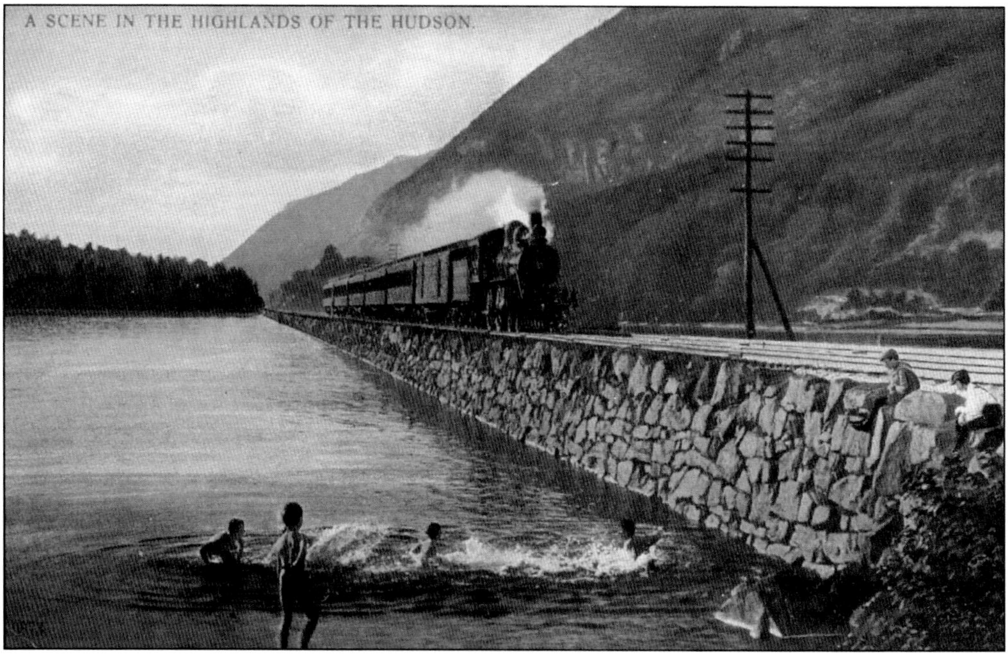

Children commonly swam in the Hudson River near Cold Spring and Garrison in times past. Here, they play in the water south of Little Stony Point while a New York Central Railroad train heads toward Cold Spring. Pollution led to a sharp decline in swimming in the river in the mid-20th century. (Courtesy of Janet Selleck Rust.)

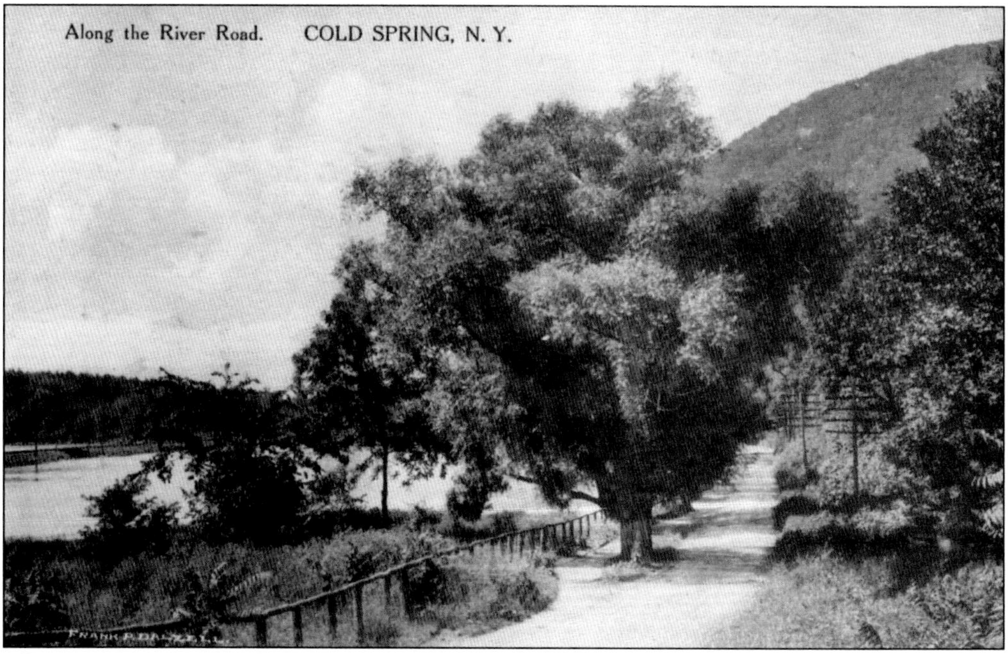

About 1906, River Road ran along the riverbank toward Little Stony Point. The small bay on the left, cut off by the railroad causeway, was once known as Smugglers' Cove. A local historian speculated that this name arose in the mid-17th century due to concerns about pirates. (Courtesy of Mark Forlow.)

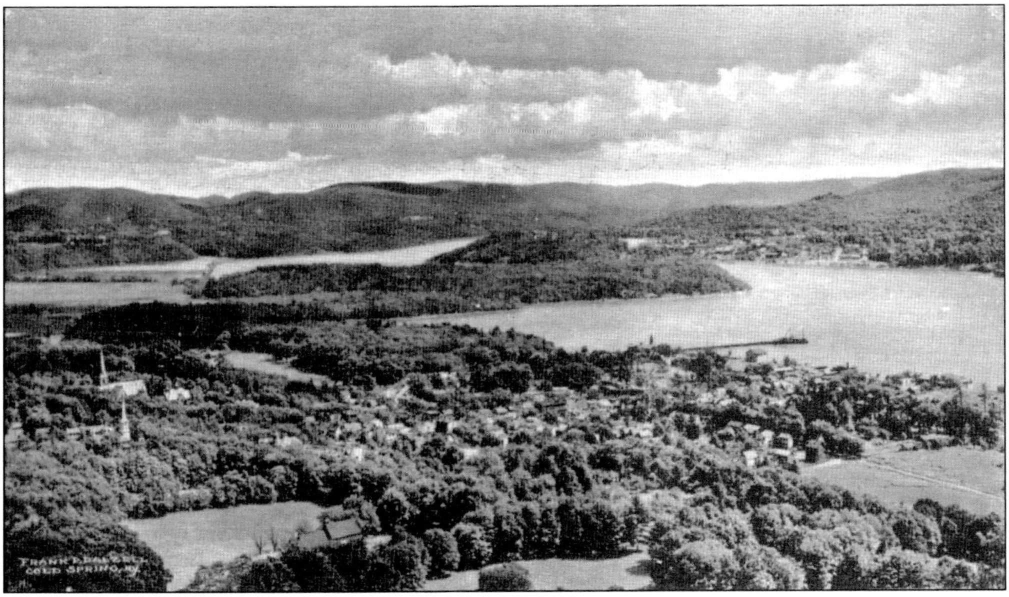

The view from Table Rock on Bull Hill shows the curve of the river around Constitution Island. Cold Spring is below. Steeples of the First Dutch Reformed Church and St. Mary-in-the-Highlands, with its parish house, are visible. The former West Point Foundry dock projects westward. The railroad causeway can be seen crossing Constitution Marsh. (Courtesy of Janet Selleck Rust.)

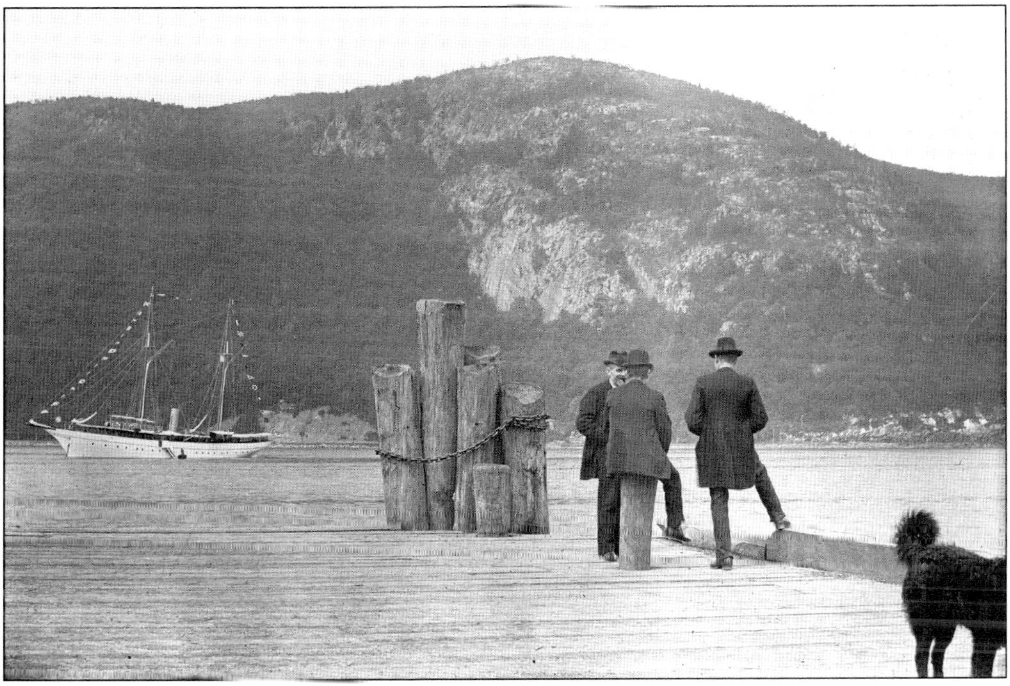

Around 1895, three men converse on the main Cold Spring dock. Crow's Nest rises across the river, and a yacht is at anchor. In 1855, the writer Nathaniel P. Willis, watching from his home, Idlewild, observed that yachts, those "dashing albatrosses," had begun to appear on the river. He lived in Cornwall-on-Hudson, above the northern flank of Storm King Mountain. (Photograph by Albert Terwilliger, courtesy of PCHS.)

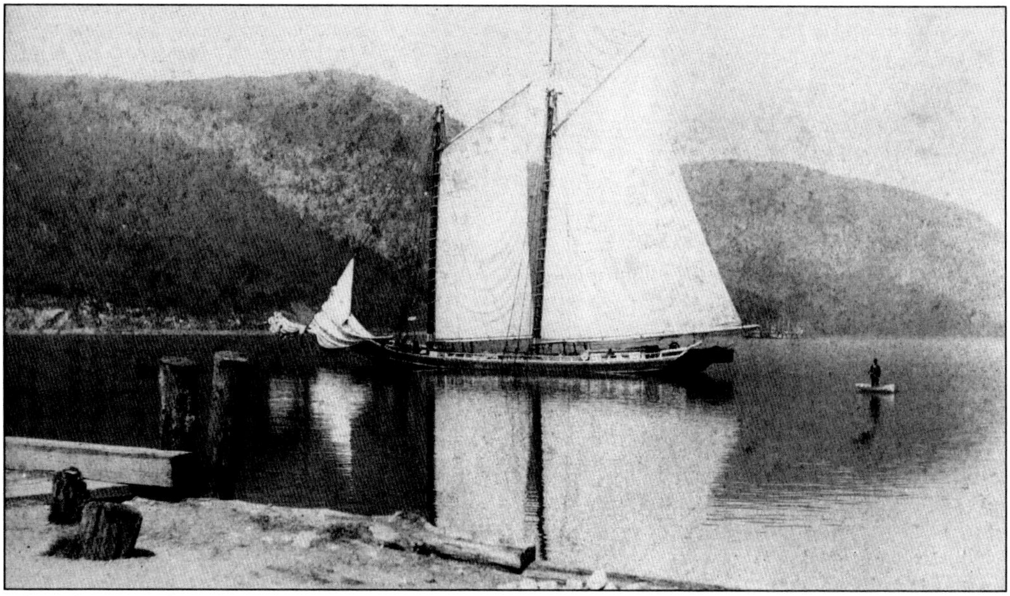

This photograph, taken about 1890, shows a schooner, with its two masts, at anchor off Cold Spring with Crow's Nest and Storm King behind. Even after the railroad came through in 1849, sloops and schooners remained an important means of cheap shipping and transportation for Cold Spring. A lumberyard on the waterfront may have used the boat. (Courtesy of PCHS.)

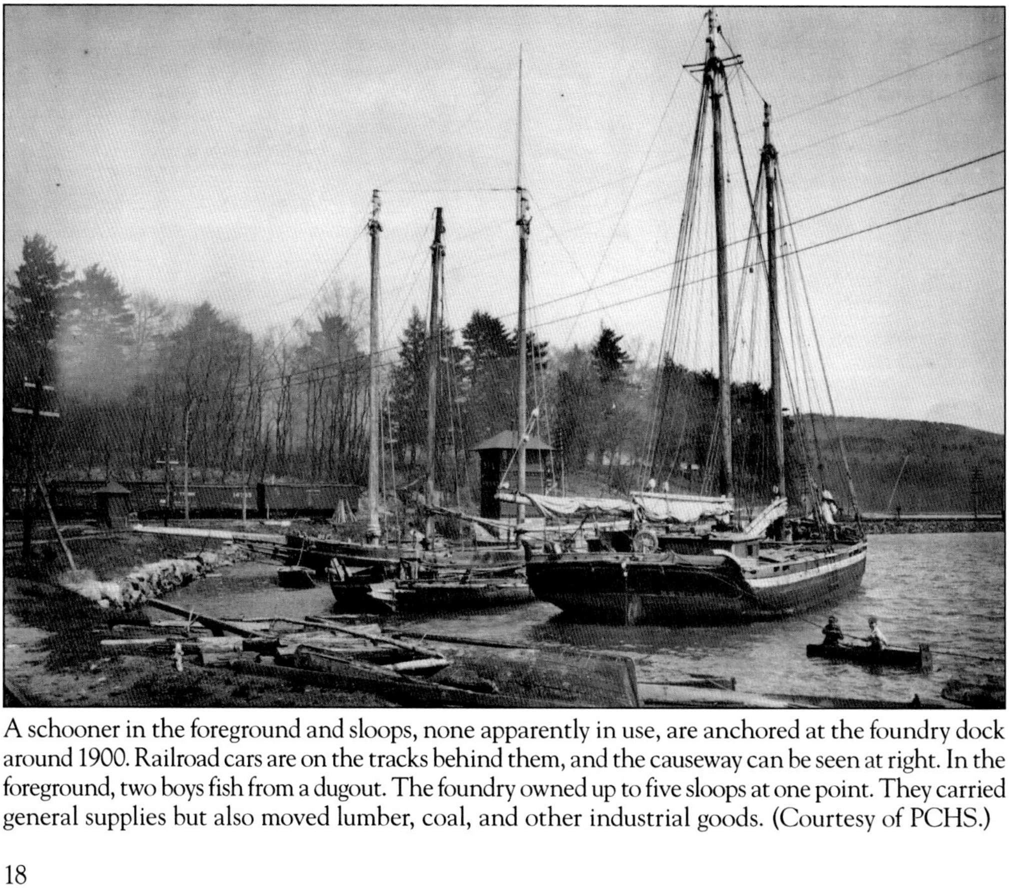

A schooner in the foreground and sloops, none apparently in use, are anchored at the foundry dock around 1900. Railroad cars are on the tracks behind them, and the causeway can be seen at right. In the foreground, two boys fish from a dugout. The foundry owned up to five sloops at one point. They carried general supplies but also moved lumber, coal, and other industrial goods. (Courtesy of PCHS.)

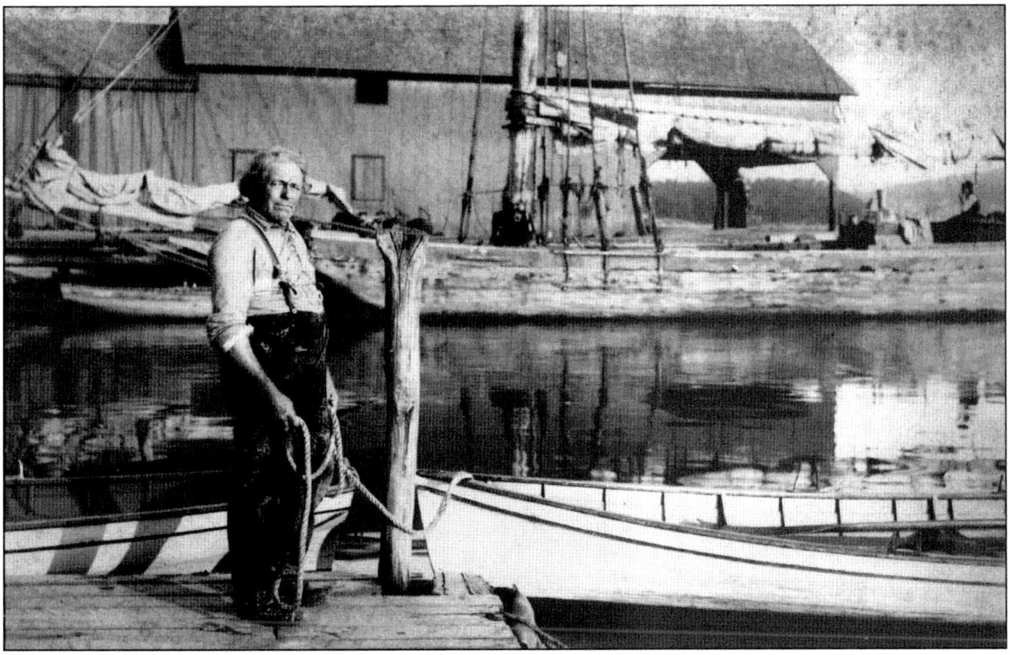

Cold Spring resident David S. Lyons, pictured around the turn of the century on a dock near Foundry Cove, was a famous sloop captain. His boat, the *Victorine*, was said to be the fastest sailing vessel on the river. A battered looking sloop, presumably not his, is anchored behind him. Constitution Island is in the distance. (Courtesy of PCHS.)

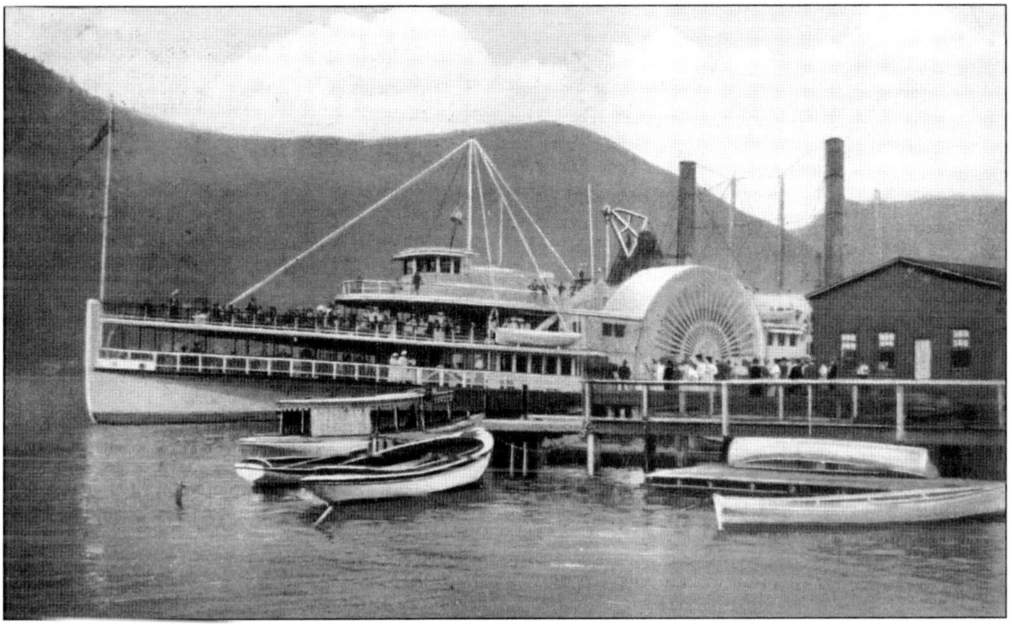

Crowds await the steamboat *Mary Powell* as she docks about 1900. Said to be the only steamboat that put in at Cold Spring, rather than anchoring mid-river, she traveled daily from Kingston to New York City and back, stopping in Cold Spring officially only from 1862 to 1864. This photograph and anecdotal reports suggest otherwise. By 1914, she was a charter boat. Built in 1861, the *Mary Powell* ended service in 1917. (Courtesy of PCHS.)

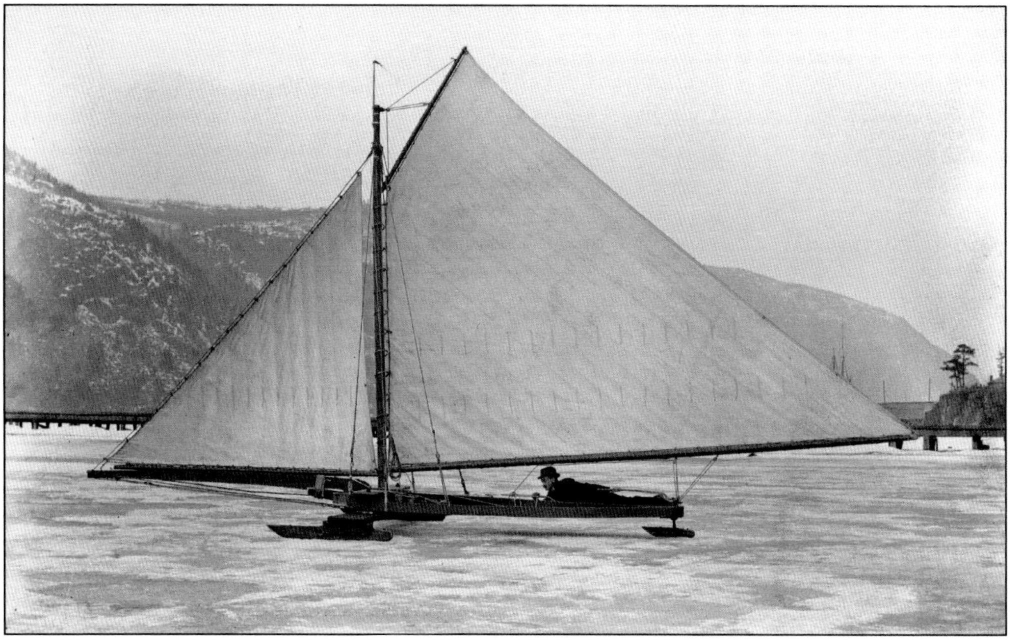

About 1893, a man sails an iceboat with a gaff-rigged mainsail from Foundry Cove toward the center of the river. On windy days, such craft could travel 60 to 70 miles per hour. Ice-sailing races were held on the Hudson River as early as 1790. The sport is said to have originated in the 17th-century Netherlands. Crow's Nest and Storm King are in the distance. (Photograph by Albert Terwilliger, courtesy of PCHS.)

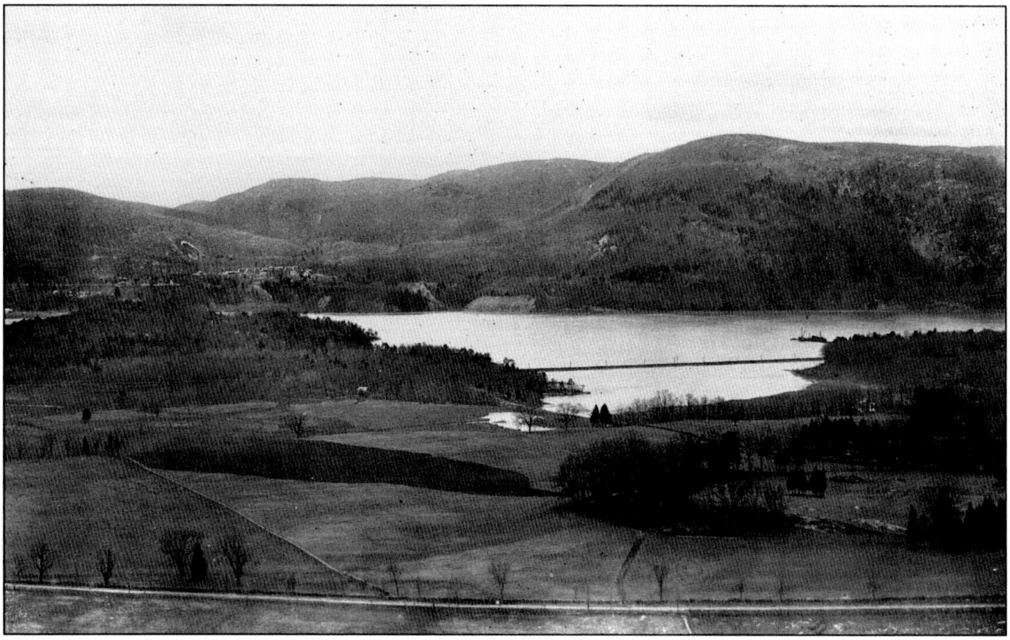

From a vantage point on Dale's Hill in Garrison, Terwilliger photographed the railway causeway across Foundry Cove, which lies south of Main Street and north of Constitution Island. Crow's Nest Mountain is across the river from the causeway. The cluster of buildings to the left is part of West Point. (Courtesy of PCHS.)

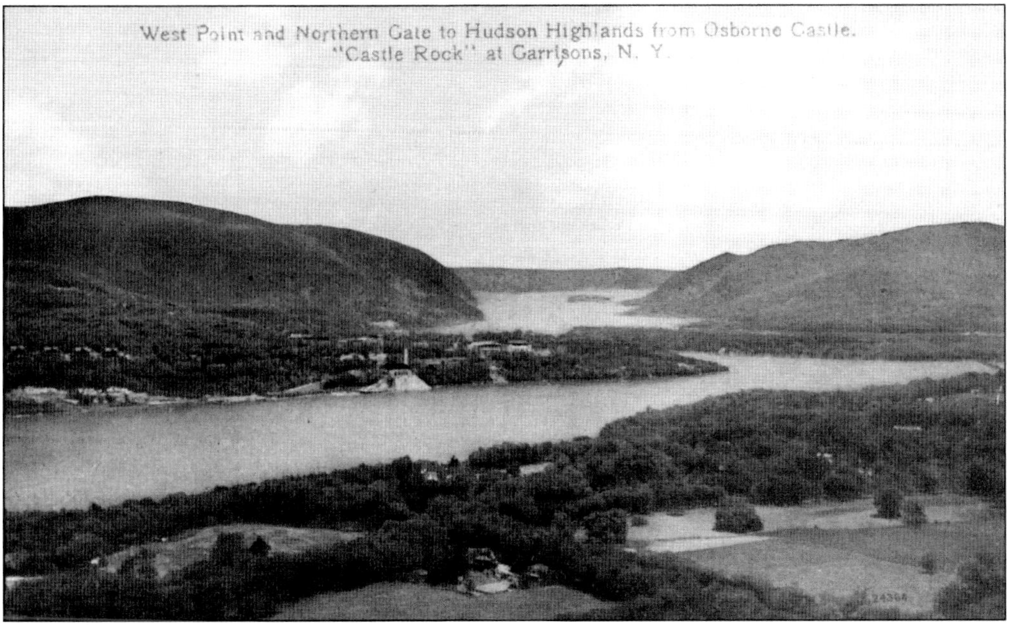

The Garrison riverfront is in the immediate foreground with West Point opposite. The river swings abruptly left around Gee's Point and then sharply right around Constitution Island. Newburgh Bay can be seen in the distance with Pollepel, now Bannerman Island, at right. The photograph was taken from Castle Rock, the estate of William Henry Osborn. (Courtesy of Antipodean Books, Maps & Prints.)

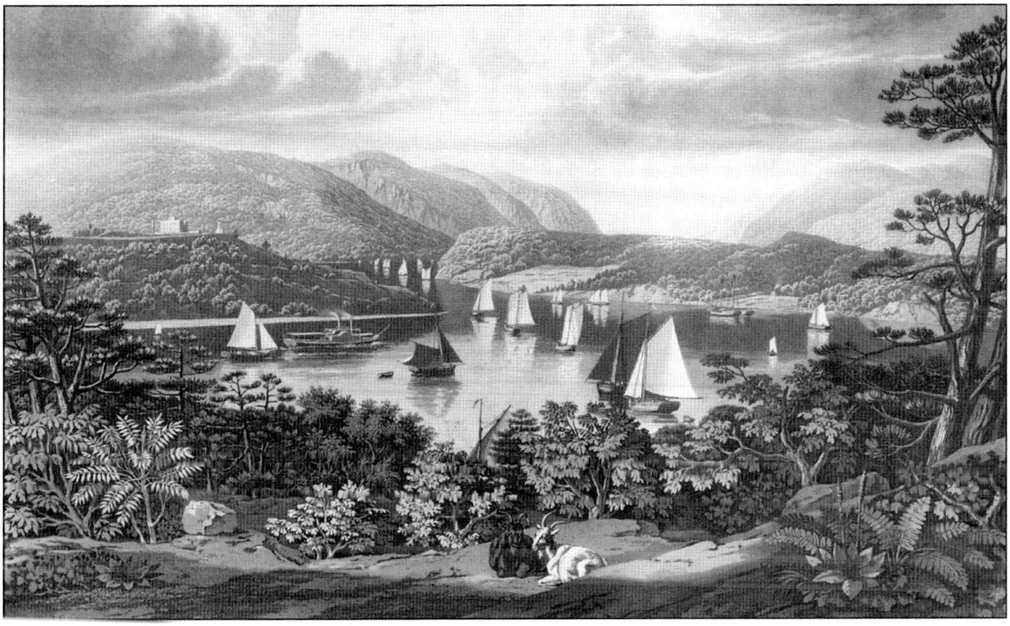

A rare print, *West Point from Phillipstown*, an aquatint by William James Bennett, hand colored by John Hill and first published in 1831, shows the river between Gee's Point at West Point and Constitution Island. Bennett was a British-born engraver and landscape painter who established himself in New York in 1836. A chain was stretched between Gee's Point and the island as a defensive barrier during the Revolutionary War. (Courtesy of PCHS.)

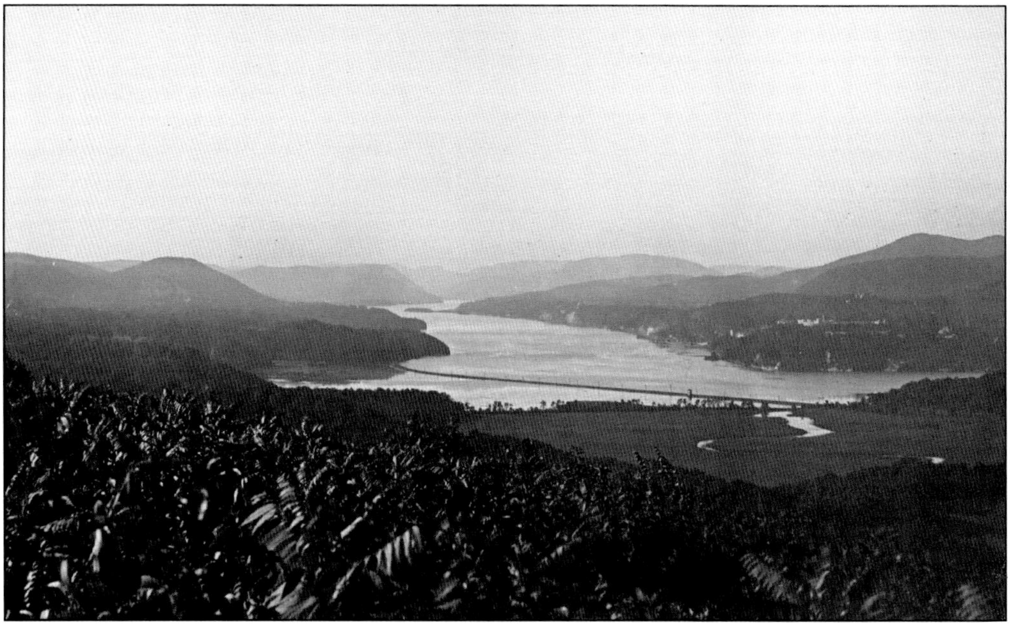

Terwilliger looked south from Dale's Hill in 1902 and captured the eastern side of the entrance to the Highlands, Anthony's Nose (elevation 900 feet). Its straight slope is in the distance to the middle left. Constitution Marsh, with its causeway, and buildings belonging to West Point are in closer view. Boscobel, the States Morris Dyckman mansion, which was relocated here and opened in 1961, has a view from the lower right. (Courtesy of PCHS.)

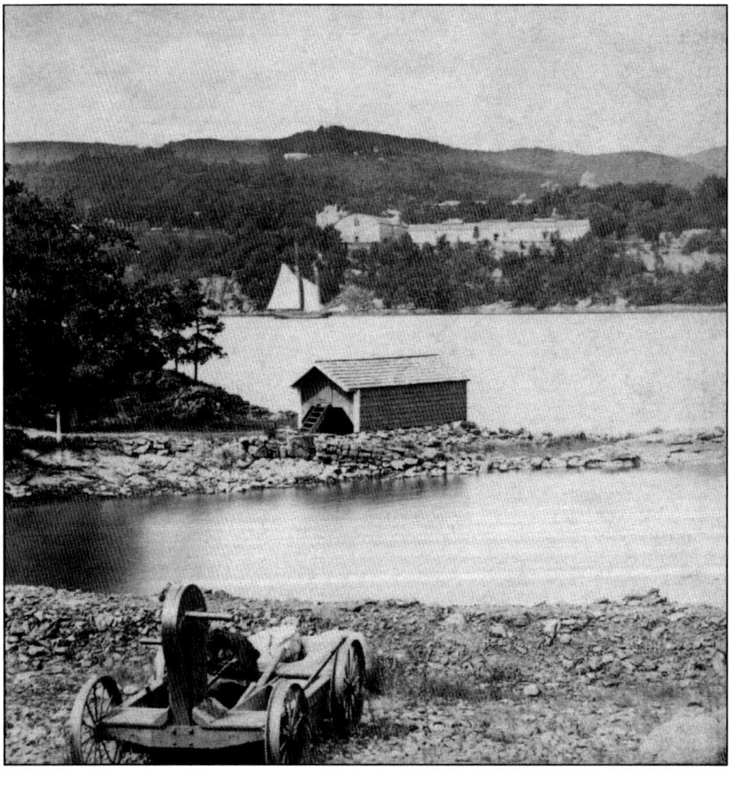

This photograph was taken near the railroad tracks at Garrison's Landing, looking across to West Point, where the arched roof of the riding hall can be seen. A rail handcart sits in the foreground, a boathouse is nearby, and a schooner sails on the river. The placement of docks and other structures at the landing has changed since the 19th and early 20th centuries. (Courtesy of the Highland Studio Inc.)

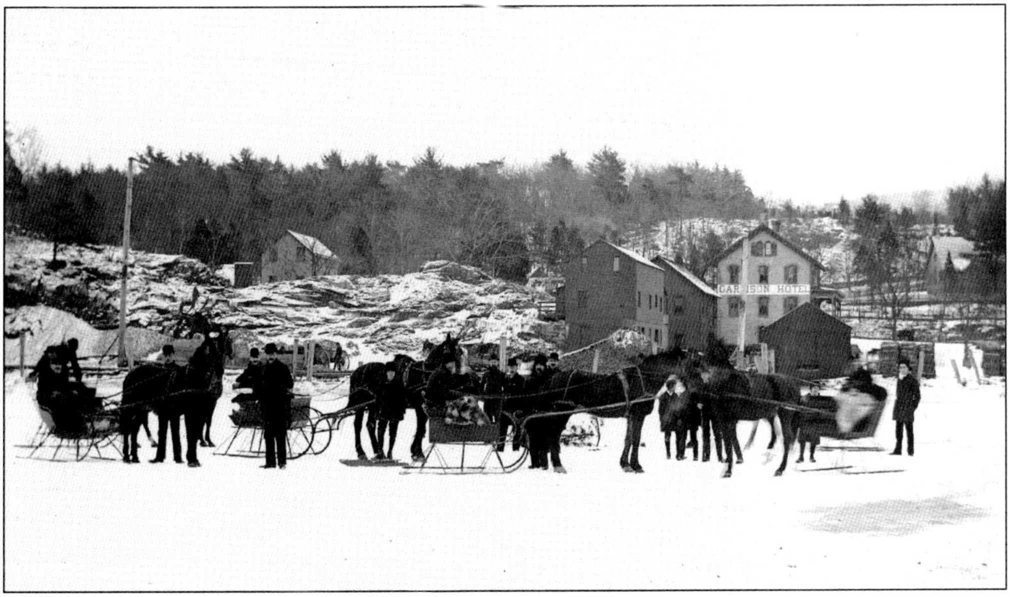

Five sleigh racers and their associates, all men, are assembled on the river at Garrison's Landing in 1892, with the Garrison Hotel behind them. Three types of cutters are being used, including an Albany cutter at the far left, which is hooked to the horse with a bellyband of bells. (Photograph by Albert Terwilliger, courtesy of PCHS.)

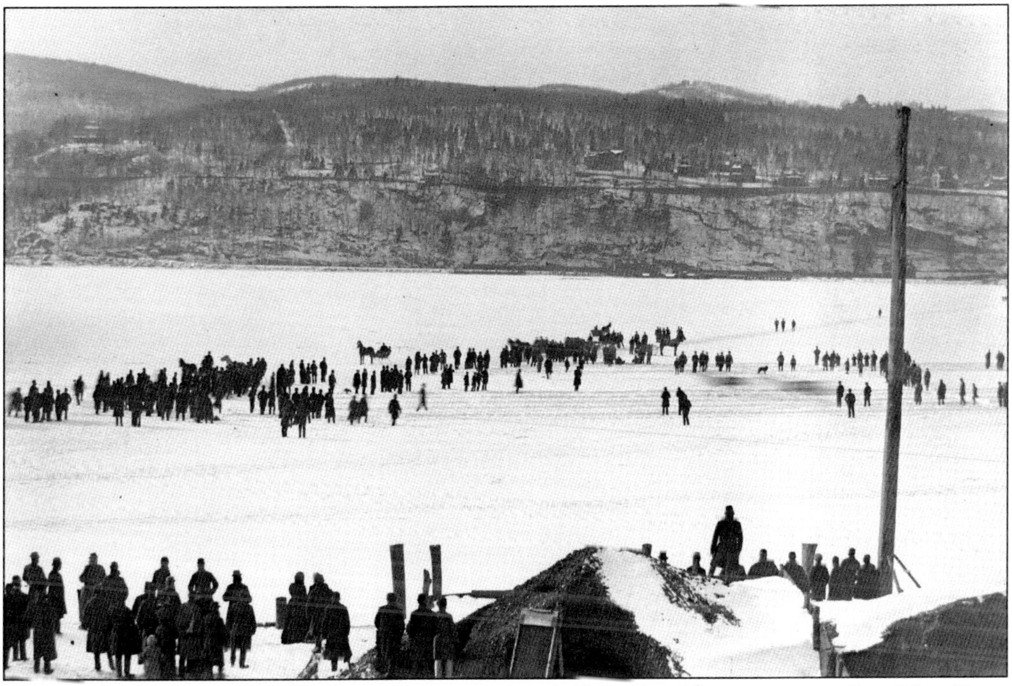

Enthusiasts await a sleigh race from Garrison to the bluffs south of the main grounds at West Point while others walk across the ice. Officers' houses can be seen in the distance. Travelers sometimes sleighed down the river from Cornwall-on-Hudson at Storm King to Cold Spring or West Point. About 1927, US Coast Guard ice-breaking boats virtually ended many winter activities on the river. (Courtesy of PCHS.)

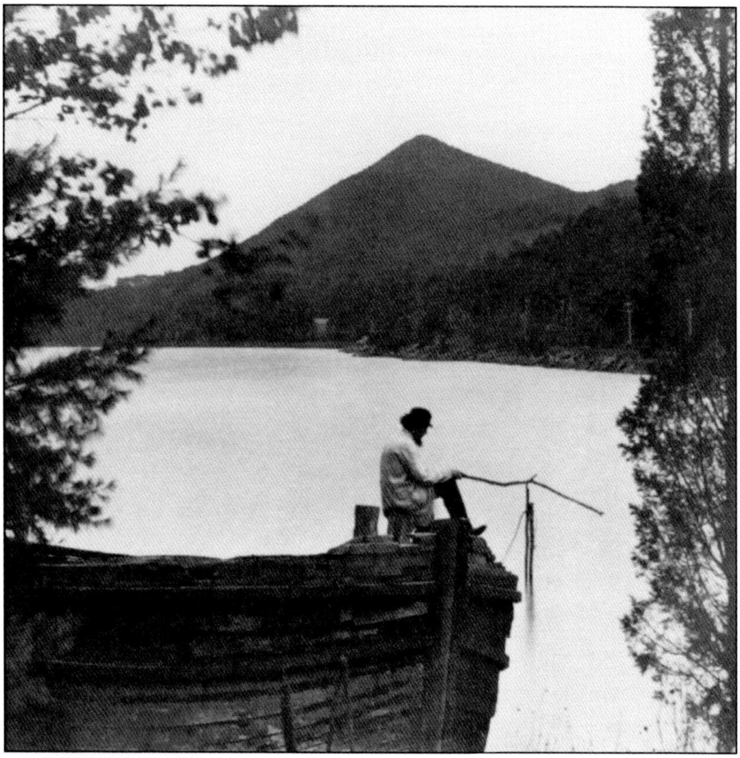

A man crabs off on an old hull. Blue crab has recently made a comeback in the Hudson River. Sugar Loaf, a hill south of Garrison's Landing, is in the distance. The location of Garrison's south redoubt during the American Revolution, Sugar Loaf has an elevation of 1,260 feet. Three hills between the Tappan Zee Bridge to the south and the northern border of Putnam County are called Sugar Loaf. (Courtesy of the Highland Studio Inc.)

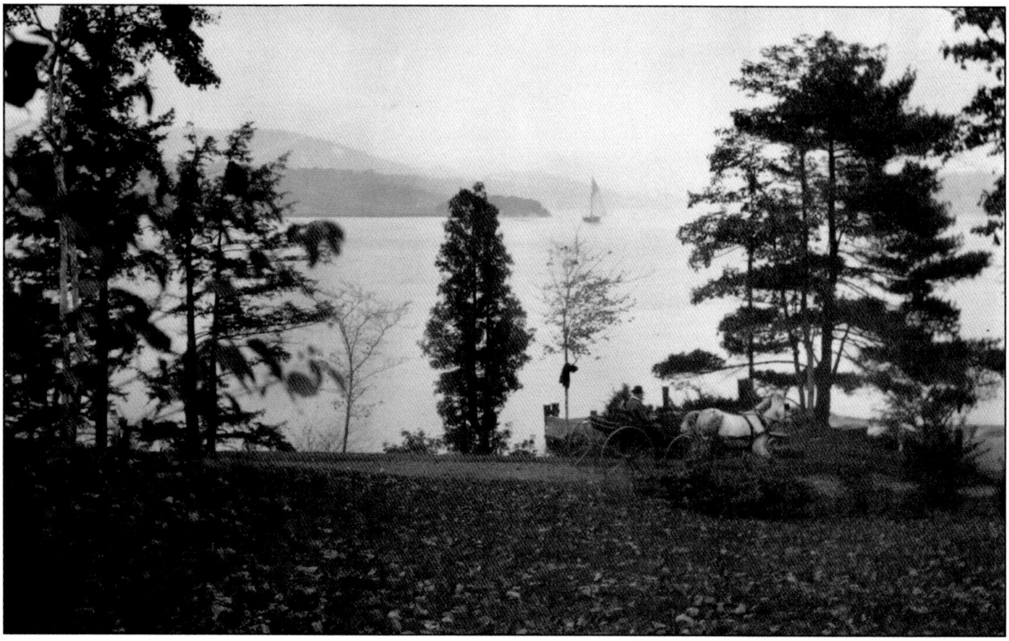

This misty view of Conns Hook is seen upriver from Edward Livingston's estate in southern Philipstown. Livingston, a New York City lawyer, built a bridge over the railroad tracks to site his house near the water. It was designed in 1897 by New York City architect George F. Pelham and built that year. Livingston's children inherited the estate. His daughter sold the property about 1937. (Courtesy of PCHS.)

Two

Doing Business Near the River and Other Locales

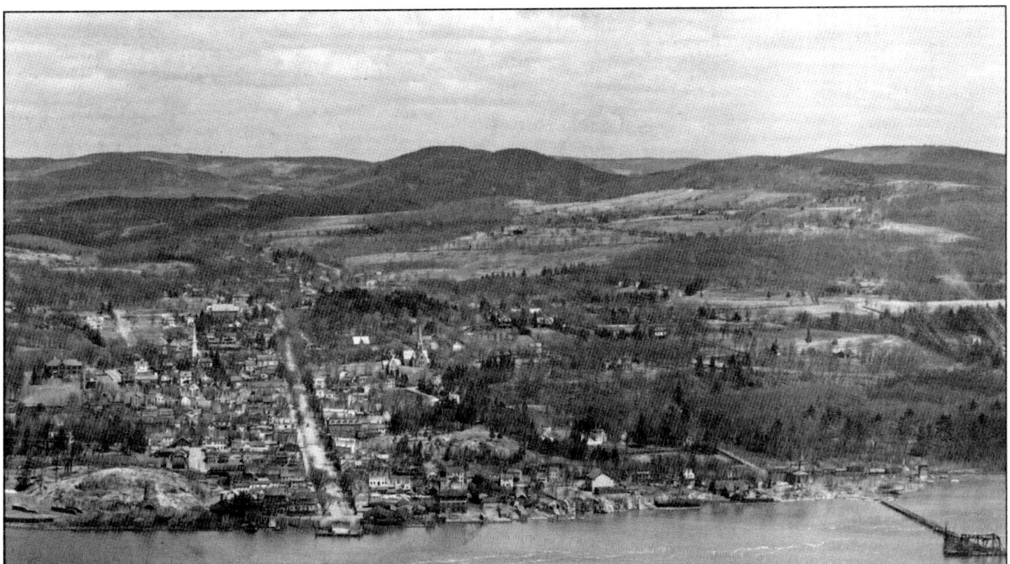

This view of Cold Spring taken between 1894 and 1906 shows its business district, which lies chiefly along Main Street. The West Point Furnace Company once stood in the open area near the river left of Main Street. In 1815, Main Street extended from the Hudson River to Connecticut as the Philipstown Turnpike. Straightened in 1838, the street continues through Nelsonville to Route 301. (Courtesy of Mark Forlow.)

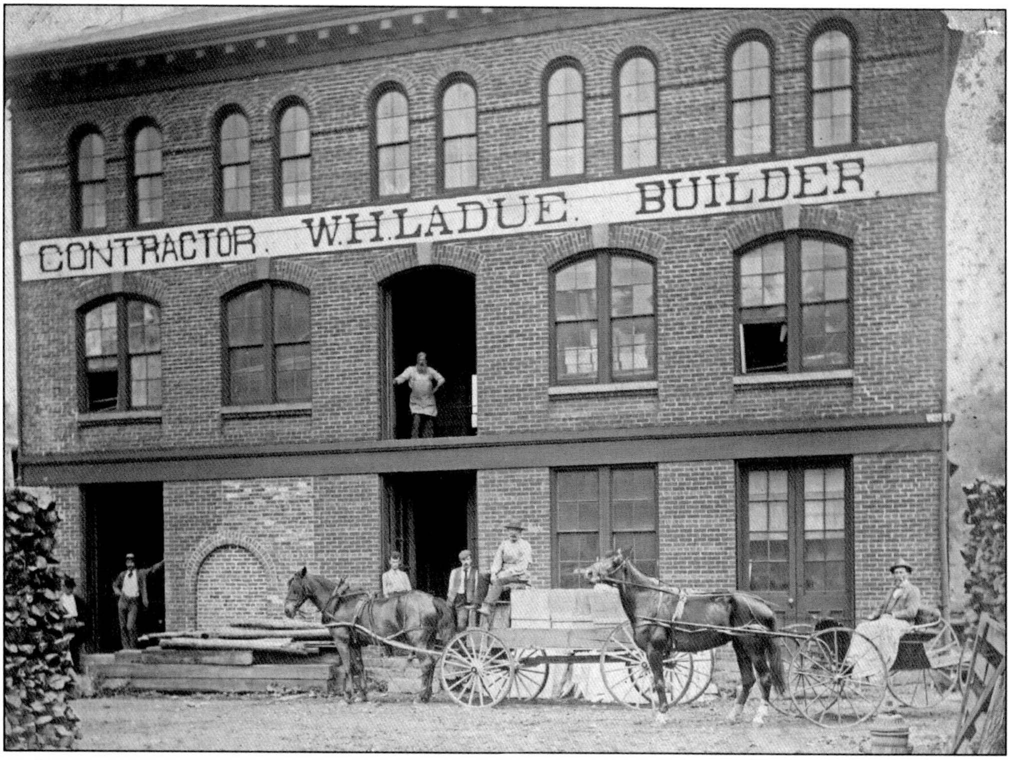

William H. La Due may be the man sitting in the buggy at right. This handsome Victorian-era building, facing the river, had segmentally arched rounded windows and smaller, rounded upper windows with a heavy, bracketed cornice. Condominiums have replaced it. A highly successful contractor, La Due was also an influential community member until his death in 1903. (Courtesy of PCHS.)

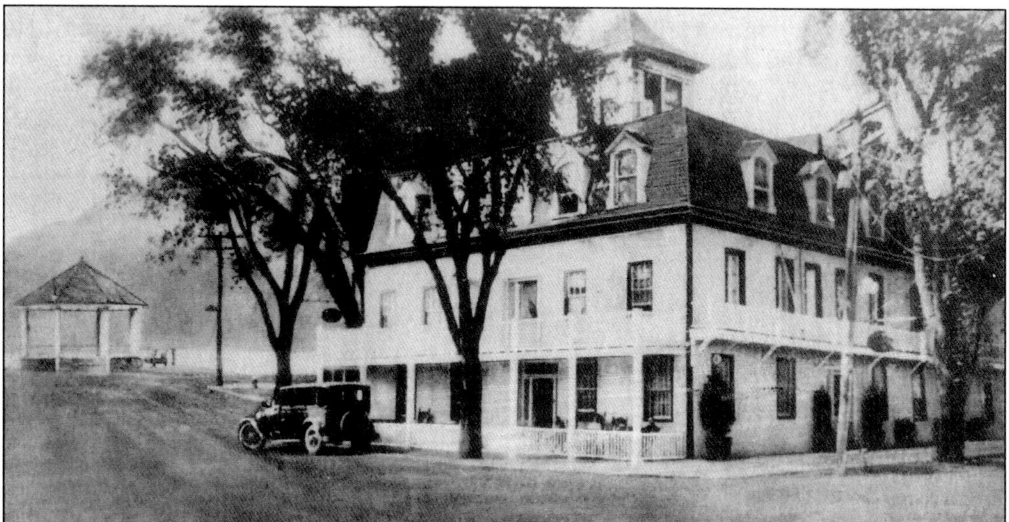

The Hudson View Hotel, probably shown in the 1930s, was in business by 1880 on this site, which has been occupied by an inn or hotel since at least 1832. The building was raised four feet in 1981 because of periodic riverfront flooding. The bandstand, an octagonal gazebo with white pillars and a red tile roof, was erected in 1928. (Courtesy of Mark Forlow.)

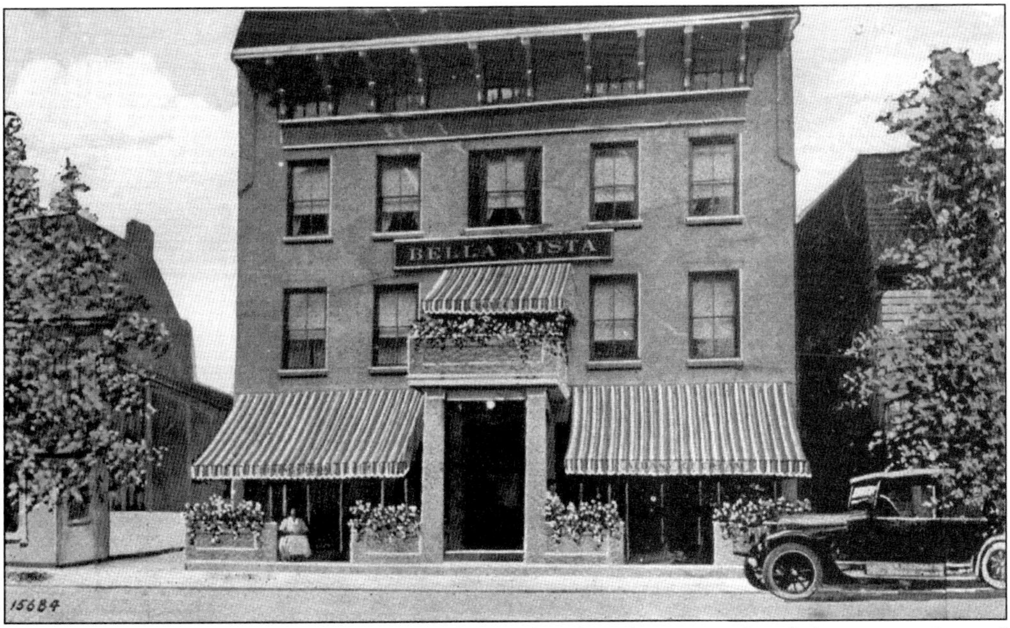

The Italianate Bella Vista Hotel, with its heavy, bracketed cornice, faced the river and stood next to the Hudson View Hotel. Its awnings indicate that the dining room was on the left. The right-hand awning advertises Albany Ice Cream. The Bella Vista operated from at least 1927 to 1937. The building remains. (Courtesy of Janet Selleck Rust.)

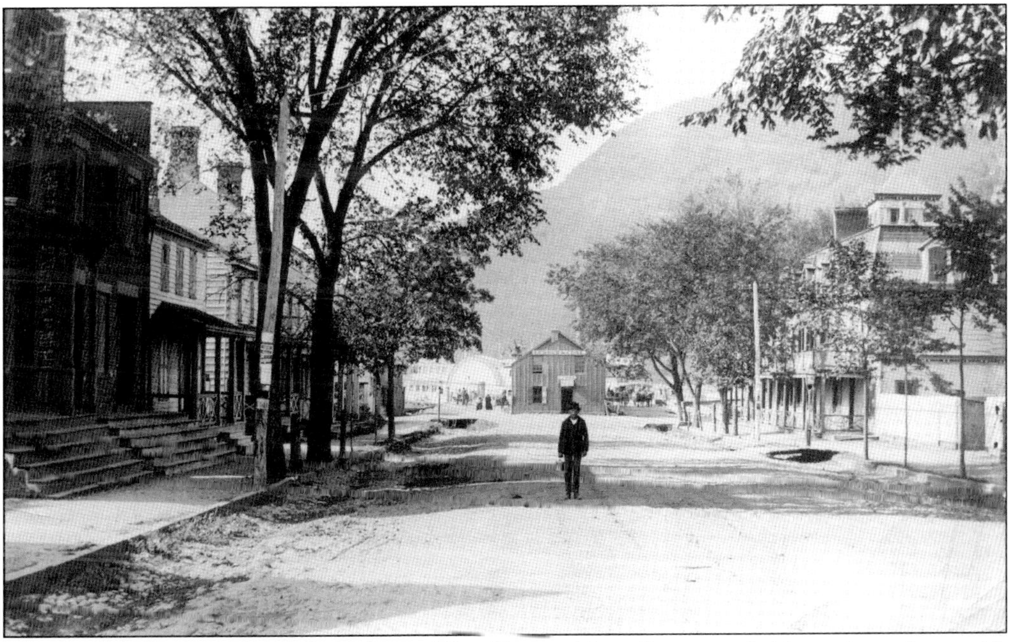

A boy with a lunch pail stands in the middle of Lower Main Street, probably in the early to mid-1890s, west of the railroad tracks. Behind him at the dock, the steamboat *Emeline* discharges passengers. Horses and buggies wait for them next to C.J. Baxter's Lumber & Coal store. The Hudson View Hotel is on the right. The houses on the left remain but with alterations. (Courtesy of PCHS.)

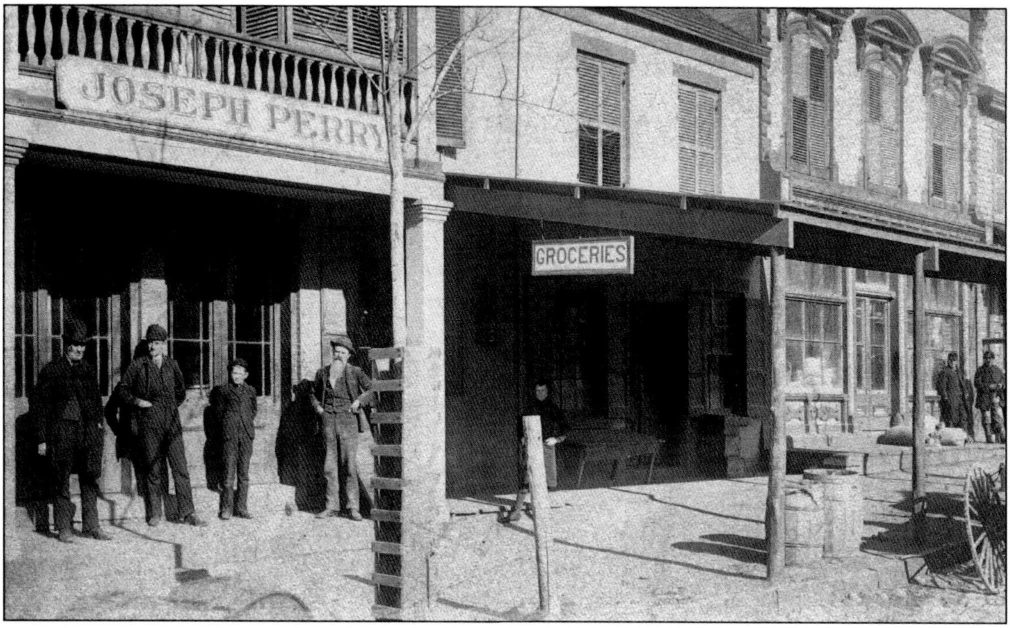

J. Hazen Perry (with long beard), photographed about 1880, sold groceries, tobacco, cigars, wines, and liquors in Cold Spring, beginning in 1860. His business occupied these three buildings, which stood between the railroad tracks and Market Street. His brothers, Wright (left) and Joseph (second from left), joined the business. In 1890, their longtime clerk, James E. Reilly, became Wright's partner. Hazen died in 1884. (Courtesy of PCHS.)

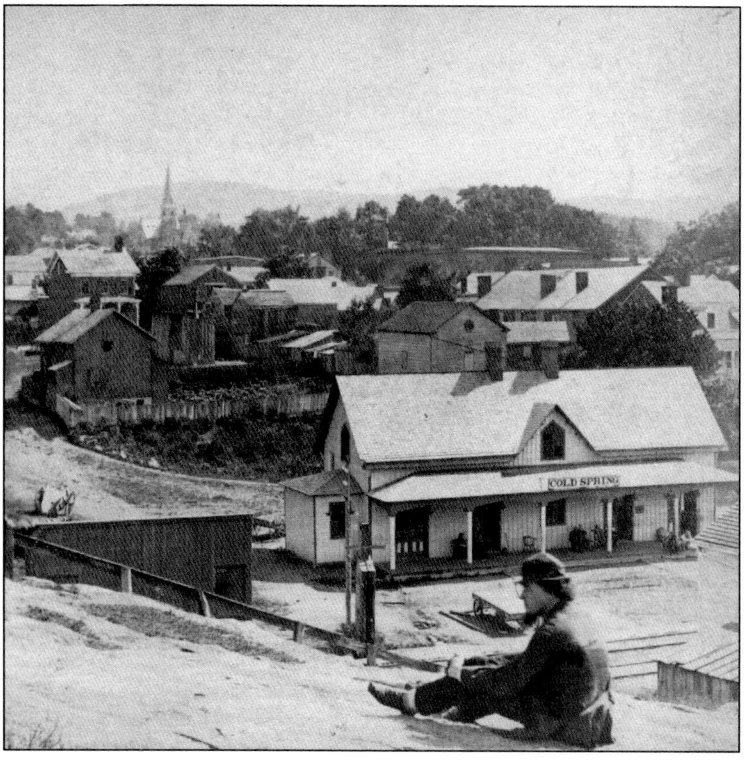

Passengers wait on the porch of an early white, gabled depot in Cold Spring sometime after 1868. The railroad track, laid in 1848, was cut through solid rock at points. Train service began in 1849. A photograph of a smaller building at this location shows what may have been Cold Spring's first depot. (Courtesy of Mark Forlow.)

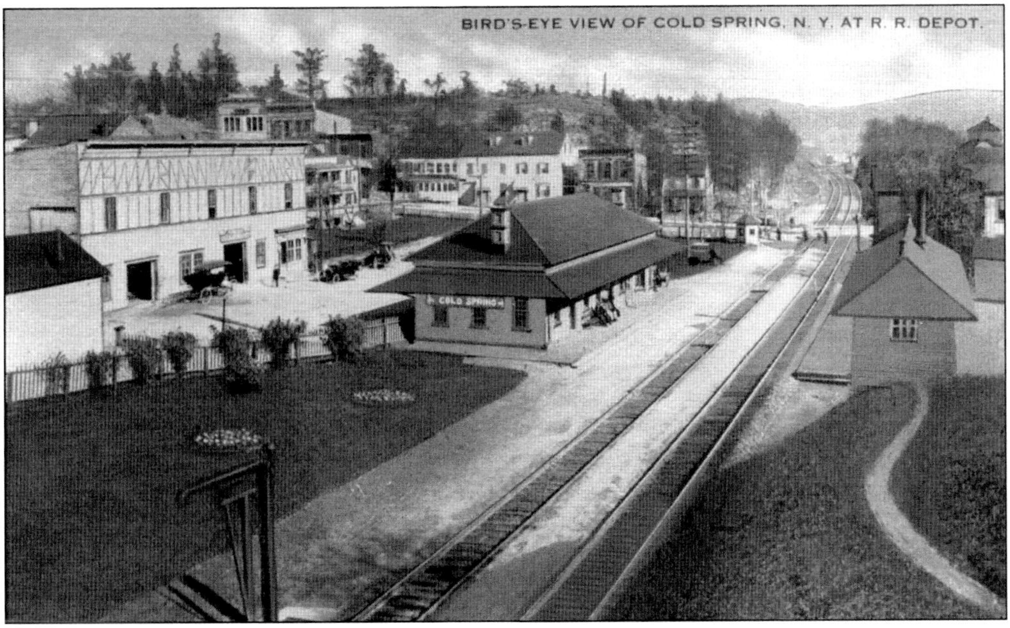

Cold Spring's brick depot (1883) was built by William La Due and is still used commercially, as is the building behind it where a car and two carriages are parked. That structure housed Henyans Livery Sale & Exchange in 1907 and Jaycox's Livery & Boarding Stable by 1909. A modern station platform was built south of Main Street in 1979. (Courtesy of Mark Forlow.)

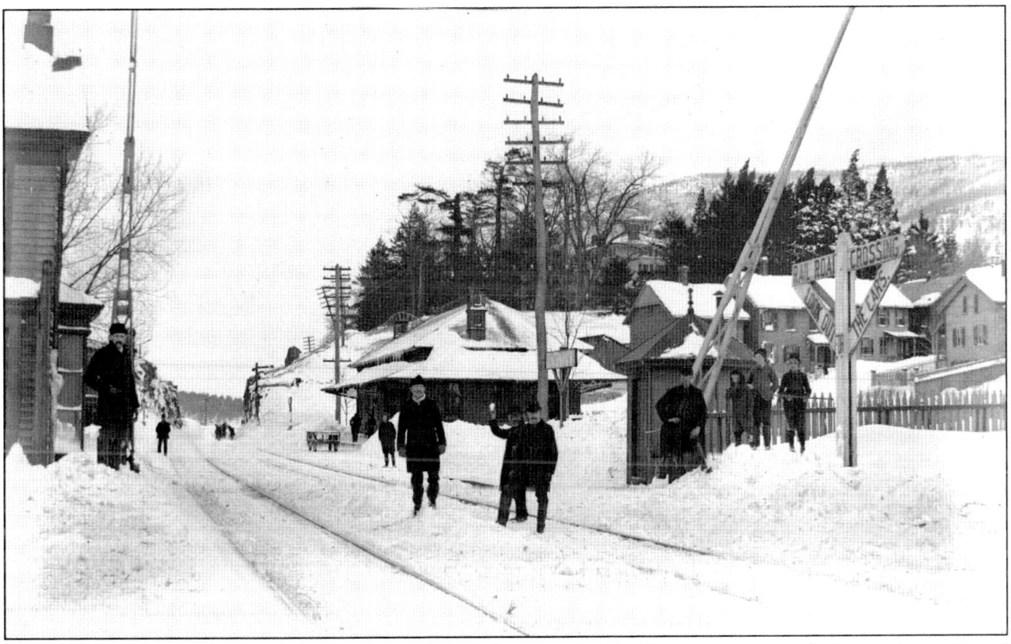

With passengers waiting at the depot behind them, men and boys are on and along the railroad tracks on the day of a record snowfall in 1893. One prepares to throw a snowball. On the rise at right is the large home of Gen. John Campbell. An underpass, built here in 1929, allows pedestrians to cross, and cars now take a nearby bridge over the tracks. (Courtesy of PCHS.)

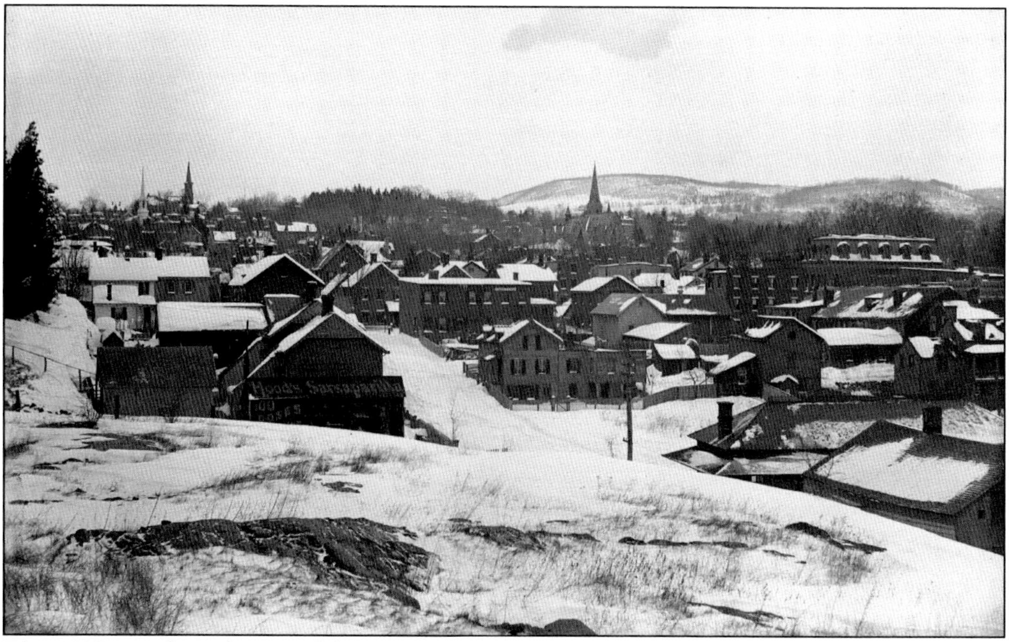

This 1893 view from the top of the cutting looks east up Railroad Avenue, which begins near the depot and runs parallel to Main Street. The depot roof is at the lower right. The Hood's Sarsaparilla sign on the building on the left advertises a soft drink made with sarsaparilla root, which tastes similar to root beer and was thought to have medicinal properties. (Courtesy of PCHS.)

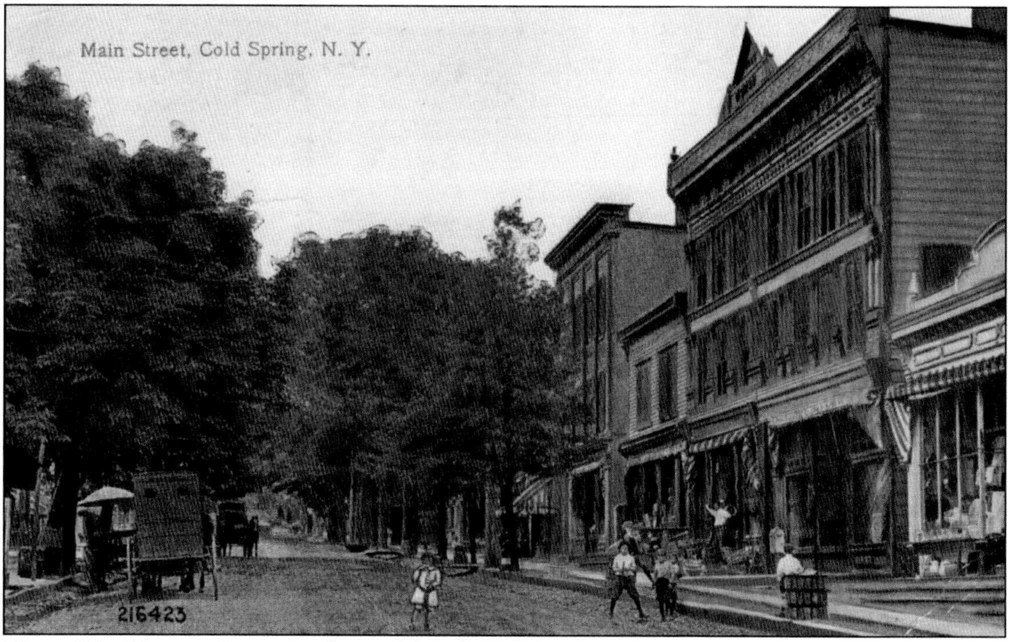

The tall building with a pressed-metal facade stands on the south side of Main Street. The date on its finial reads 1900. The moldings imitating wood enable the front to blend with neighboring buildings. A fire down the street in 1875 destroyed about 15 structures, from Rock Street to the railroad tracks, including a saloon, hotel, jewelry and shoe stores, and a doctor's office. (Courtesy of Mark Forlow.)

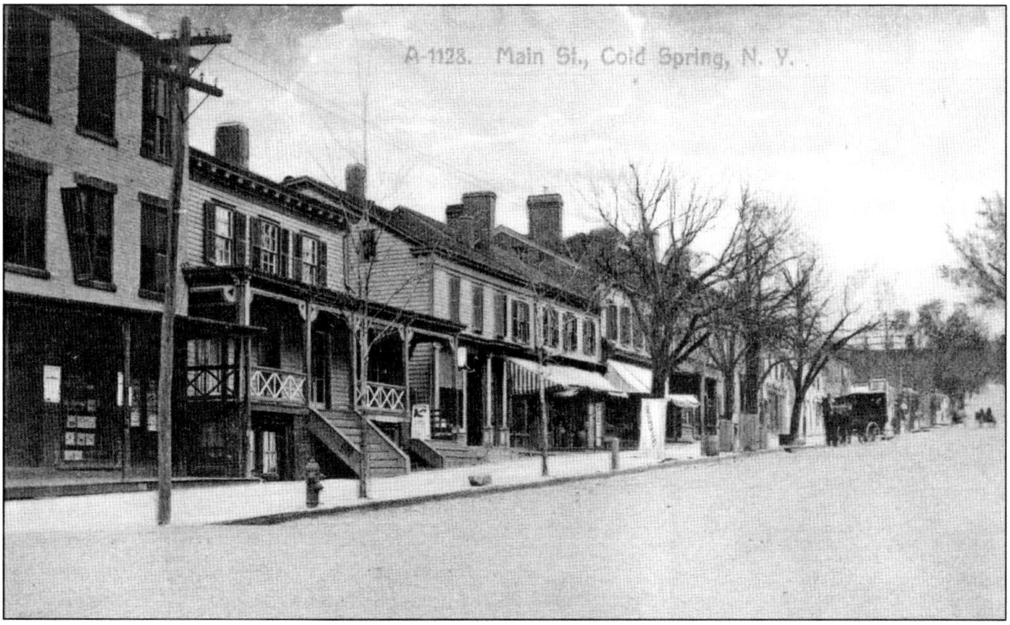

Businesses were interspersed with residences on the north side of Main Street about 1906. An undertaker advertises on the large sign leaning against a tree. The house with an ornamental porch has a lower second porch and a placard showing a shoe, perhaps advertising a cobbler's stall. Several of the buildings have since been removed, and at least one has been destroyed by fire. (Courtesy of PCHS.)

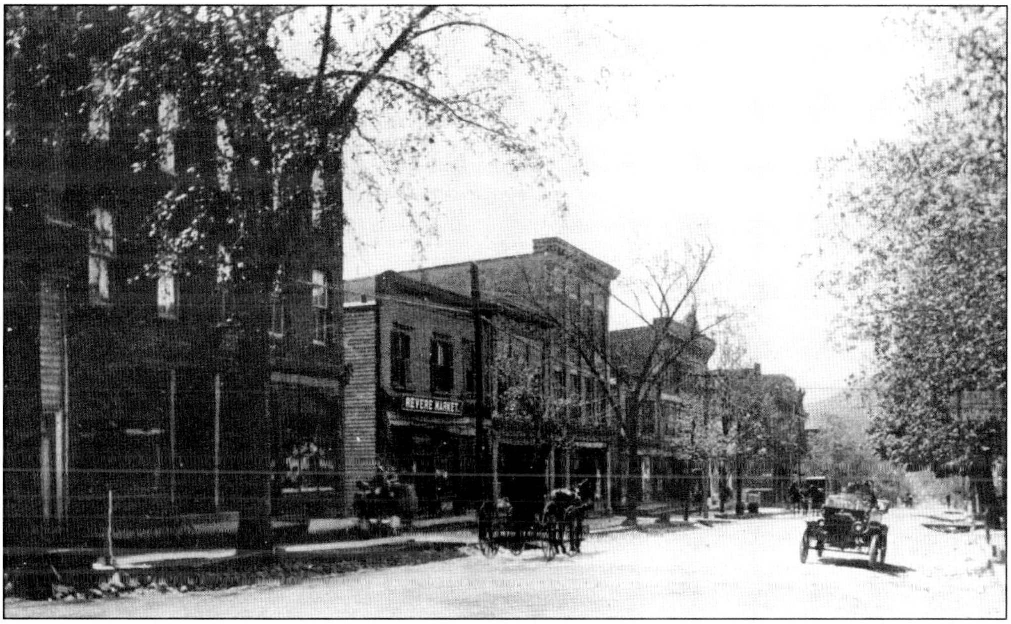

Horses, a buckboard, a carriage, and a car share the road in this undated view of the south side of Main Street. Each conveyance hugs its side of the street. Before 1903, American towns and cities had no rules for driving. Once automobiles were mass-produced, traffic rules began to emerge. The sign on the second fully viewed building at the left marks the Revere Market. (Courtesy of Janet Selleck Rust.)

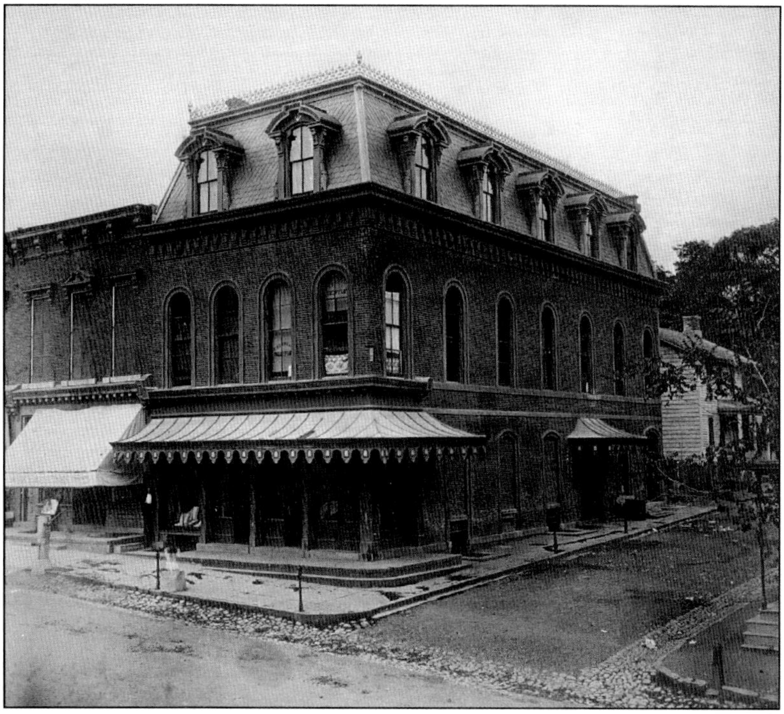

Constructed in 1864 to house the McCabe Dry Goods store, this Second Empire brick building stands on the east corner of Main and Rock Streets. It has heavily molded broken arches on the upper windows. Signs on the second floor advertise a dentist. A drugs and medicines maker occupied the building at left. (Courtesy of Cold Spring Antiques Center.)

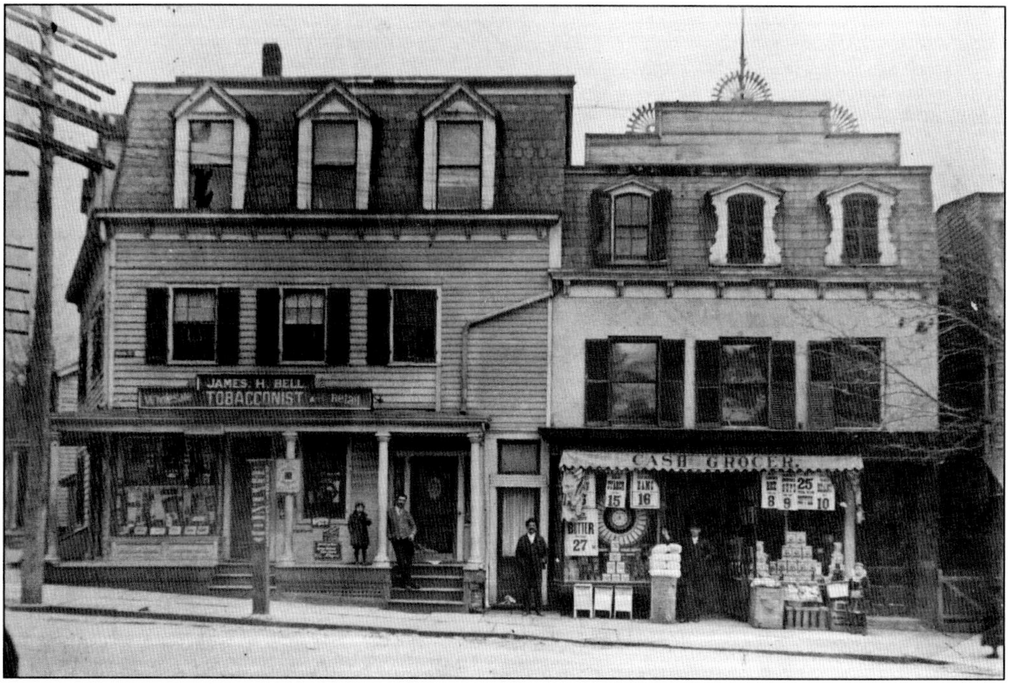

James H. Bell stands on the steps of his tobacconist shop at the corner of Main and Furnace Streets around 1910. The pole in front of Bell's shop advertises postcards. His son Bert, on the porch behind him, became village historian during the 1970s. One proprietor of Cash Grocer rests his arm on bags of goods. Both buildings appear to have undergone multiple alterations. (Courtesy of Francis J. Lahey.)

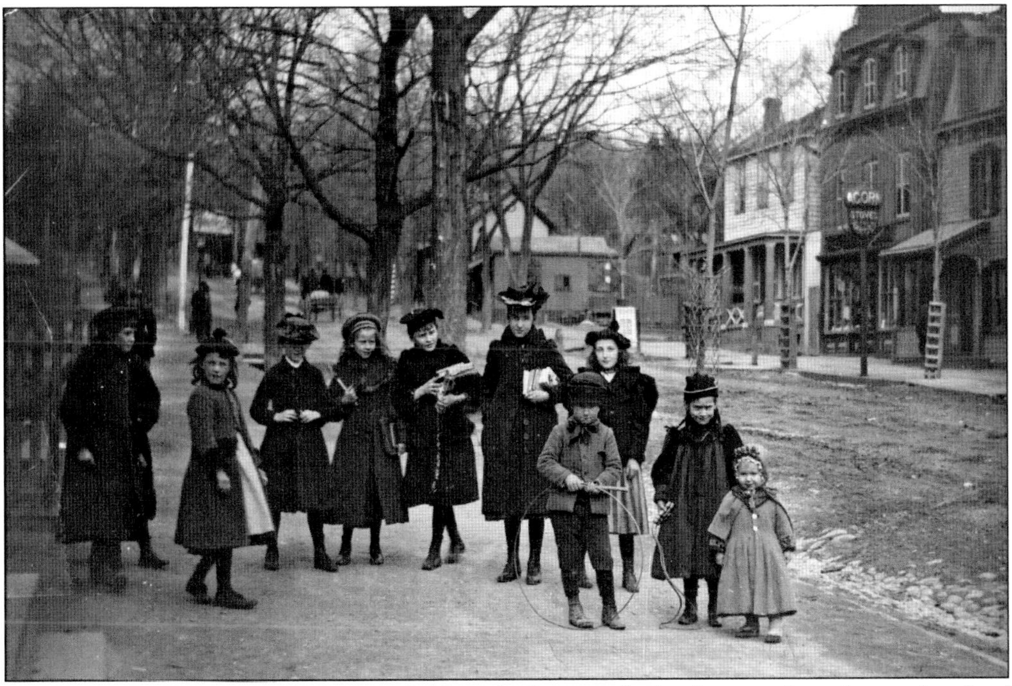

About 1895, schoolgirls and younger children, looking ready for play, stand on the north side of Main Street. Behind the boy is a girl wearing the full sleeves popular then. Hats were socially necessary accessories. A sign across the street advertises Acorn stoves and ranges. Protectors jacket trees on both sides of the street, which was paved in 1926. (Courtesy of PCHS.)

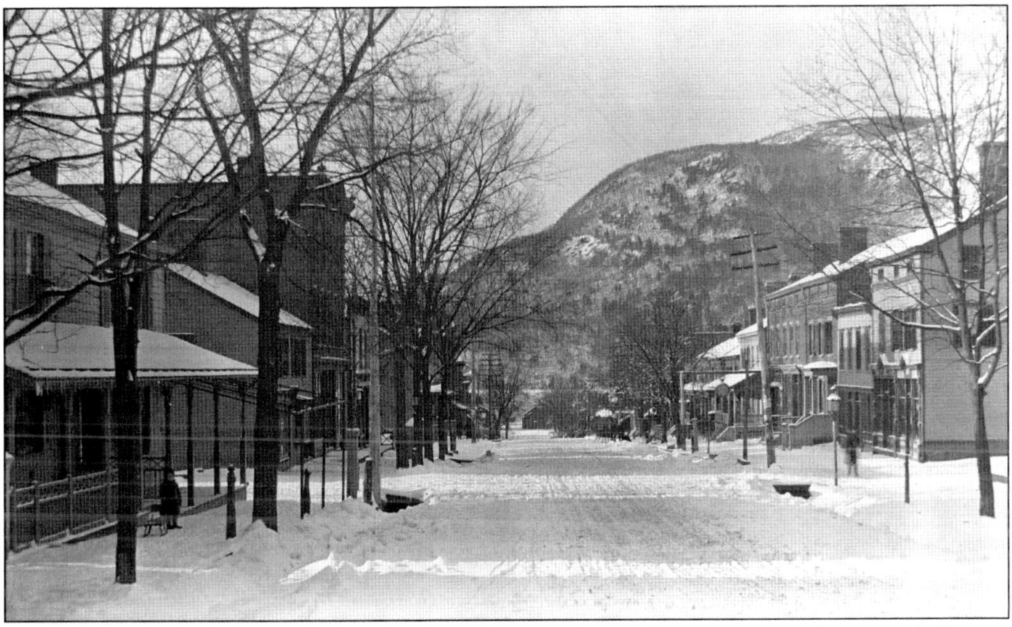

This photograph of a quiet, snowy Main Street captures Crow's Nest across the river. A blurred figure, at right, crosses Garden Street. The suspended replica of a watch advertises a watchmaker, and further down the street, a horse and sleigh wait. Above the junction of Kemble Avenue and Main Street, a child with sled pauses to observe the photographer. (Courtesy of PCHS.)

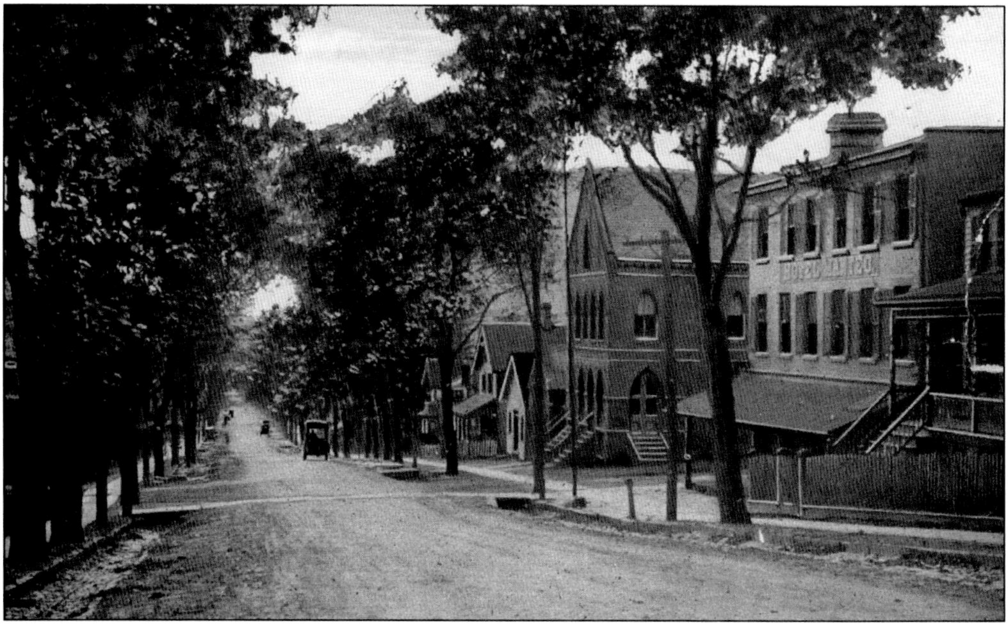

This view west down Main Street, still a dirt road about 1912, shows the Hotel Manteo on the right. The high-gabled brick building next door with arched entry porch and windows, on the other corner of Morris Avenue, was then the P.R. Hoag Co. Knitting Mills, a glove manufacturer. A gas station now stands in its place. (Courtesy of Mark Forlow.)

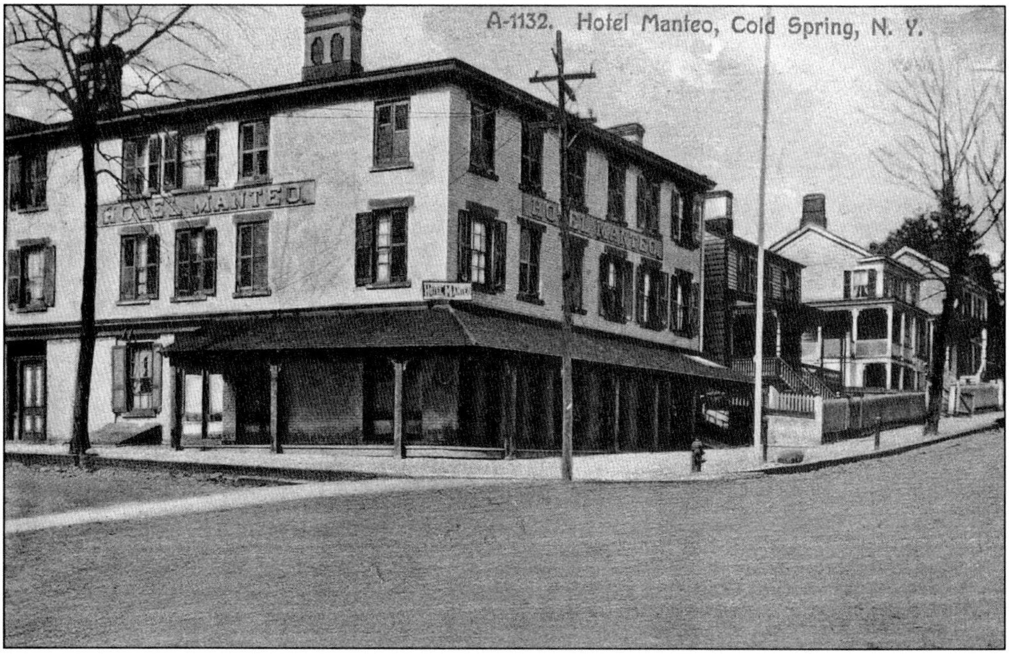

This later photograph of the Hotel Manteo has a utility pole and fireplug clearly in view. Cold Spring installed water mains about 1896 and electricity in 1898. The building housed the Diamond Hotel in 1849 and served as a veterans' hospital during and after the Civil War. It has since served as both a bar and a restaurant. Currently, an awning has replaced the columned porch. (Courtesy of Mark Forlow.)

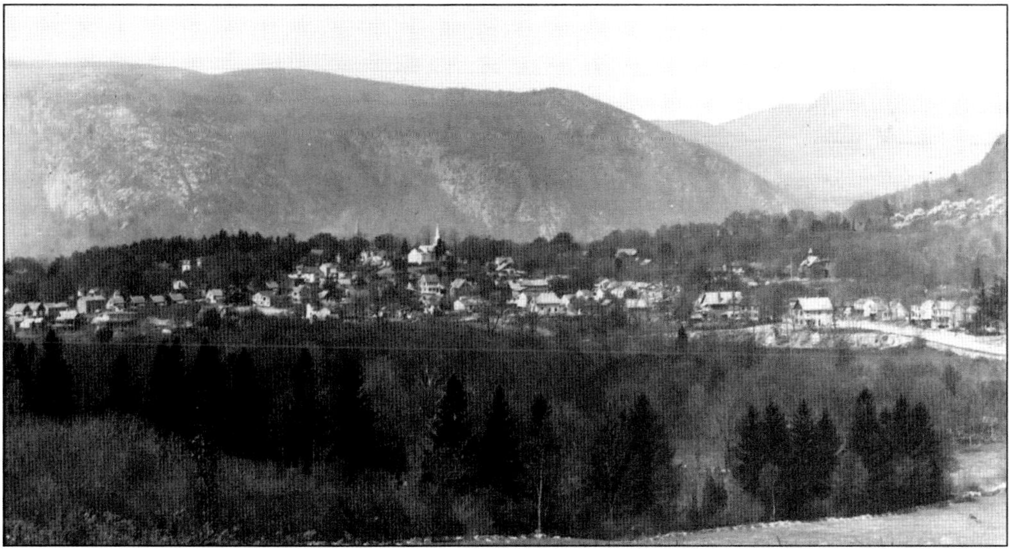

This view looking northwest, taken about 1895, shows part of Cold Spring and most of Nelsonville, which is one square mile in size. The boundary lies just left of the large, white Baptist church, center left, standing on a hill on Main Street. The broad face of Crow's Nest lies across the river. (Courtesy of PCHS.)

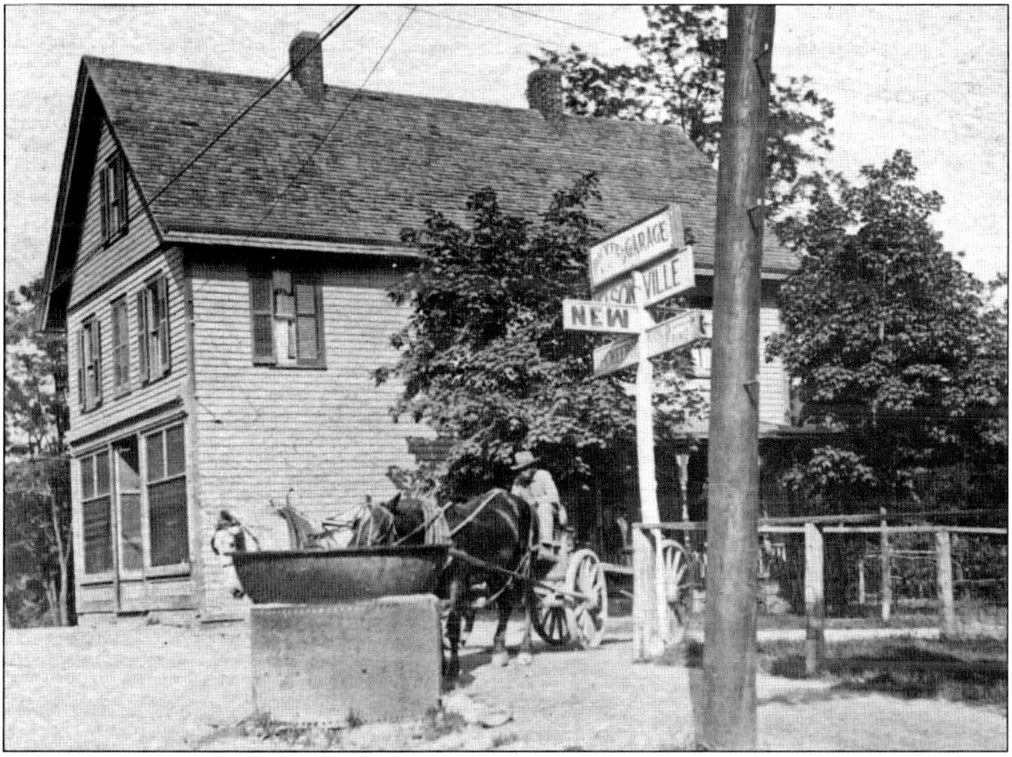

About 1907, a farmer waters his horses at a drinking trough in Nelsonville that was set up at the corner of Main Street and Garrison (now Peekskill) Road around 1896, when a water line was laid along Main Street. The trough was removed when the street was paved about 1925. Three children watch from the porch of the house and store behind. (Courtesy of Josephine Doherty.)

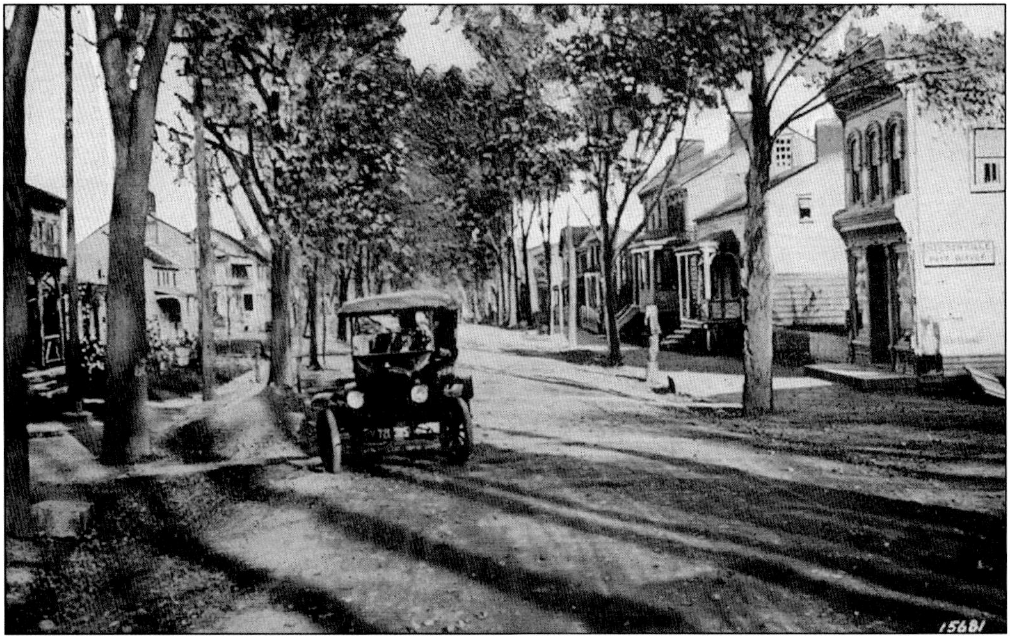

Nelsonville's Main Street, the village's primary business area, is a continuation of Cold Spring's Main Street. On the left is the Fish and Fur Club, which is now the Nelsonville Village Office. The lines of trees are gone. A car has been parked with wheels askew, a precaution against rolling when cars were not equipped with emergency brakes. (Courtesy of Josephine Doherty.)

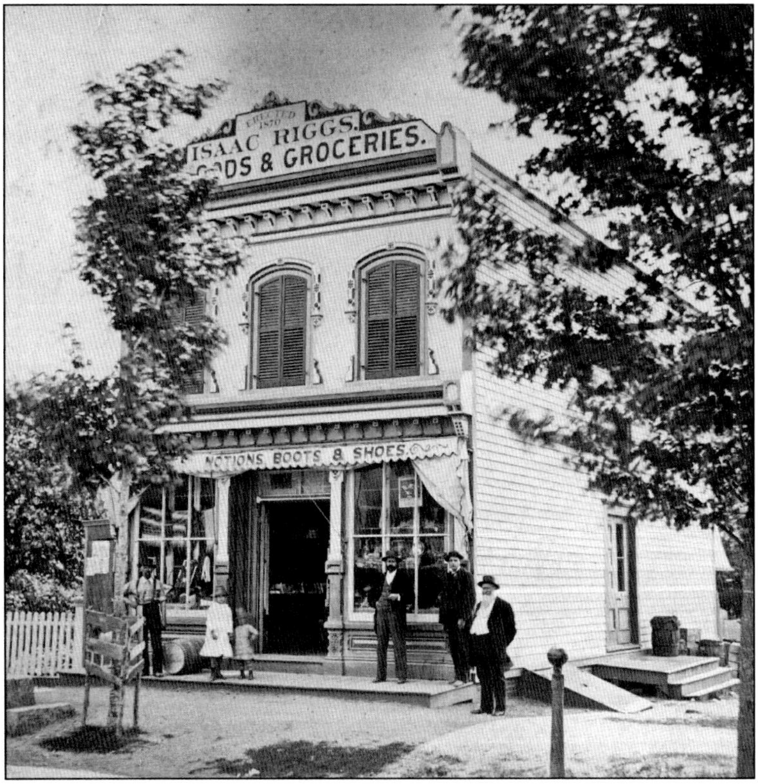

Adults and children pose about 1880 in front of Isaac Riggs's store, established in 1870. Riggs, who was also the postmaster, sold "Goods & Groceries," including "Notions, Boots, & Shoes." A noteworthy example of Nelsonville architecture, the building was in the Italianate style, with a bracketed cornice. Ornamental carving is visible at the base of the right-hand pilaster. (Courtesy of PCHS.)

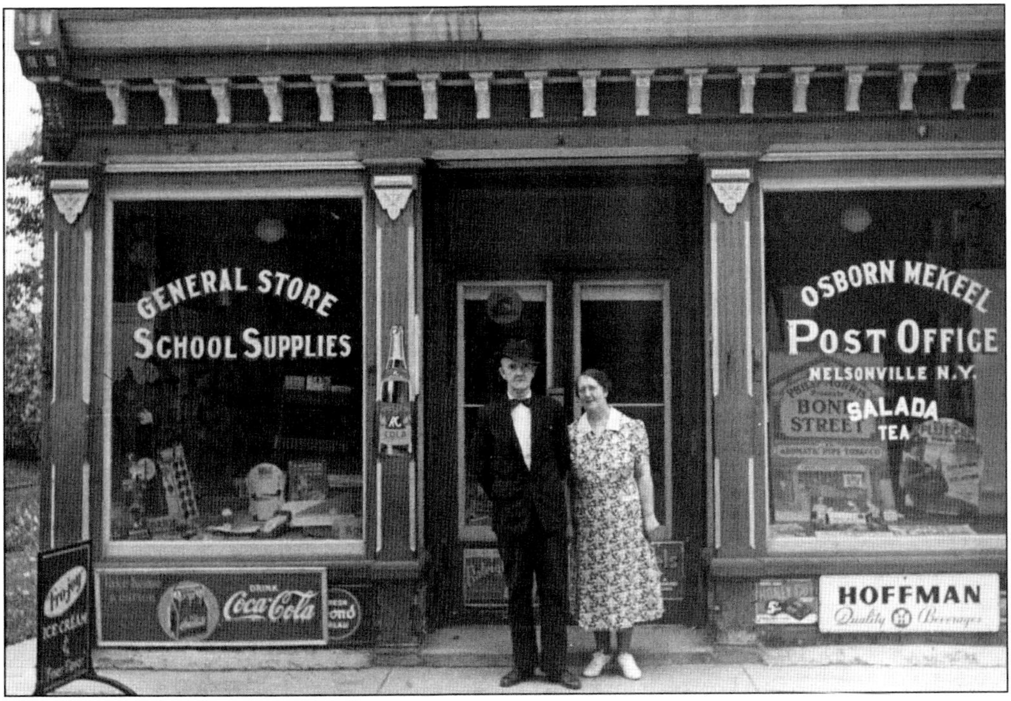

In 1924, Osborn "Ossie" and Catherine Mekeel stand in front of the Osborn Mekeel General Store and Nelsonville Post Office, formerly Riggs's, located at the corner of Main and Pearl Streets. Some Italianate details can be seen in this close-up. The building burned down in 1996 and was replaced by the Village Green. (Courtesy of PCHS.)

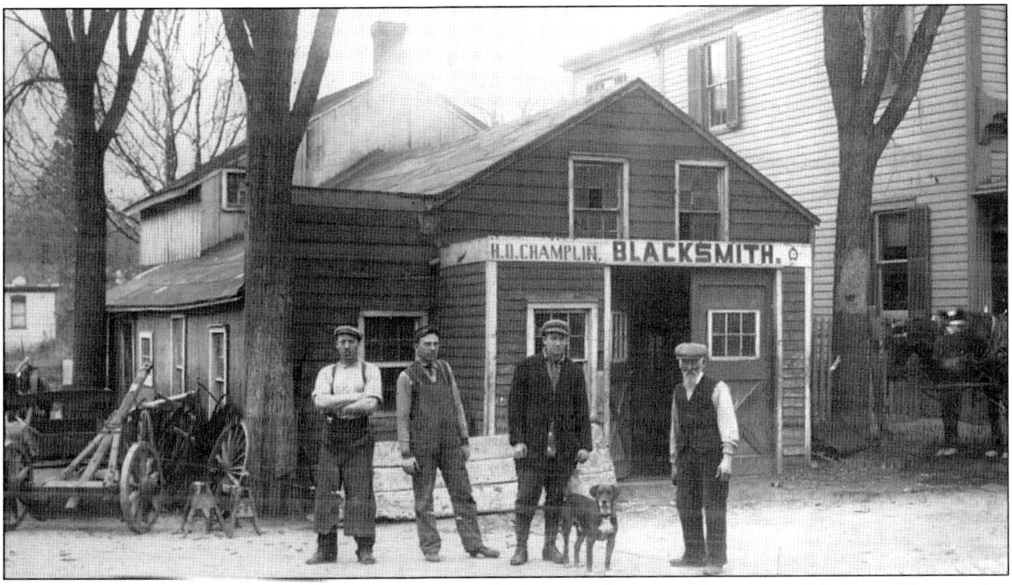

A smith occupied this site, now the corner of Main and Spring Streets in Nelsonville, in the early 1800s. Henry D. Champlin (far right in this 1912 photograph) took over the business in 1858 and was later joined by his son Norman (far left). The business' formal name became H.D. Champlin & Son Horseshoeing and Wagonmaking. Norman Jr. continues the business. (Courtesy of Josephine Doherty.)

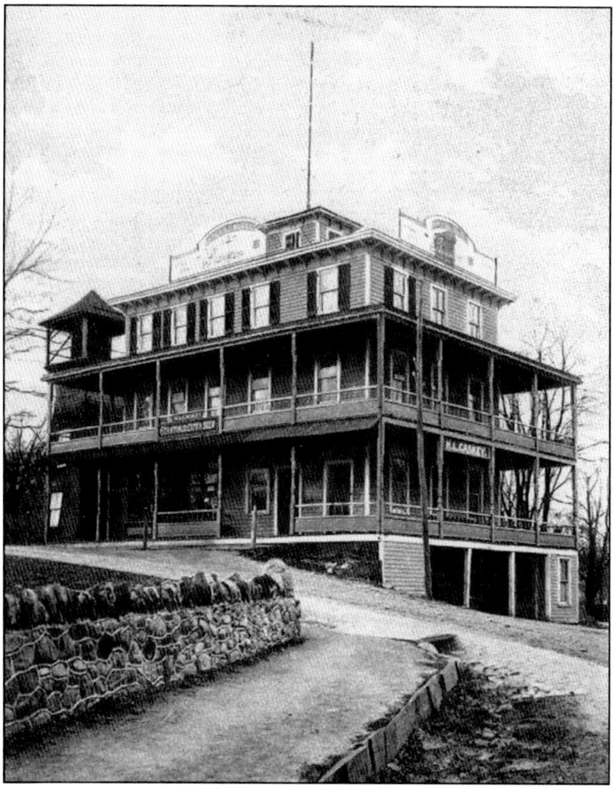

The Imperial Hotel, shown about 1908, was popular with wealthy patrons. It stood at the intersection of Division and Bank Streets in Nelsonville and was noteworthy for its two-story wraparound porch. It also had a bracketed cornice at the top of the third floor. The hotel was destroyed by fire a few years after this photograph was taken. Another Nelsonville hotel was the Alhambra. (Courtesy of Josephine Doherty.)

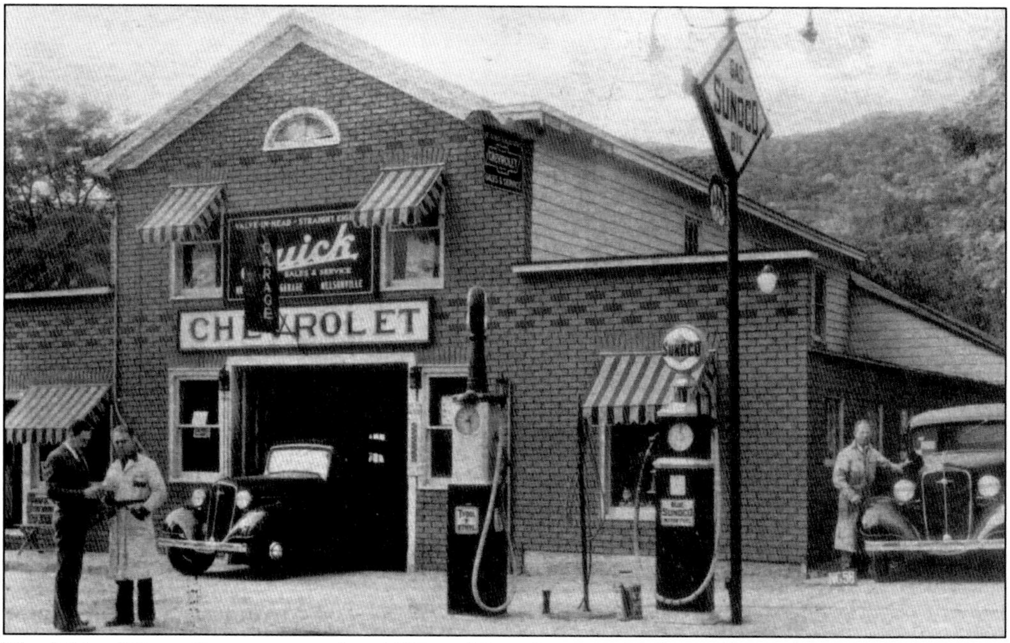

The Mekeel Bros. Garage opened in 1923 on Main Street in Nelsonville. A showroom was added in 1933, and remodeling was done 1945. The Mekeel brothers, Winslow in a white coat and Harry on the left, used this photograph as a business card. The building had once housed the post office, which opened in 1888. (Courtesy of Josephine Doherty.)

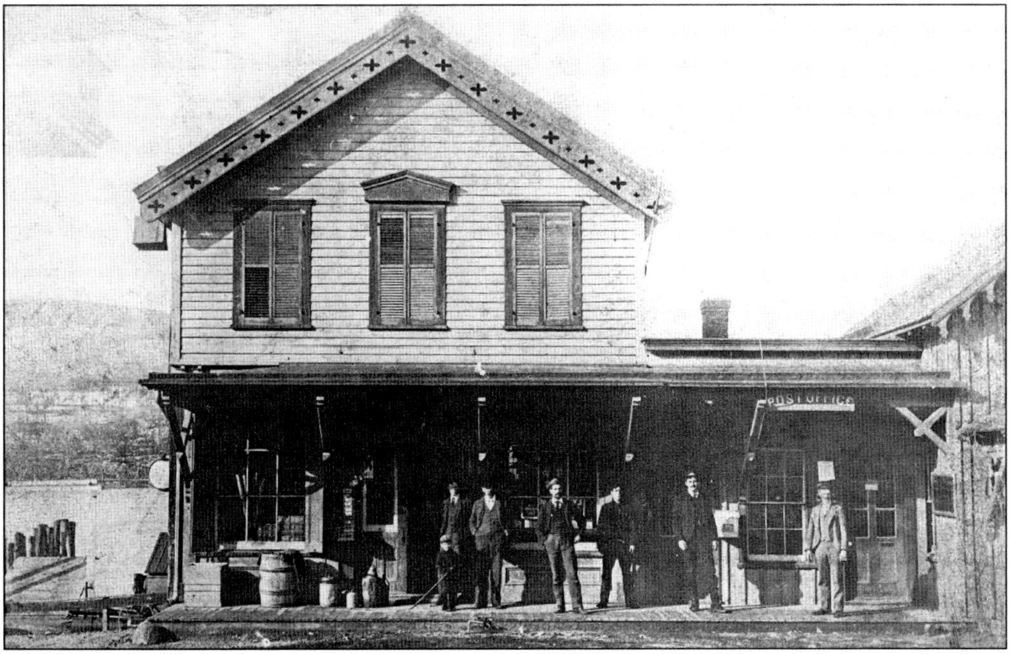

Garrison's Landing, opposite West Point, was, and still is, the main business location in Garrison. The Forson Brothers General Store, shown in 1910, was to the right of one of the ferry and boat docks. The store operated from 1898 to 1963. Bargeboard decorative detail along the building's gable gives it visual interest. The Garrison Post Office to the right shares the porch. (Courtesy of PCHS.)

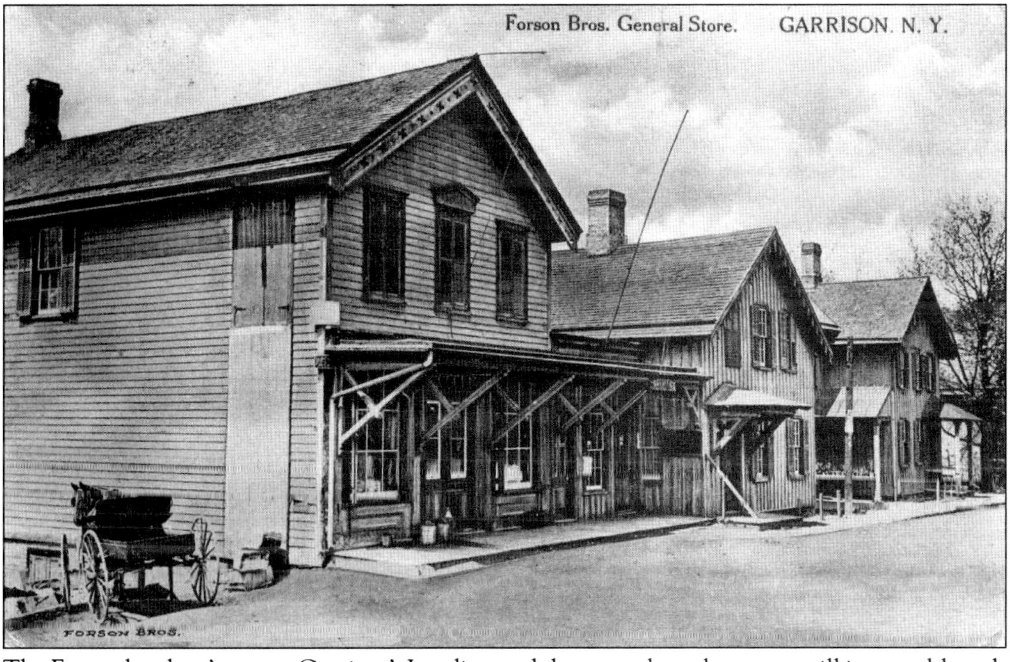

The Forson brothers' store at Garrison's Landing and the two others shown are still in use, although their appearances have been slightly altered over the years. The Garrison Art Center occupies the former Forson store. This area was transformed to portray Yonkers, New York, during the 1968 filming of *Hello, Dolly!* (Courtesy of Antipodean Books, Maps & Prints.)

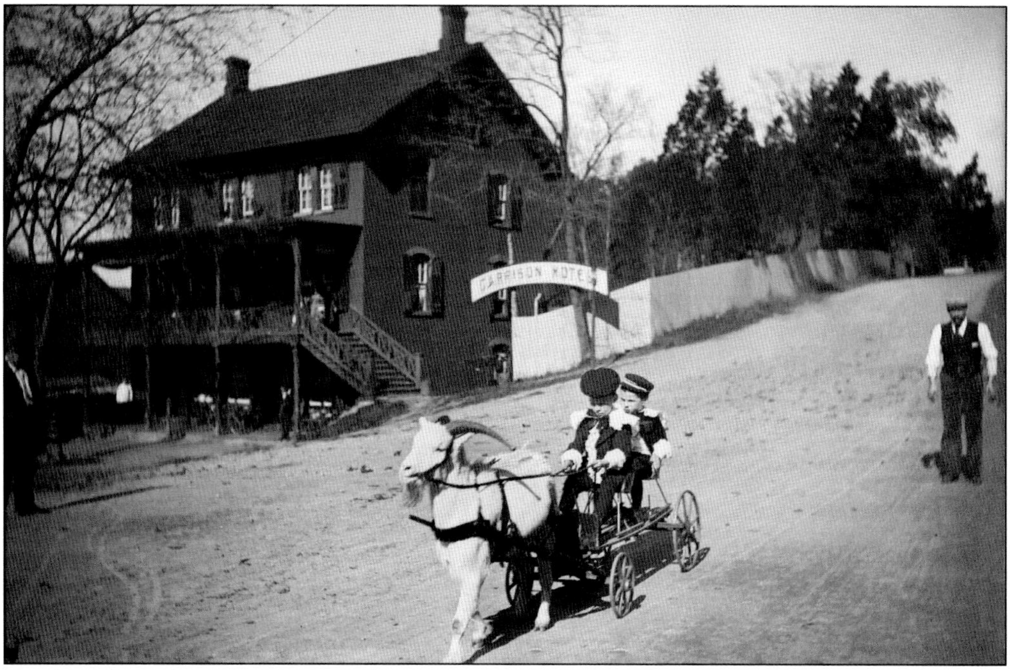

Two boys drive their goat cart past the Garrison Hotel on Dock Street in Garrison. The building was used as a hotel from about 1854 to 1923. The Garrison was in business from at least 1881 to 1923. Before that, Ganung's Hotel & Livery Stable occupied the building. It has been home to many businesses, including a speakeasy during Prohibition. (Courtesy of PCHS.)

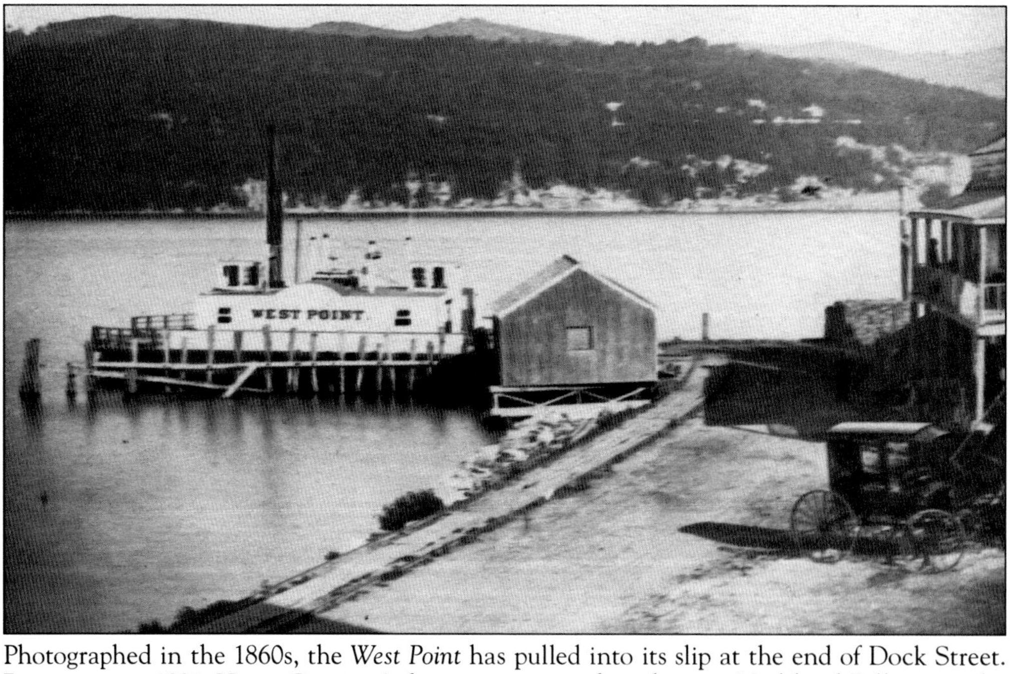

Photographed in the 1860s, the *West Point* has pulled into its slip at the end of Dock Street. Beginning in 1821, Harry Garrison's ferry service ran from here to Highland Falls, near the main part of West Point. The two-story Dock House is at the right. A number of 19th-century photographs and prints have similar views. (Courtesy of Antipodean Books, Maps & Prints.)

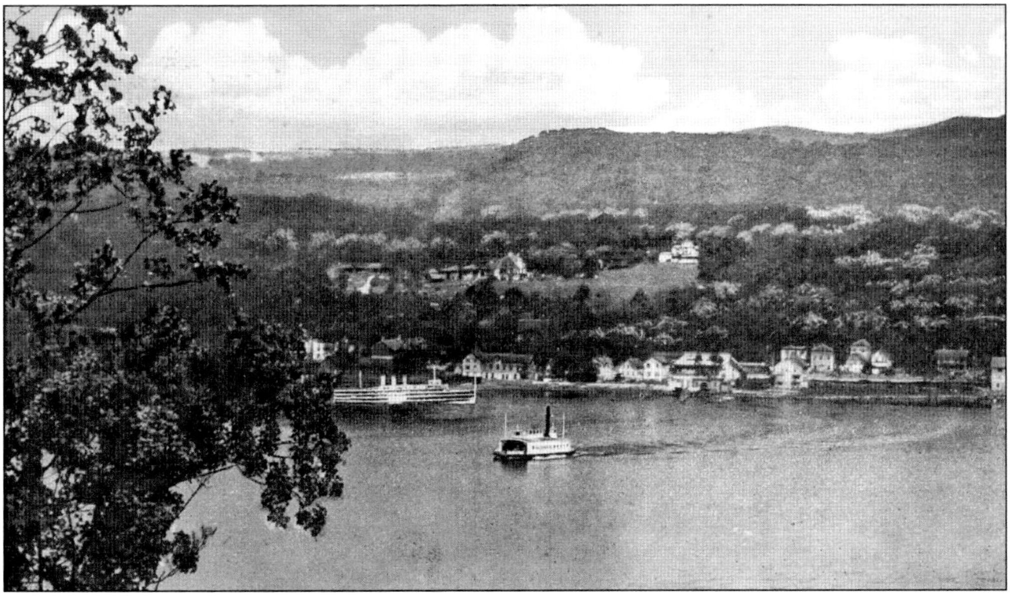

A view from the west bank of the Hudson River shows the *Highlander*, a ferry that crossed the waterway between 1878 and 1928. A new ferry slip was built for it in 1878, south of the dock area pictured here. The Bear Mountain Bridge, constructed in 1924 about 4.5 miles to the south, put the ferries out of business. (Courtesy of PCHS.)

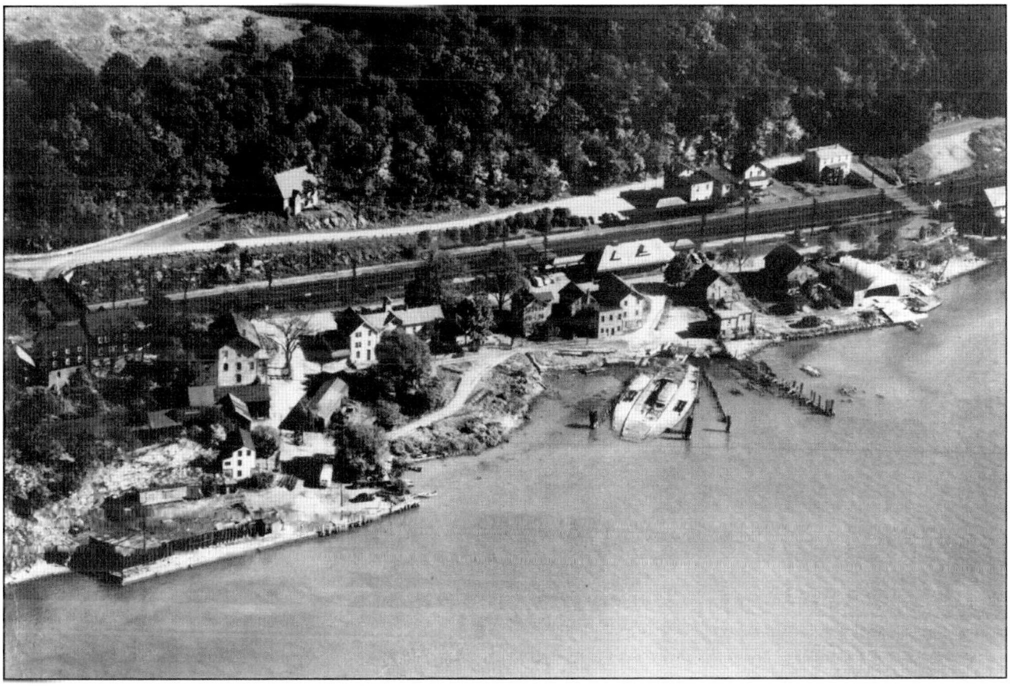

In 1928, the *Highlander* sprang a leak and sank at Garrison's Landing. Her superstructure was partially dismantled and her engine sold for scrap during World War II. For many years, her skeleton was visible during low tide. In 1957, Osborn Marine Park was created here in honor of William Church Osborn, the first president of the Hudson River Conservation Society. A gazebo was built in 1968. (Courtesy of PCHS.)

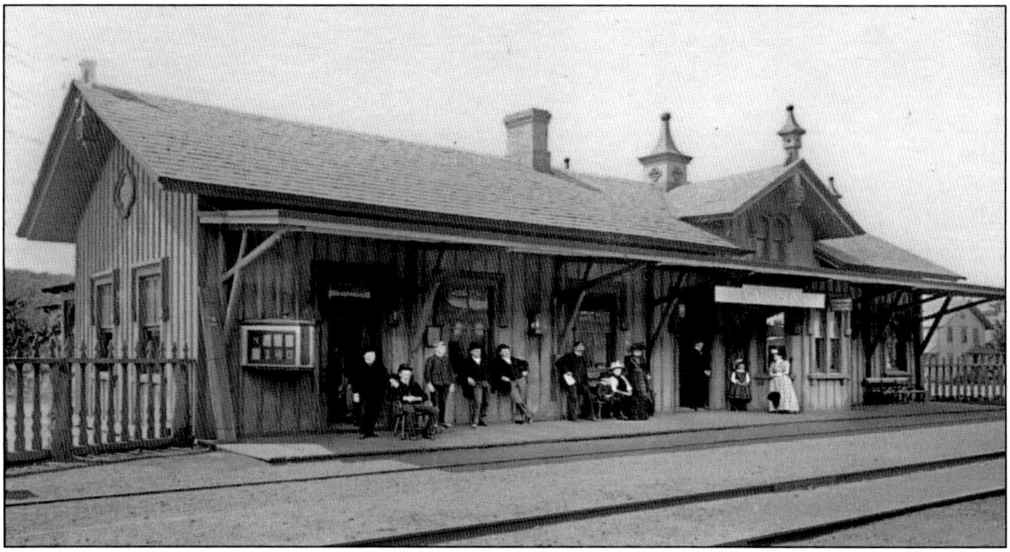

The Garrison Depot, with board-and-batten siding, was moved down the track slightly to this location in 1870. In 1892, the building was purchased, moved to its present site near the corner of Dock Street, given additions, and used as a library until 1942. It now houses businesses. (Courtesy of Antipodean Books, Maps & Prints.)

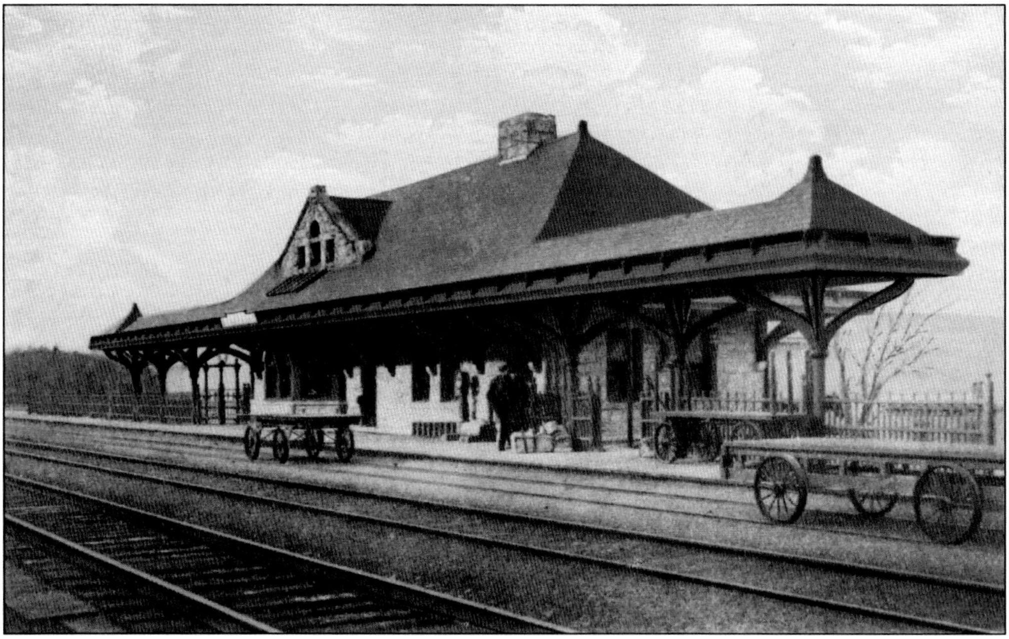

Cold Spring contractor William La Due completed this station in 1893. Although the heavy stone suggests the Romanesque Revival style, graceful columns split into S-curves, and bracketing connects the facade to the roof. The quality of construction may have been partly due to the influence of prominent railroad men who were summer residents, including John M. Toucey and Samuel Sloan. (Courtesy of Antipodean Books, Maps & Prints.)

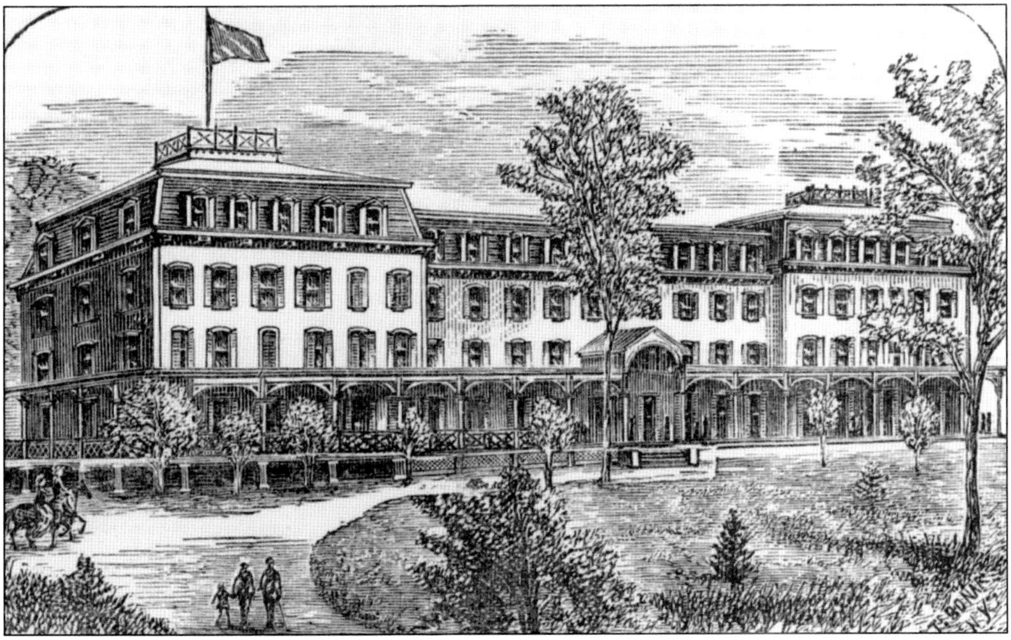

The Highland House in Garrison, shown on an 1879 receipt, stood across from St. Philip's Church. It was a joint venture of the brothers William and George Garrison. Dates vary as to its opening, but its heyday seems to have been from 1866 to 1888. William Garrison was well regarded in the hotel business. Demolition began on the building in 1908. (Courtesy of PCHS.)

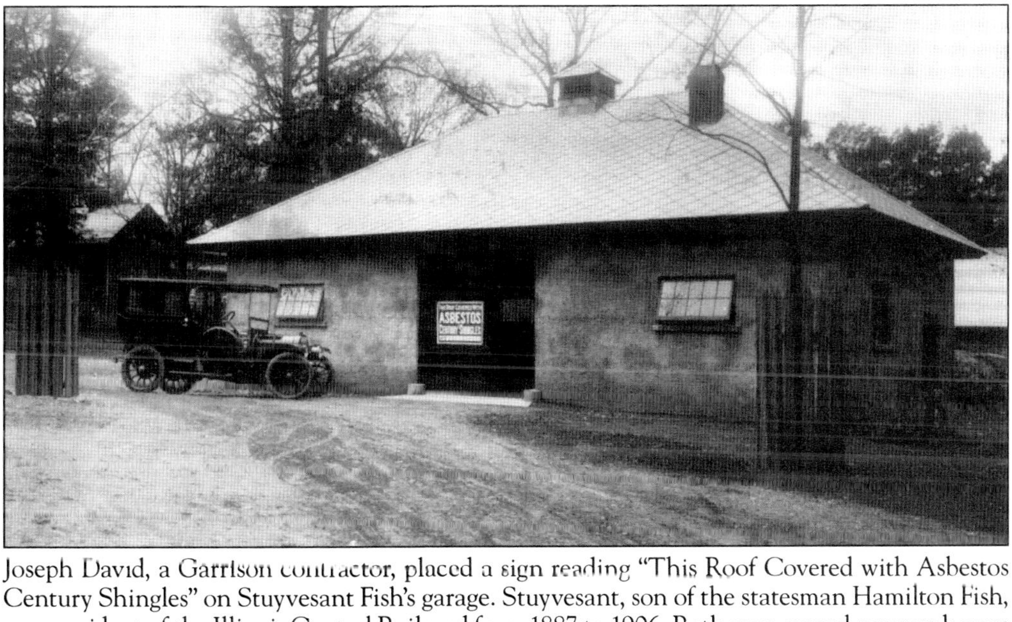

Joseph David, a Garrison contractor, placed a sign reading "This Roof Covered with Asbestos Century Shingles" on Stuyvesant Fish's garage. Stuyvesant, son of the statesman Hamilton Fish, was president of the Illinois Central Railroad from 1887 to 1906. Both men owned summer homes in Garrison. (Courtesy of Mark Forlow.)

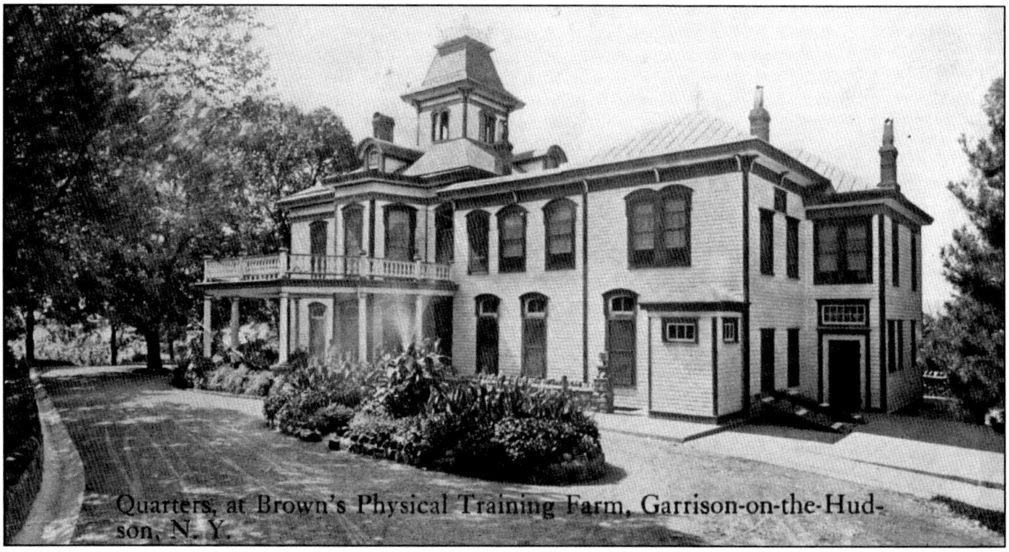

Bill Brown's Physical Training Farm, on what is now Route 9 in Garrison, operated from about 1909 to 1943, primarily catering to wealthy men from New York City. The main building, with Italianate windows and a porte cochere, housed a dining room and sleeping quarters. Brown had inherited a well-known gym in New York in 1904. The 180-acre tract was sold in 1959 and became the Garrison Golf Course. (Courtesy of PCHS.)

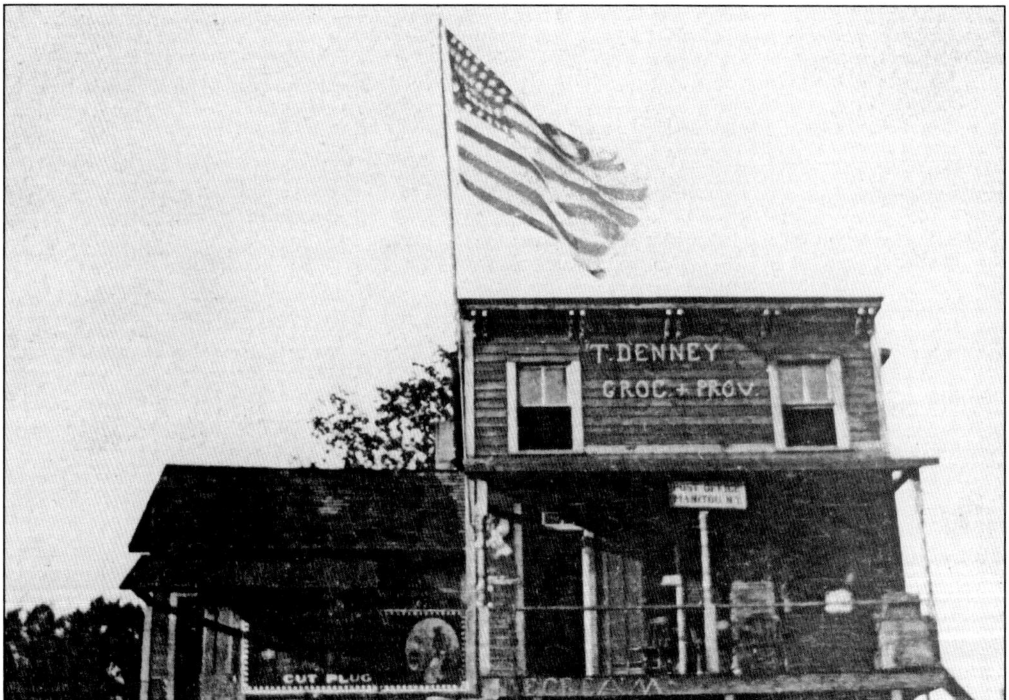

The T. Denney Grocery & Provisions Store in Manitou stood near present-day Route 9D and Manitou Station Road on property now owned by the Polhemus family. Miners working for the Hudson River Copper Company, which closed about 1900, bought their provisions here. The building was torn down in the 1960s. (Courtesy of the Polhemus family.)

Three

Putting Resources to Work

West Point Foundry and Other Industries

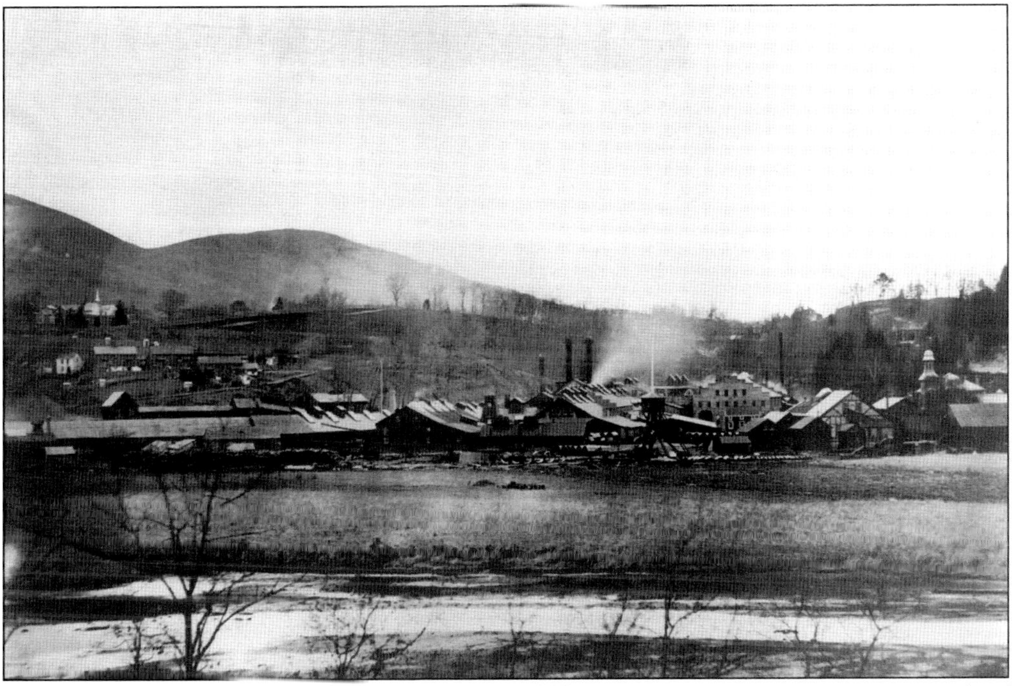

The West Point Foundry, shown not long after 1865, was located on Foundry Cove, south of Cold Spring's Main Street. It opened in 1818 and became one of America's major 19th-century industrial sites. During the Civil War, it produced rifled cannons designed by Robert Parrott, the superintendent at the foundry. Other iron products included steam engines, sugar mills, and the first iron ship made in the nation. (Courtesy of PCHS.)

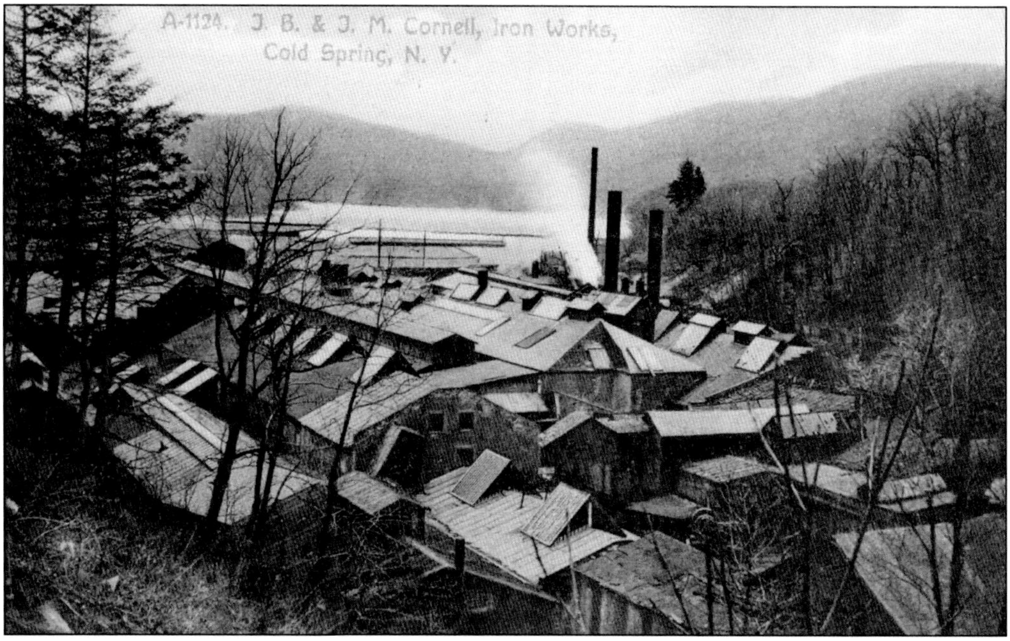

In 1897, the J.B. & J.M. Cornell Company, photographed looking toward Foundry Cove, took over the West Point Foundry, where production had dwindled, and increased output. The local newspaper called the change "a great boon for Cold Spring." Cornell ceased production in 1909. Recent archaeological work has helped to preserve the site's industrial history. (Courtesy of PCHS.)

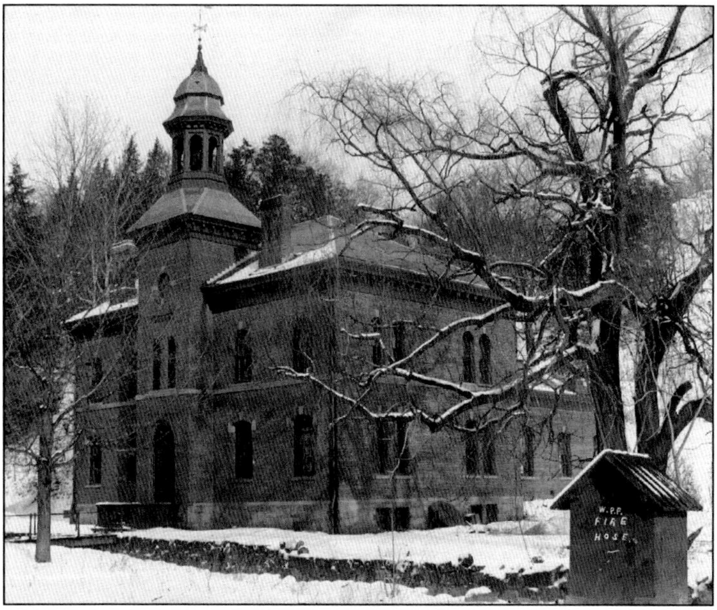

The brick administrative building (1865) of the West Point Foundry has been saved thanks to Scenic Hudson, which stabilized the structure and is developing the site as the West Point Foundry Preserve. Additions and alterations were made to the building's core. Foundry Brook flows in front of it. Pres. Abraham Lincoln visited the foundry in 1862 during the Civil War. (Courtesy of PCHS.)

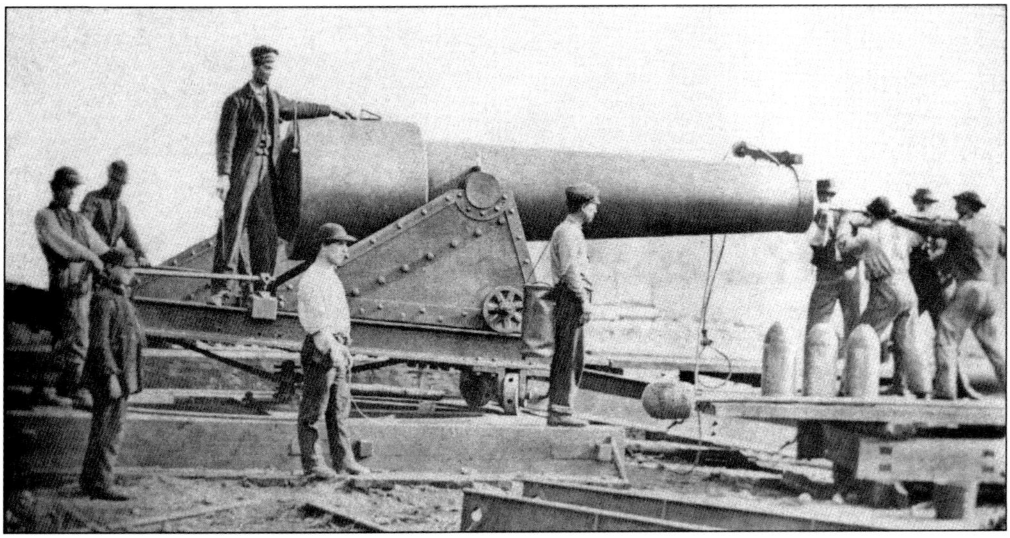

On May 1, 1864, West Point Foundry workers prove a 300-pounder Parrott gun, firing at Crow's Nest. The gun's name refers to the weight of the projectile. The gun was also known as a 10-inch rifle and was the largest of the Parrott guns made during the Civil War period. Few of them were produced, and their utilization was limited. Smaller versions witnessed widespread use. (Courtesy of PCHS.)

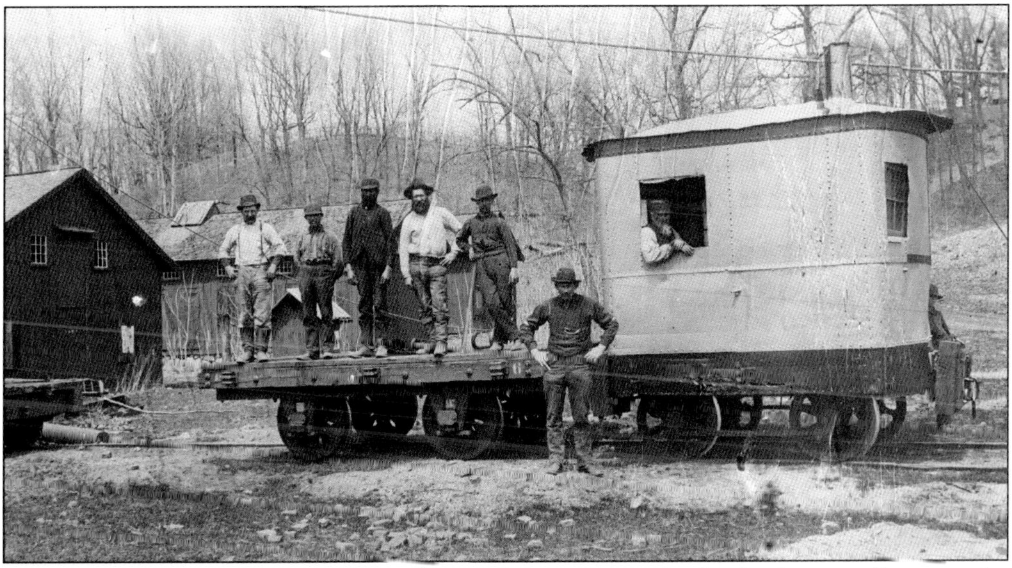

Workmen pose with *The Pioneer*, a small steam locomotive said to be the first to pull cars on the Ninth Avenue El (elevated line) in New York City. Put into use at the foundry, it carried materials from the production area onto the foundry dock, which extended from the north side of Foundry Cove. Note the foreman's watch chain and aggressive pose. (Courtesy of PCHS.)

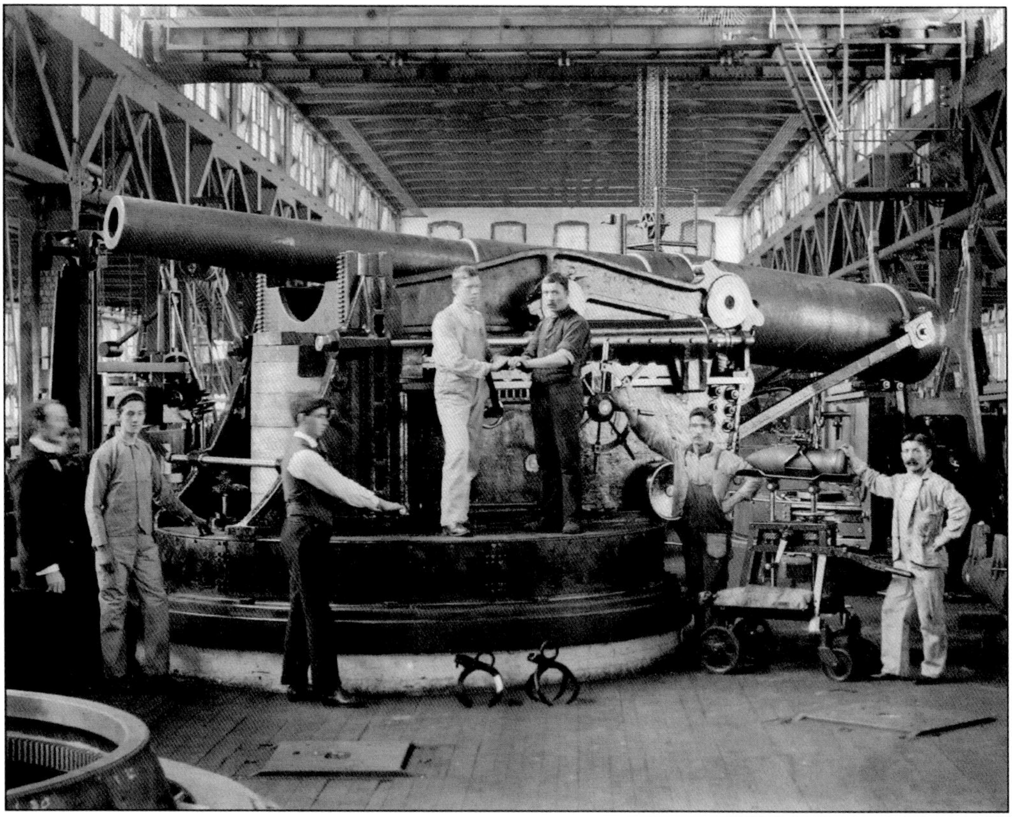

Workmen display an 1896, LF model eight-inch disappearing gun, so named because it shot shells eight inches in diameter and was mounted on a carriage that could be rotated backwards and down into a pit. Parts produced at the West Point Foundry were assembled here at the Pond Machine and Tool Company in Plainfield, New Jersey, probably for shipment to Sandy Hook, the site of batteries to protect New York Harbor. (Courtesy of PCHS.)

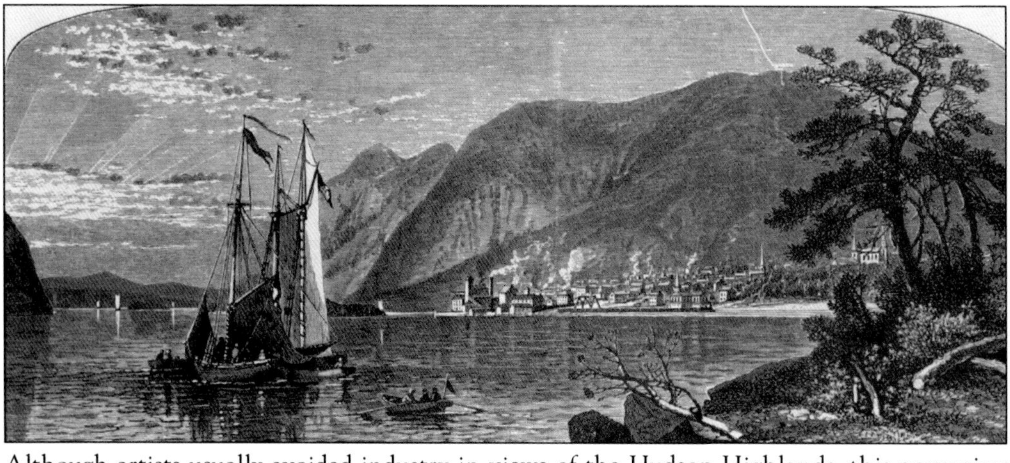

Although artists usually avoided industry in views of the Hudson Highlands, this engraving dating after 1867 depicts the industrial presence in Cold Spring. The view is from the western end of Constitution Island. The artist also shows the Victorian Chapel of Our Lady, located on the waterfront, and many of Cold Spring's other churches. (Courtesy of Hudson Rogue Co.)

Smoke rises from the Beek & Tower Blast Furnace Company, constructed about 1864 at the river's edge on West Street. An 1867 map identifies it. Maps from 1876 and 1891 identify the site as that of the West Point Furnace Company. The triangular sail visible at the photograph's left edge belongs to a sloop at the Cold Spring dock. (Courtesy of Mark Forlow.)

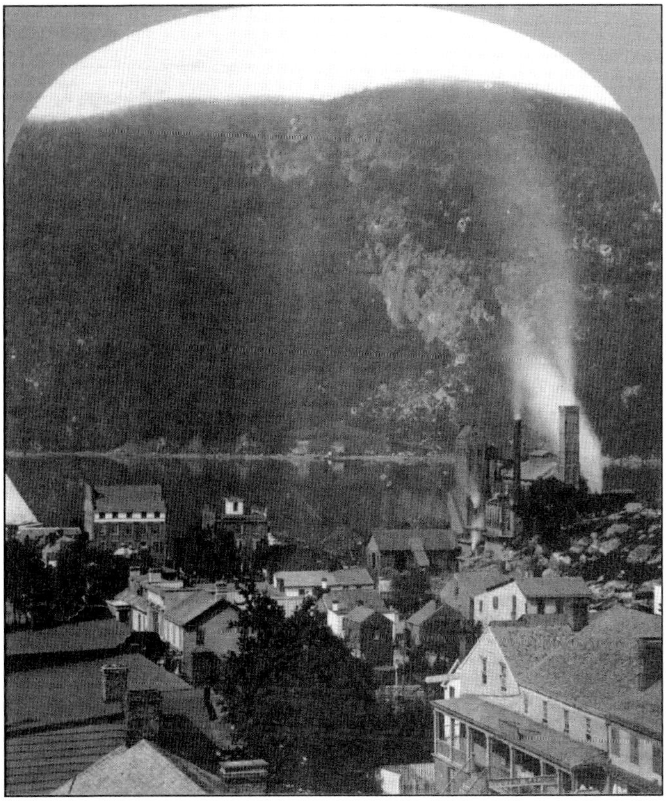

The West Point Furnace Company is seen from the river before 1894, when the buildings were razed except for one of the furnaces. Anthracite, or hard coal, which burned cleanly, was used in the facility. Views of Cold Spring are dated after 1894 if a virtually empty area exists here. (Courtesy of PCHS.)

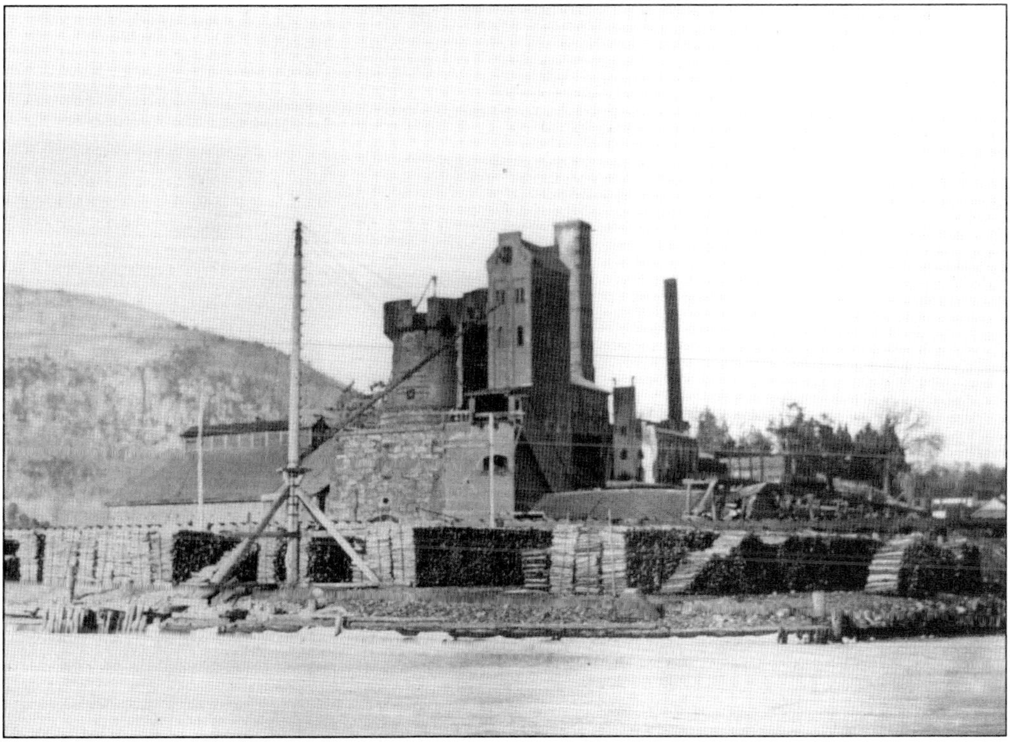

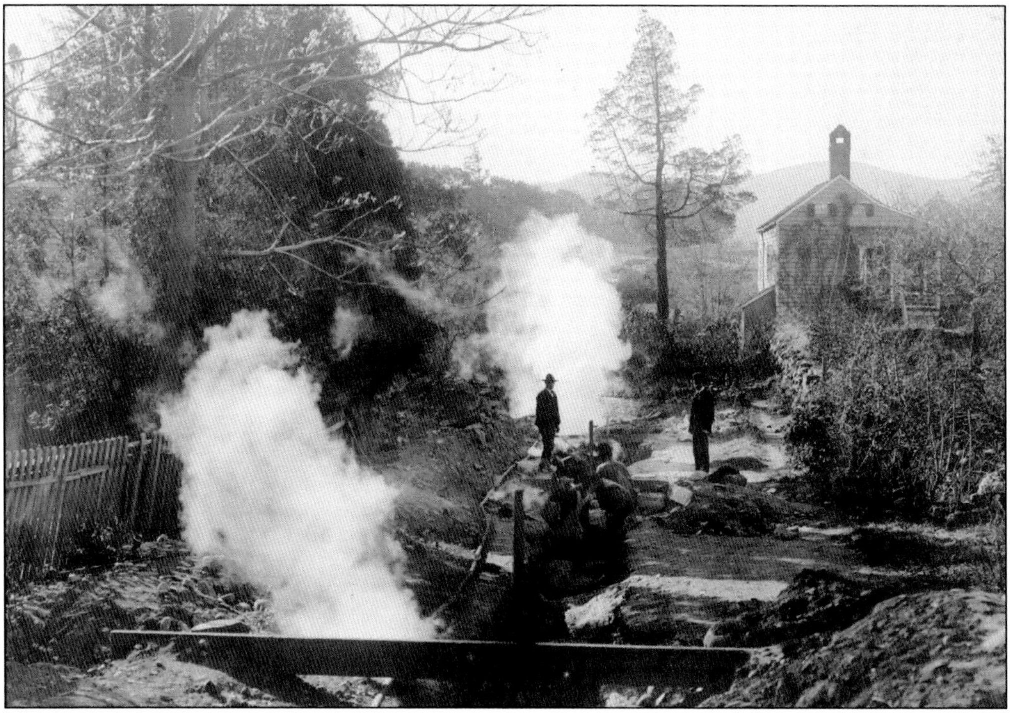

Under the eyes of supervisors, workmen break up stone as they deepen a ditch along Kemble Avenue for water pipes about 1895. That date is relatively early for a village water system, but Cold Spring needed water to prevent the spread of fire at industrial sites, among them the West Point Foundry. (Courtesy of PCHS.)

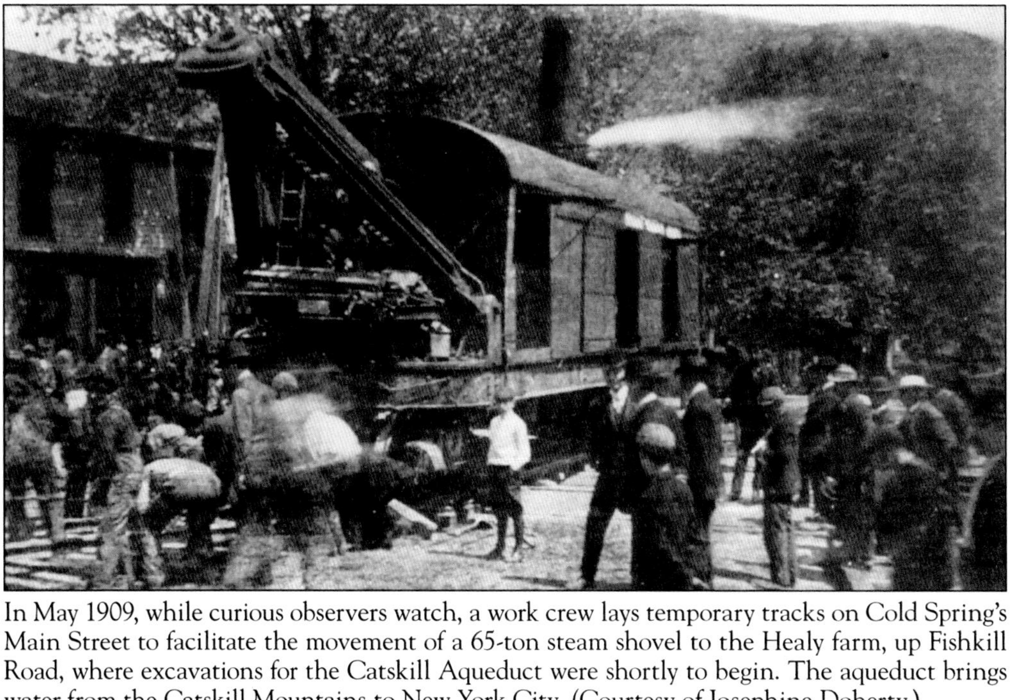

In May 1909, while curious observers watch, a work crew lays temporary tracks on Cold Spring's Main Street to facilitate the movement of a 65-ton steam shovel to the Healy farm, up Fishkill Road, where excavations for the Catskill Aqueduct were shortly to begin. The aqueduct brings water from the Catskill Mountains to New York City. (Courtesy of Josephine Doherty.)

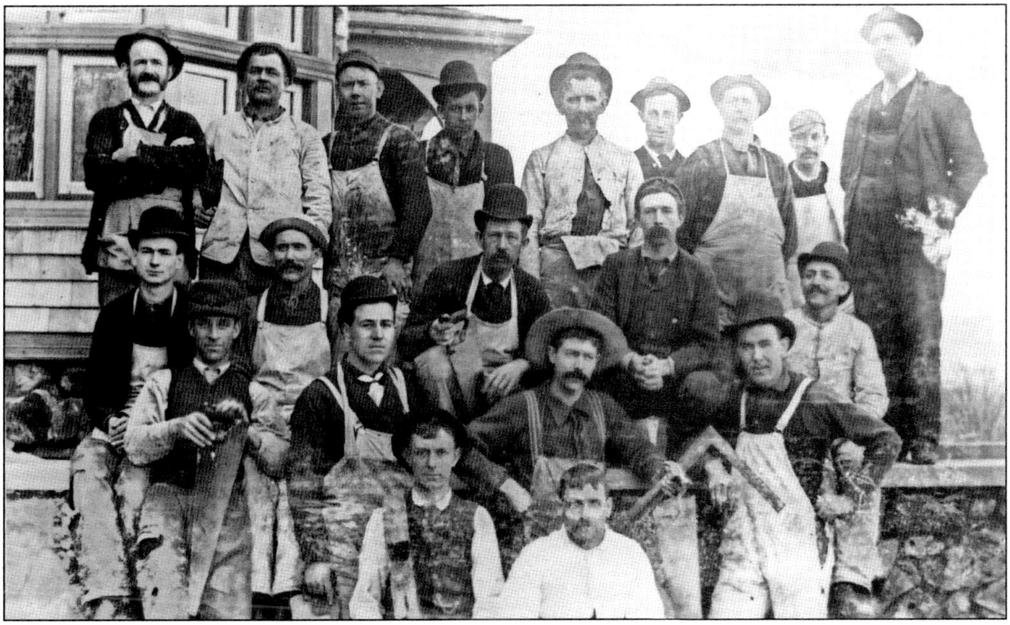

Carpenters, many of them wearing the aprons of their trade, have a variety of hats and expressions. One man holds a carpenter's square, a hammer, and his saw, one of four in the photograph. The detached looking man at the top right may be the foreman. The building behind the men is likely their latest project, a shingled Philipstown house with a projecting bay. (Courtesy of PCHS.)

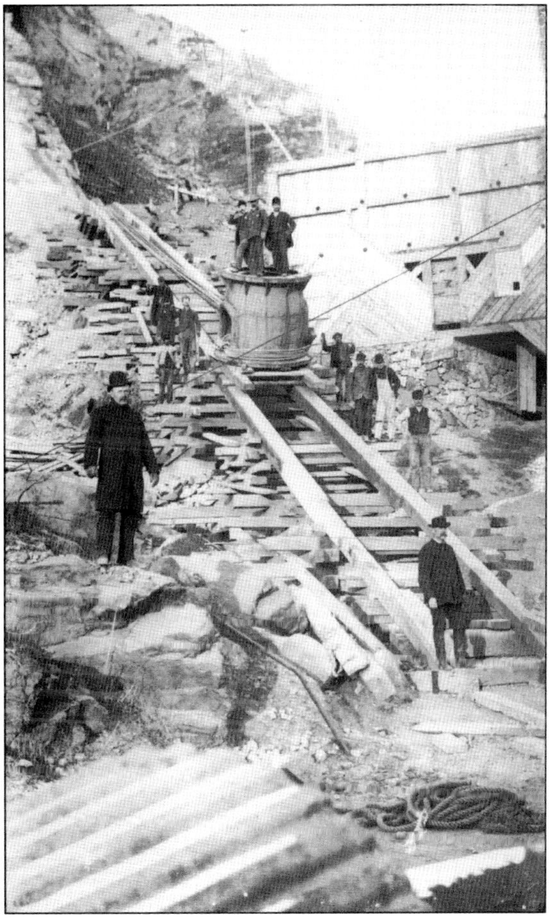

Bull Hill at Little Stony Point and Breakneck were quarrying sites. Although identification on the back of this photograph indicates quarrying on Breakneck, some researchers think that it may show work on the Catskill Aqueduct, which was begun in 1907. Part of the construction involved sinking shafts into Storm King and Breakneck to build a tunnel about 1,100 feet under the Hudson River. (Courtesy of PCHS.)

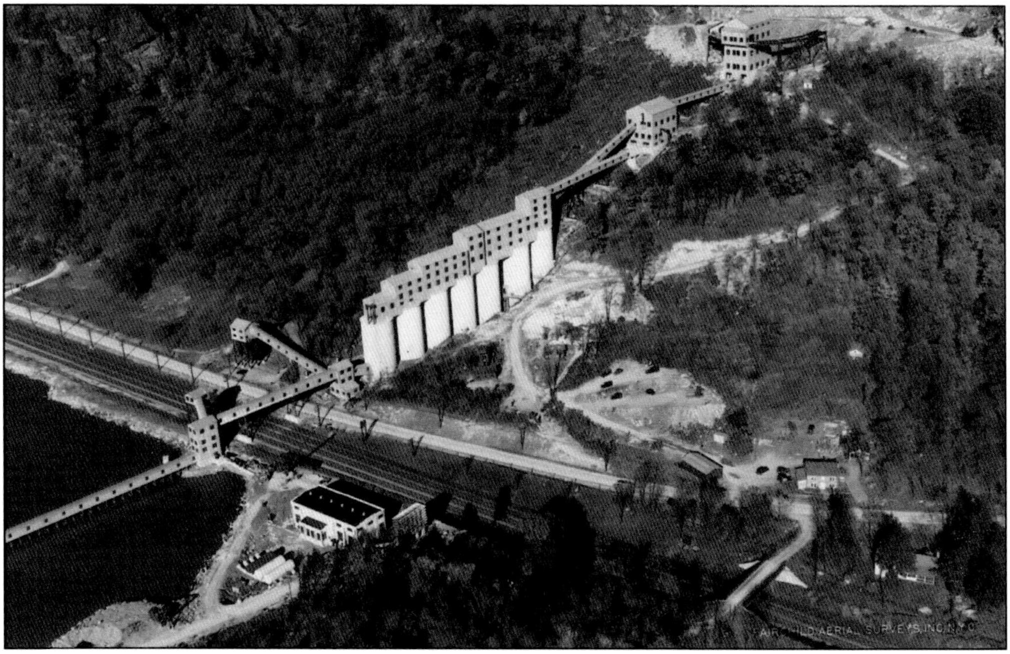

During the 1930s, a large employer, the Hudson River Stone Company, bought 1,000 acres of Bull Hill, blasted a gash across it, and filled some 20 acres of underwater land with rubble. Stone was crushed to varying sizes and sorted by silo as it descended. Prominent citizens formed the Hudson River Conservation Society, purchased land, and negotiated contracts with property owners to protect other areas from destruction. (Courtesy of Francis J. Lahey.)

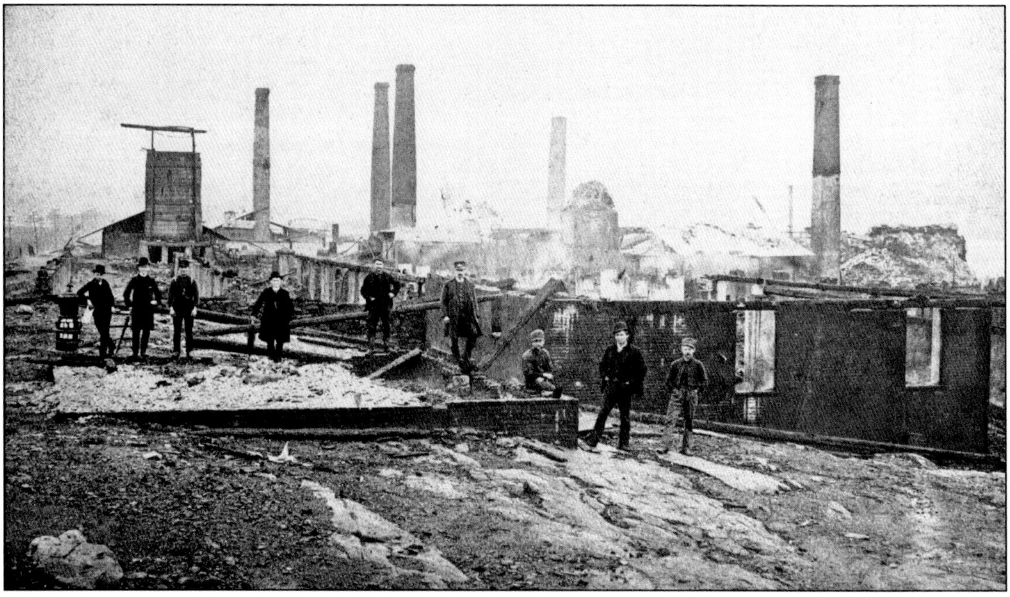

Employing men at its plant and in nearby mines, the Highland Chemical and Mining Company at Manitou Landing in southern Philipstown, established in 1873, made sulfuric acid from iron sulfide it mined. An 1889 fire that consumed 17 of its 20 buildings caused local hardship. After rebuilding in 1892, the plant continued under a new name, Waugh Chemical Company. It merged with General Chemical in 1900 and closed in 1913. (Courtesy of PCHS.)

Four

Getting Together
Associations, Socializing, and Celebrations

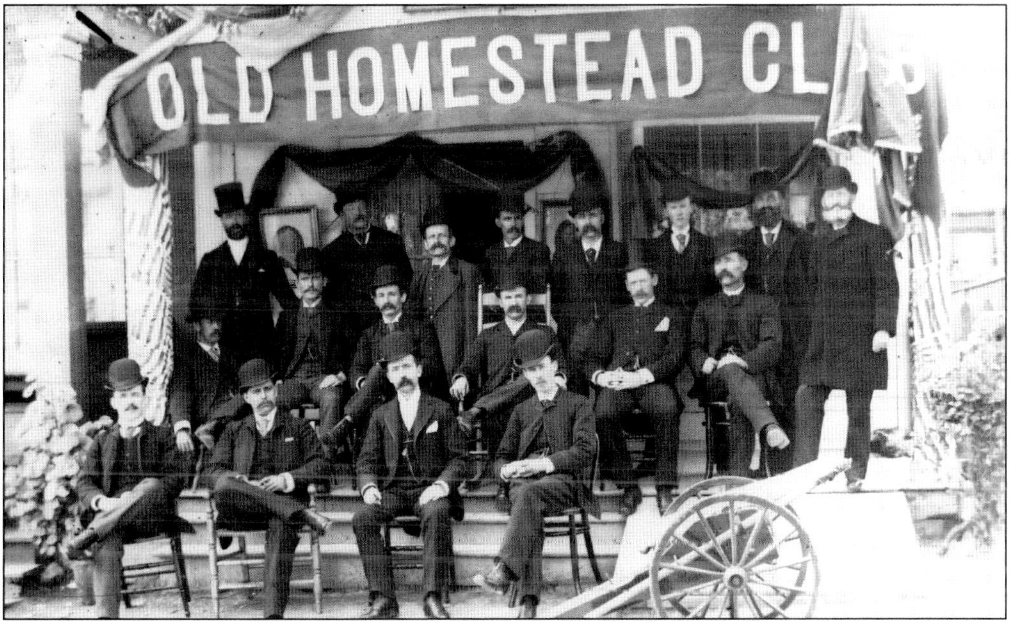

Members of the Old Homestead Club pose on the porch and steps of their clubhouse in Cold Spring. Most of them wear the high-crowned bowlers and mustaches popular in the 1880s. The club started around 1882 when local residents, mainly businessmen, began meeting in Spaulding's Pharmacy. They later built this clubhouse on Main Street. The saluting gun, probably from the West Point Foundry, was used in parades. (Courtesy of PCHS.)

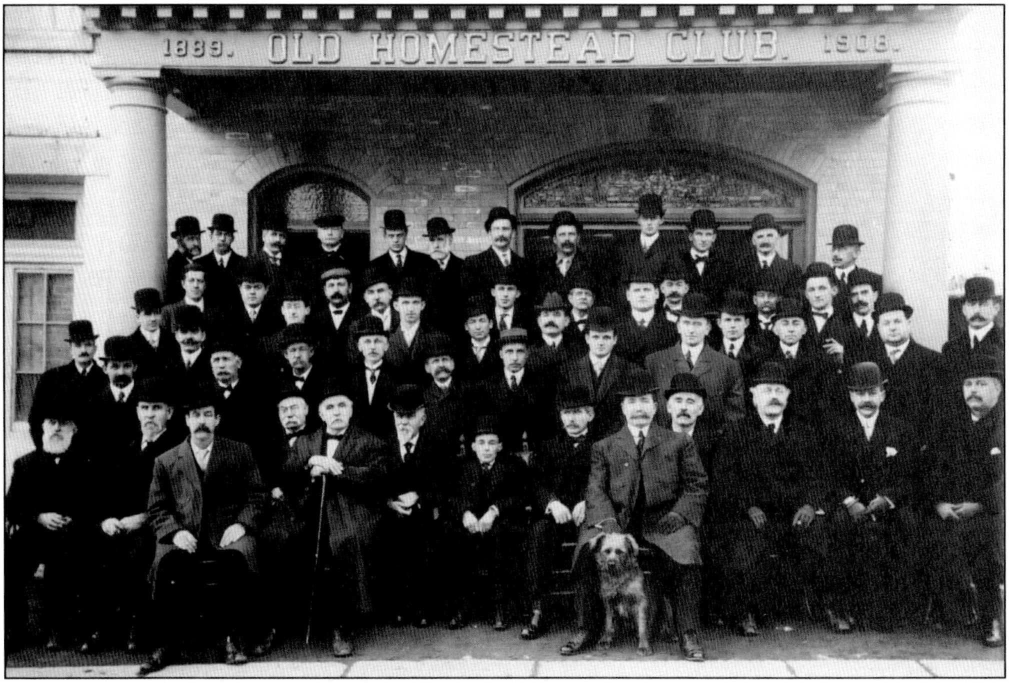

In 1909, the Old Homestead Club dedicated its second and larger clubhouse at the same location as its first. Members were photographed in front of it at the ceremony. Judge William Wood, an influential politician and club president, sits in the first row (left) with a cane. He emigrated from Ireland as a child, worked for a time at the foundry, and later became a judge. (Courtesy of PCHS.)

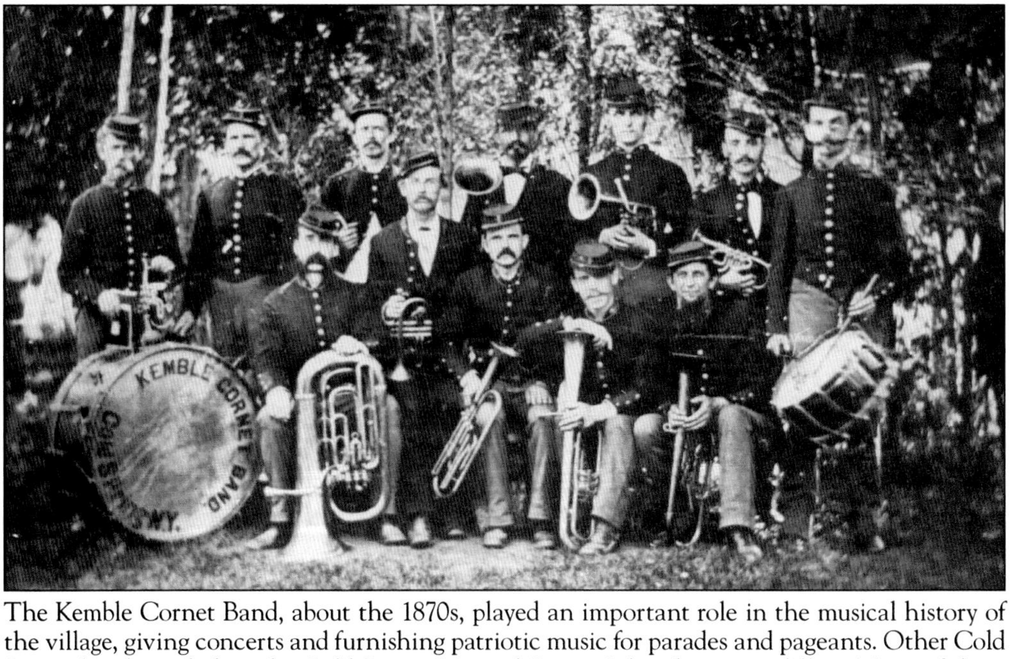

The Kemble Cornet Band, about the 1870s, played an important role in the musical history of the village, giving concerts and furnishing patriotic music for parades and pageants. Other Cold Spring bands, including the Cold Spring Musical Society's band, were to follow. Many of them played at the bandstand erected in 1928 at the foot of Main Street. (Courtesy of PCHS.)

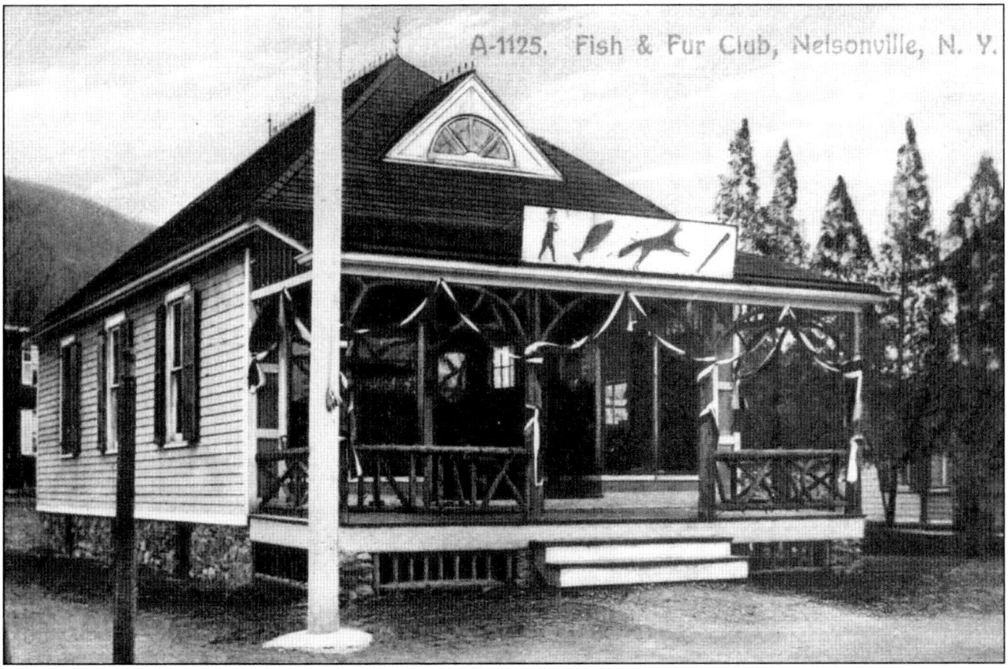

Local sportsmen created the Fish and Fur Club in 1895. This clubhouse on Main Street in Nelsonville was built in 1905 and adorned with a sign in the form of a pictograph, showing a man, a fish, a fur, and a club. The club moved to the building next door in 1955, and Nelsonville began using the original clubhouse as its village hall. (Courtesy of Mark Forlow.)

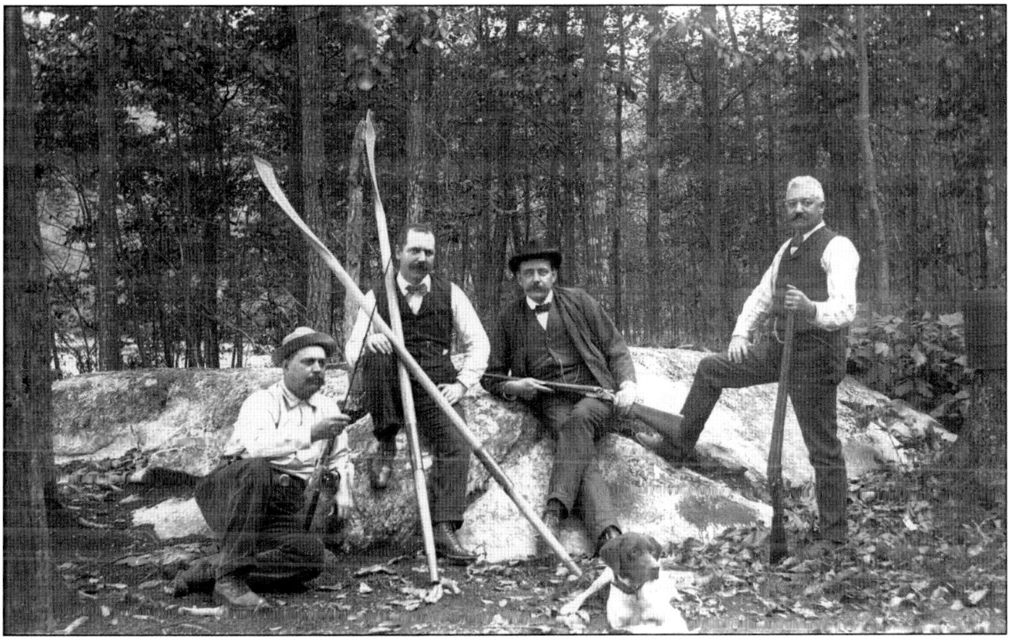

About 1920, local sportsmen show off equipment used by members of the Fish and Fur Club. Two men hold 12 gauge, double barreled shotguns, a third grasps a fishing pole, and a fourth sits with oars leaning against his upraised knee. A restful but alert shorthaired pointer lies in the foreground. (Courtesy of PCHS.)

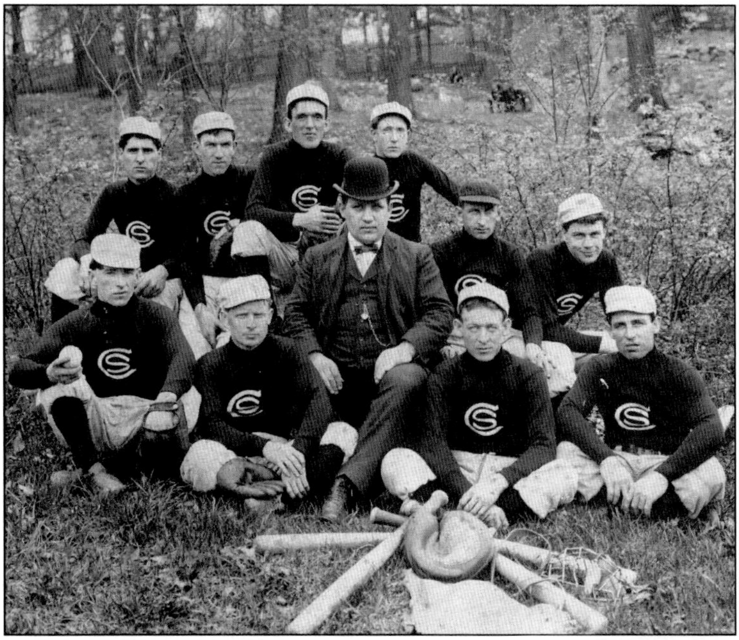

Cold Spring's history of baseball clubs began by at least the 1860s. This team, with "CS" on its shirts poses with the coach, probably between 1900 and 1910. Another team, the Undercliffs, played for several seasons in the 1860s, practicing near Undercliff, the George Pope Morris estate. The Kellogg Ball Club played in the 1870s, and the Pastime Baseball Team was active during at least 1908 and 1909. (Courtesy of PCHS.)

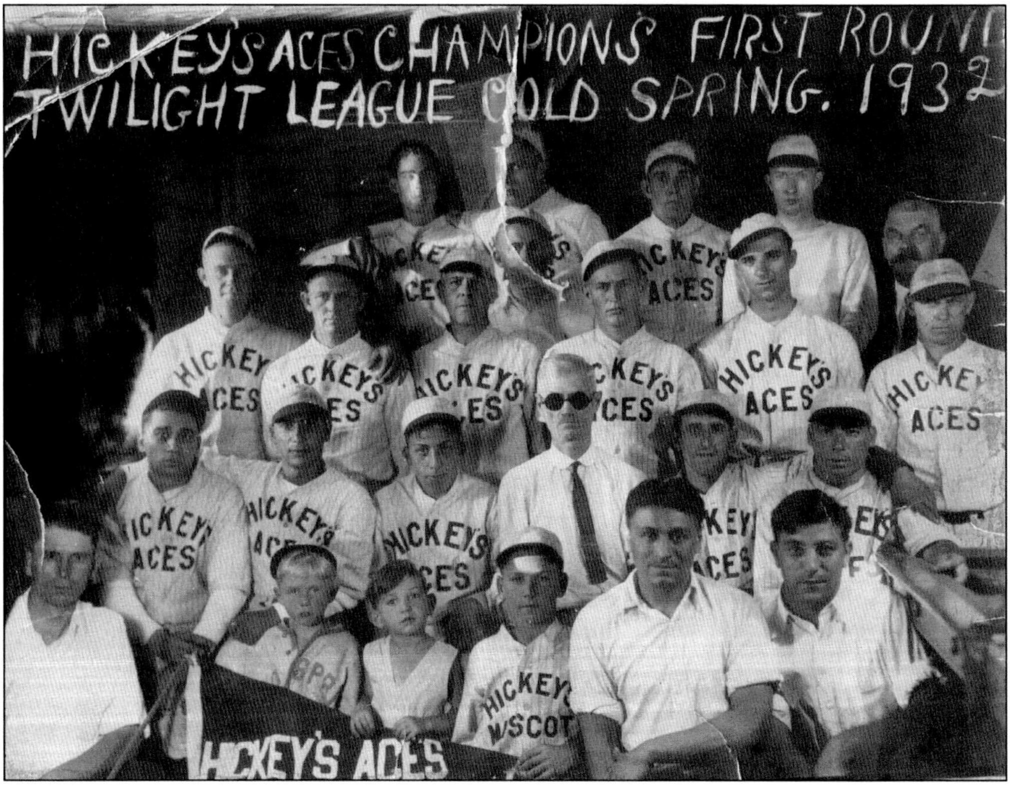

William H. Hickey, shown at center with a tie, was blind and owned a pool parlor on Main Street. Like many businesses in Cold Spring and elsewhere, Hickey's had its own baseball team, Hickey's Aces. The team was Cold Spring's first-round Twilight League champion in 1932. Hickey's mascots hold the team flag. (Courtesy of Francis J. Lahey.)

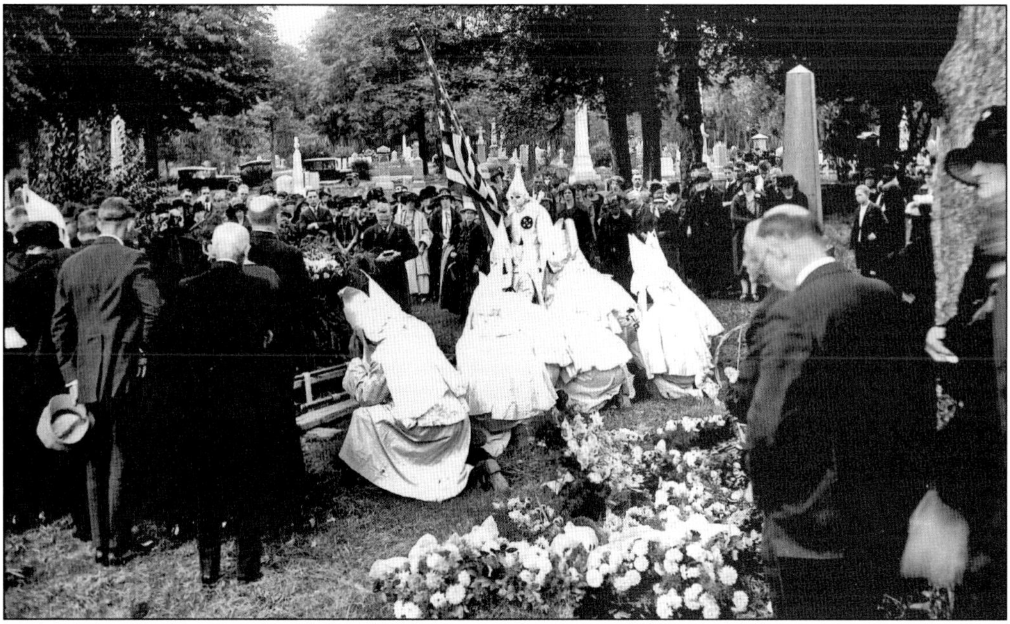

Members of the Ku Klux Klan pray during the funeral of a fellow Klansman at the Cold Spring Cemetery in 1924. One holds the American flag. The Klan began recruiting aggressively in 1921 and grew rapidly nationwide, its membership peaking in the mid-1920s. Meetings and rallies were held in Putnam County and in nearby Putnam Valley and Peekskill. Klan support was narrowly repudiated during the 1924 Democratic National Convention. (Courtesy of a private collector.)

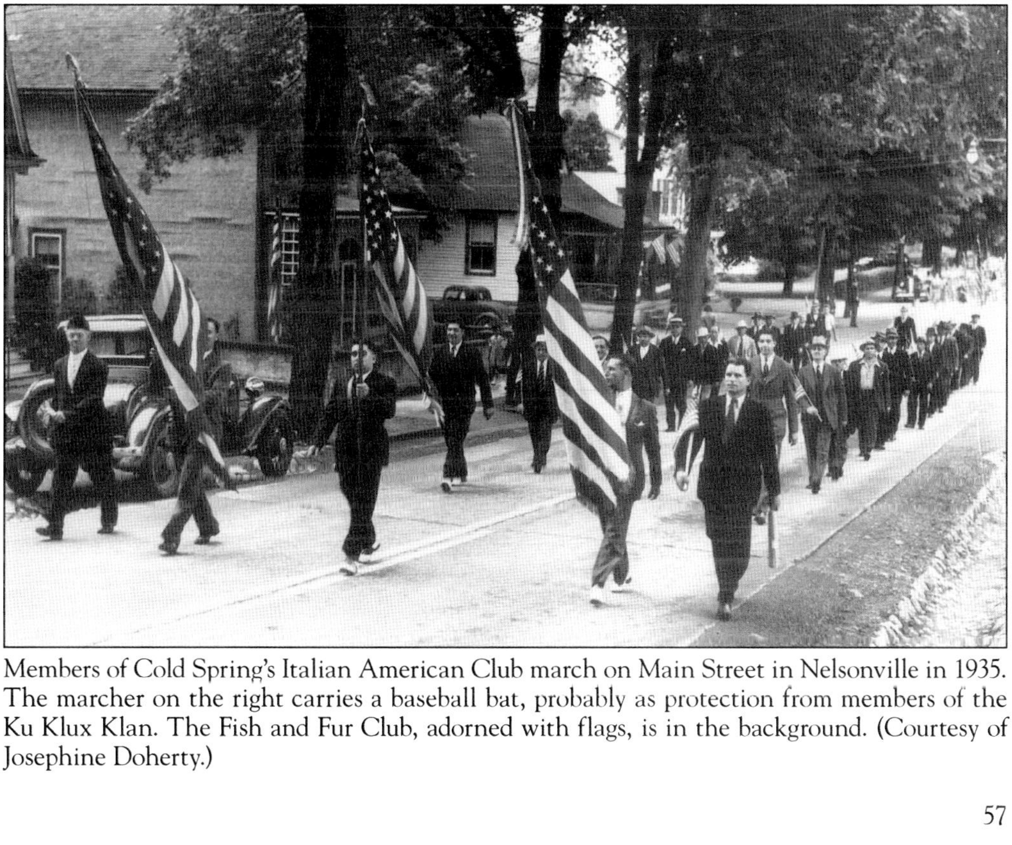

Members of Cold Spring's Italian American Club march on Main Street in Nelsonville in 1935. The marcher on the right carries a baseball bat, probably as protection from members of the Ku Klux Klan. The Fish and Fur Club, adorned with flags, is in the background. (Courtesy of Josephine Doherty.)

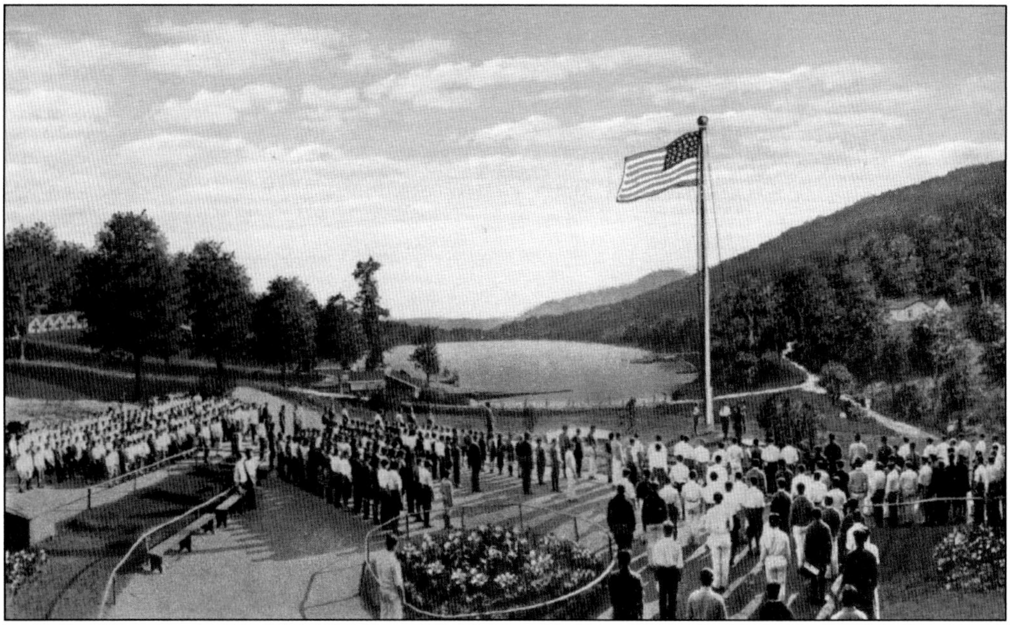

Campers gather for an assembly and flag salute at Surprise Lake Camp in northern Philipstown. The name was adopted in 1917. The Educational Alliance, which founded the camp in 1902, offered joint sponsorship to the 92nd Street Young Men's Hebrew Association in New York City in 1911. The nation's oldest Jewish sleepaway camp, the Alliance Camp, as it was first called, served boys from Manhattan's Lower East Side. (Courtesy of Mark Forlow.)

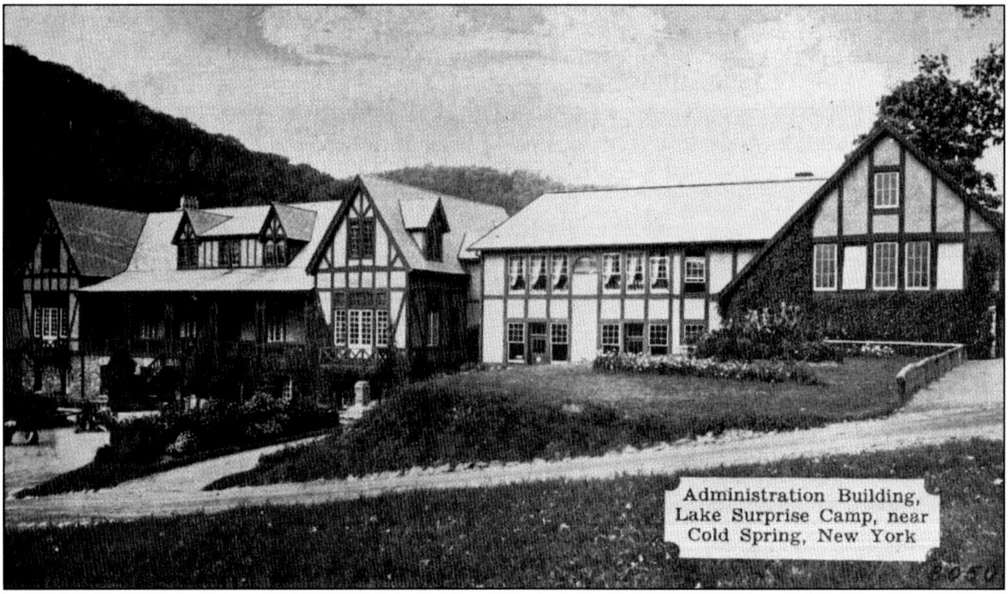

Surprise Lake Camp's Tudor-style main building contained offices, a dining hall, kitchen, gym, library, and storage area. Eddie Cantor was among the first campers; singer-songwriter Neil Diamond, television host Larry King, and comedian Jerry Stiller also attended. The camp now serves children from around the world. Another long-established camp near Cold Spring, Camp Eden (later Moonbeam Camp), was reorganized recently as Eden Village Camp. (Courtesy of Mark Forlow.)

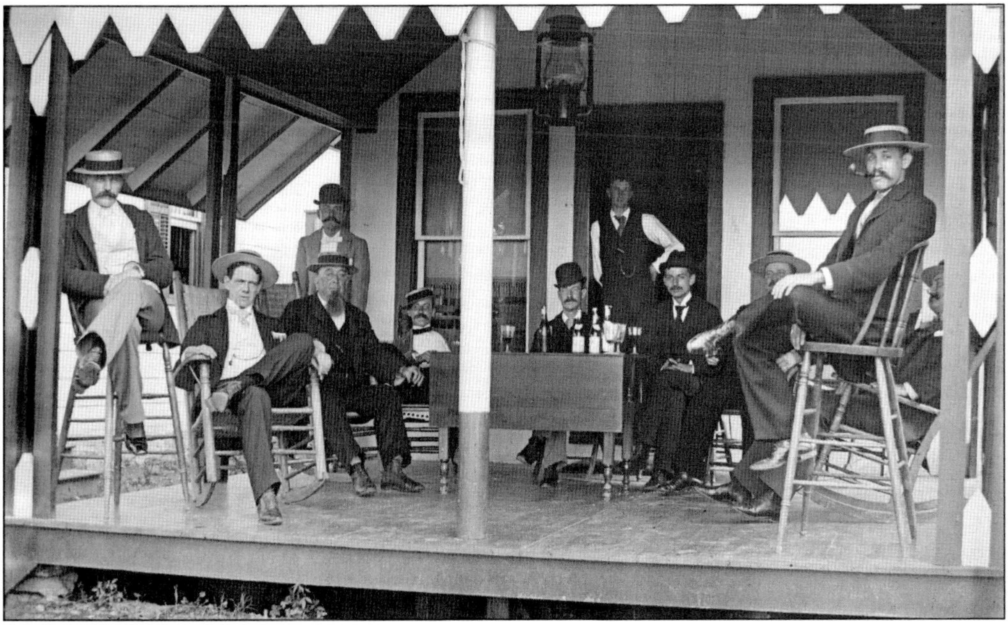

Between 1900 and 1915, a group of men socializes on a front porch, a common gathering place in Cold Spring, where porches were plentiful. The ornamentation across the porch top was typical of the Carpenter Gothic style popular then. Many of the men wear boaters, which gave them a debonair, informal look, which was also popular then. The flat crown and brim derived from the shape of sailor's hats. Working men favored bowlers. (Courtesy of PCHS.)

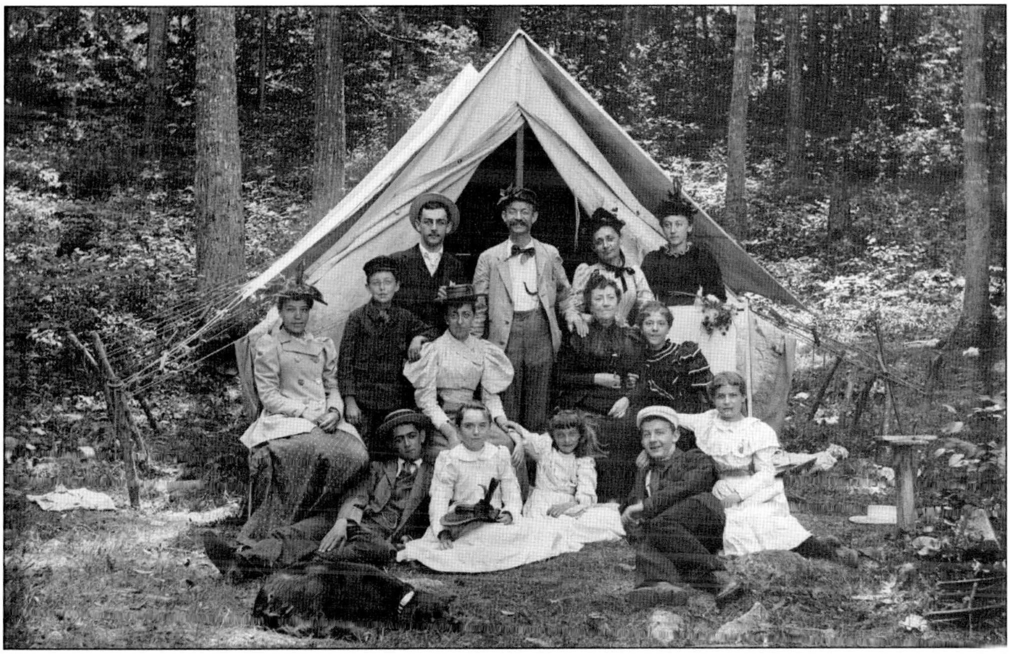

Outside gatherings were frequent in the 1890s. This formally dressed group may be an extended family attending a church picnic or camp meeting. Tents provided a place to nap as well as protection against rain or too much sun. Note the women's elaborate leg-of-mutton sleeves, popular about 1895, heavily ruffled dresses, and corseted waists. (Courtesy of PCHS.)

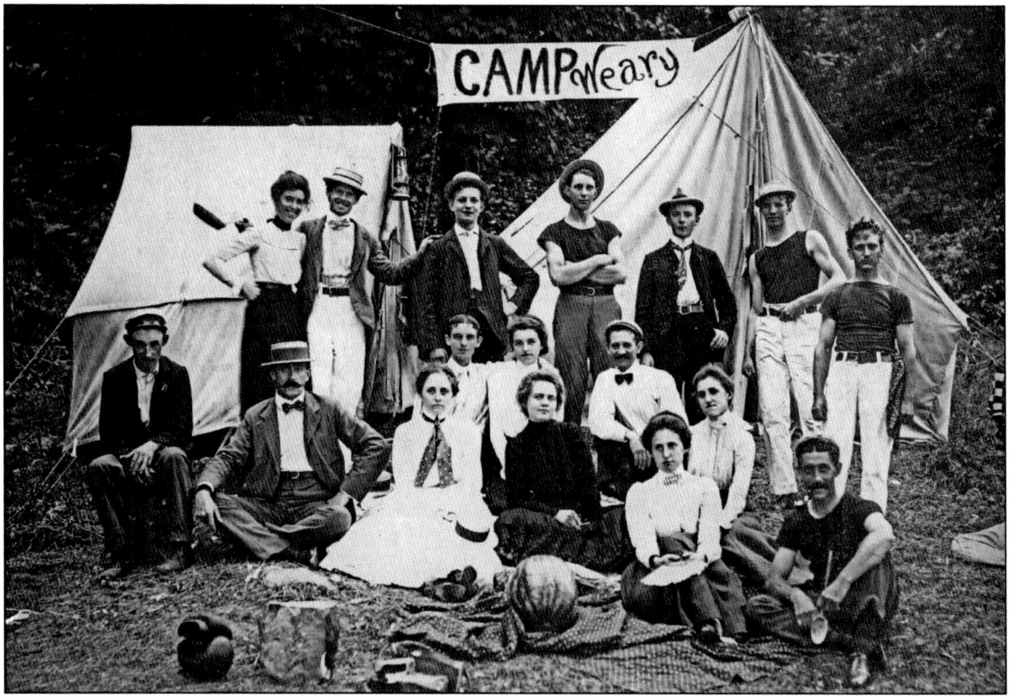

These young adults have strung a banner, "CAMP Weary," at their tent site about 1900. High necklines on shirtwaist blouses closed with brooches or neckties were de rigueur for women. A pair of boxing gloves (bottom left) and the short-sleeved or sleeveless attire of several of the young men suggest a boxing exhibition. A large watermelon is in the foreground. (Courtesy of PCHS.)

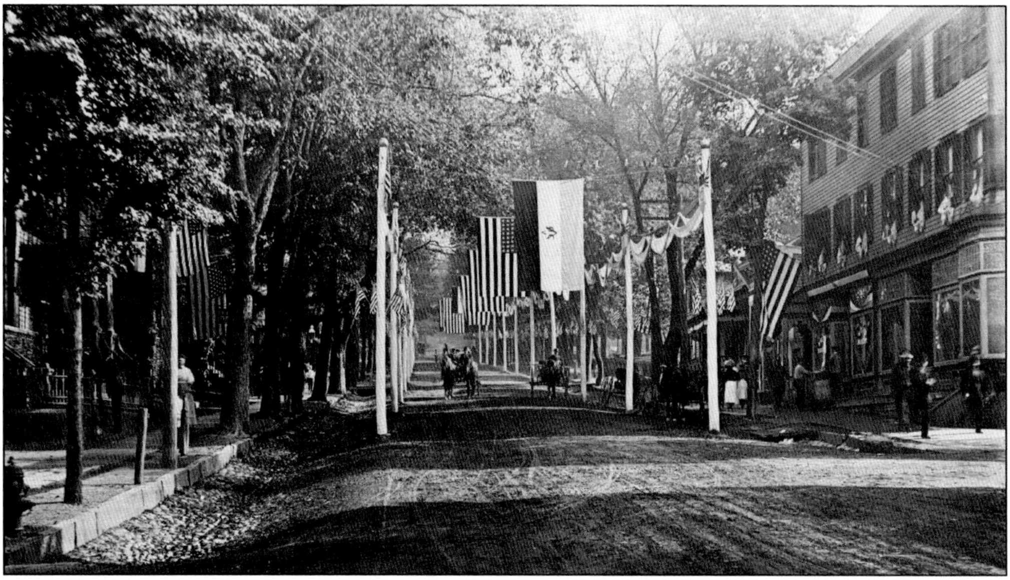

Residents are gathering on a flag-arrayed Main Street for Cold Spring's Hudson-Fulton Tercentenary Celebration parade on October 9, 1909. The two-week event, which was centered in New York City and celebrated in towns and villages throughout New York State, marked Henry Hudson's 1609 journey up the river named for him and honored Robert Fulton for his successful commercial use of a steamboat on the Hudson River in 1807. (Courtesy of PCHS.)

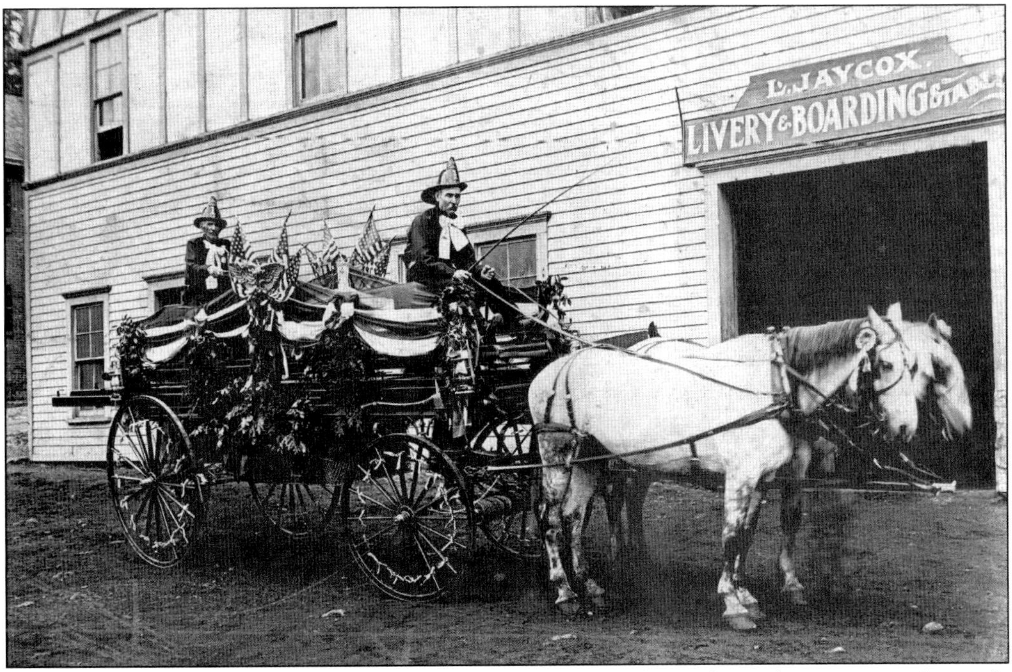

Decorated with bunting for the tercentenary celebration parade, a horse-drawn fire wagon stands outside Leonard Jaycox's Livery & Boarding Stable, located near the railroad tracks at Depot Square off Main Street. The volunteer firemen on the rig wear helmets and enormous neck bows, the same uniform as the brigade of their fellows marching in the parade in the photograph below. (Courtesy of PCHS.)

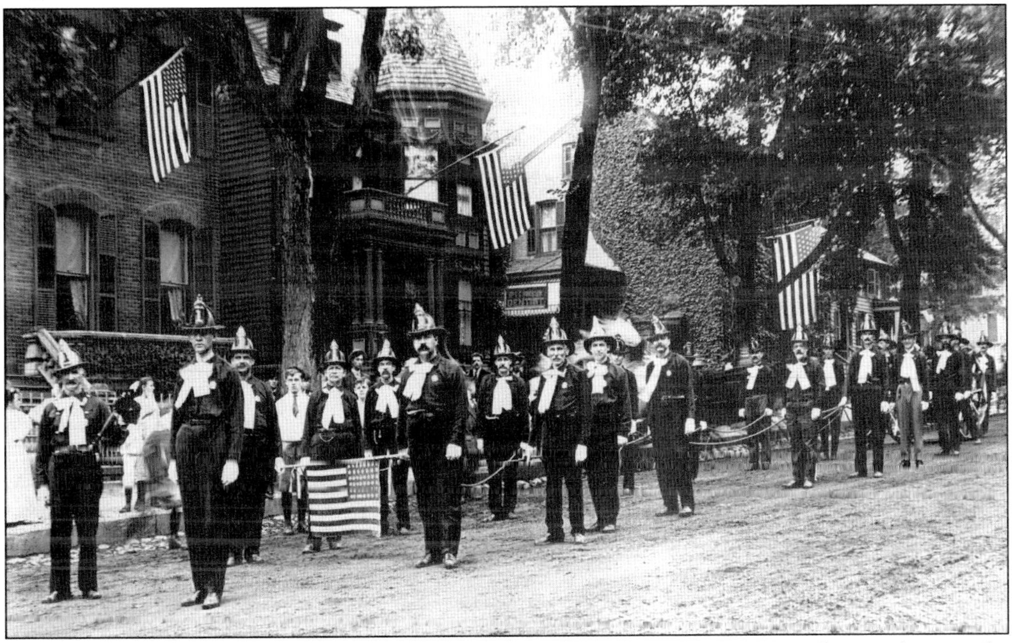

Helmeted firemen of the volunteer Cold Spring Fire Company No. 1 pause during the parade. They are pulling a hose cart. The houses behind them on the left along the north side of Main Street still stand. The sign on the second building from the left reads, "Dr. C.C. Robinson. Dentist." (Courtesy of PCHS.)

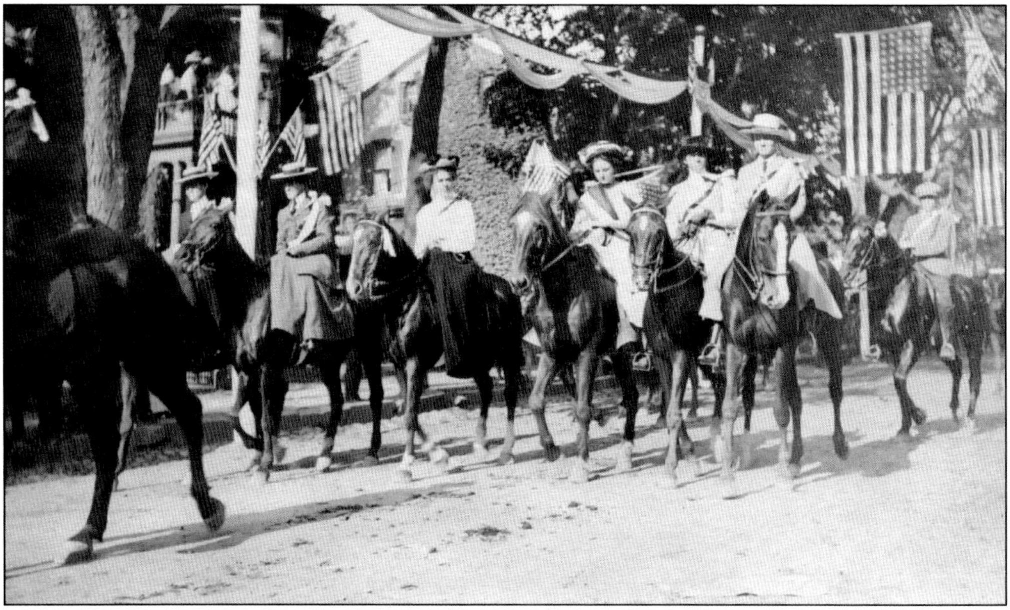

Women on horseback, some riding sidesaddle and others with split skirts, were part of the parade. Two of them wear feminine versions of men's boaters. The parade began at Depot Square and followed Main Street to Pearl Street, then Pine Street to Paulding Avenue, then on to Chestnut Street and over to the Haldane Athletic Field via Morris Avenue. (Courtesy of PCHS.)

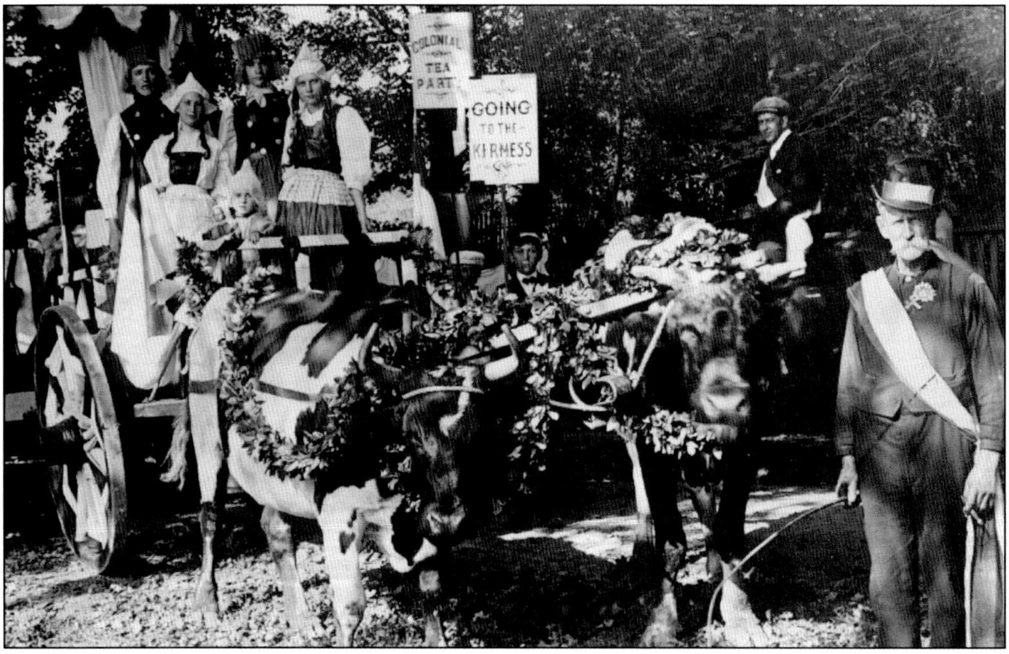

A gaily-decorated farm cart pulled by long-horned oxen, yoked together and garlanded for the parade, carries children in Dutch costume who are "Going to the Kermess." The word derives from the Middle Dutch *kercmisse*, which was a church festival. The Dutch were the first European settlers in the Hudson Valley. (Courtesy of PCHS.)

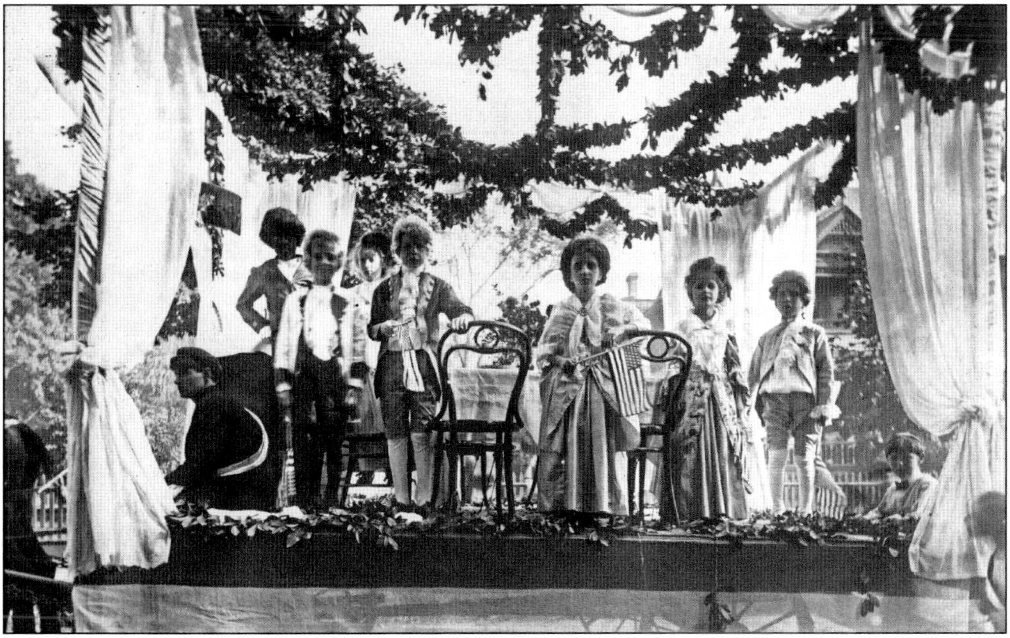

The Colonial Tea Party float shows a tableau of decorous children. This is probably a reference to the Boston Tea Party in 1773, during which the tea carried by three British ships was thrown into Boston Harbor. The British Parliament responded with the Intolerable Acts, which closed the Port of Boston, among other measures, and incited broader rebellion. (Courtesy of PCHS.)

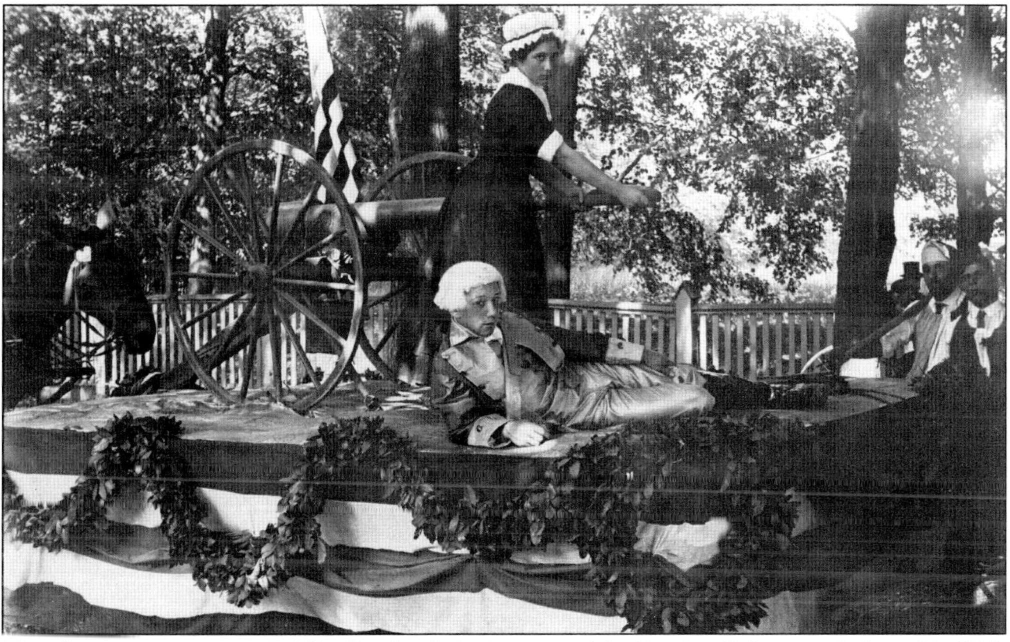

This float commemorates Molly "Pitcher," the heroine of the Battle of Monmouth, June 28, 1788. Under heavy fire, Molly Hays carried water to the artillerymen, her husband among them. When he was wounded, she operated his cannon until the battle ended. George Washington acknowledged her courage by making her a noncommissioned officer. Laurel garlands and wreaths, symbols of victory, decorate the float. (Courtesy of PCHS.)

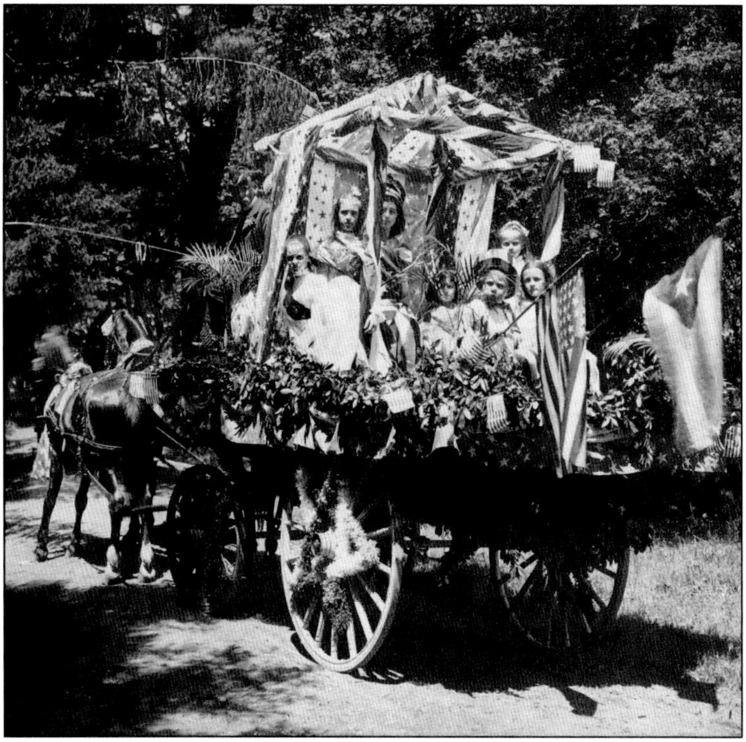

Draped in the flag, Lady Liberty, a popular figure of the era, rides beneath a canopy of bunting on a wagon laden with laurel, flags, and little girls. The woman may also represent a "daughter of the regiment," often an officer's daughter, who provided the soldiers' food and tended the wounded. The driver sports a tricorne, the three-cornered hat worn during the American Revolution. (Courtesy of Mark Forlow.)

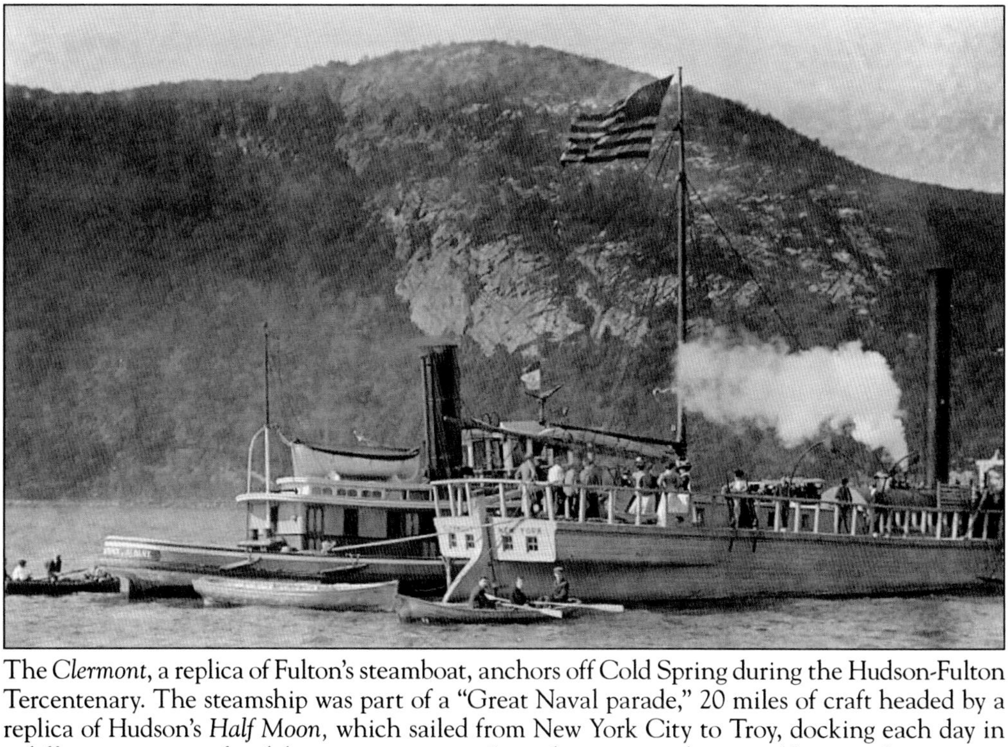

The *Clermont*, a replica of Fulton's steamboat, anchors off Cold Spring during the Hudson-Fulton Tercentenary. The steamship was part of a "Great Naval parade," 20 miles of craft headed by a replica of Hudson's *Half Moon,* which sailed from New York City to Troy, docking each day in a different river port for elaborate ceremonies. In each city, a newly minted historical statue was unveiled. (Courtesy of Josephine Doherty.)

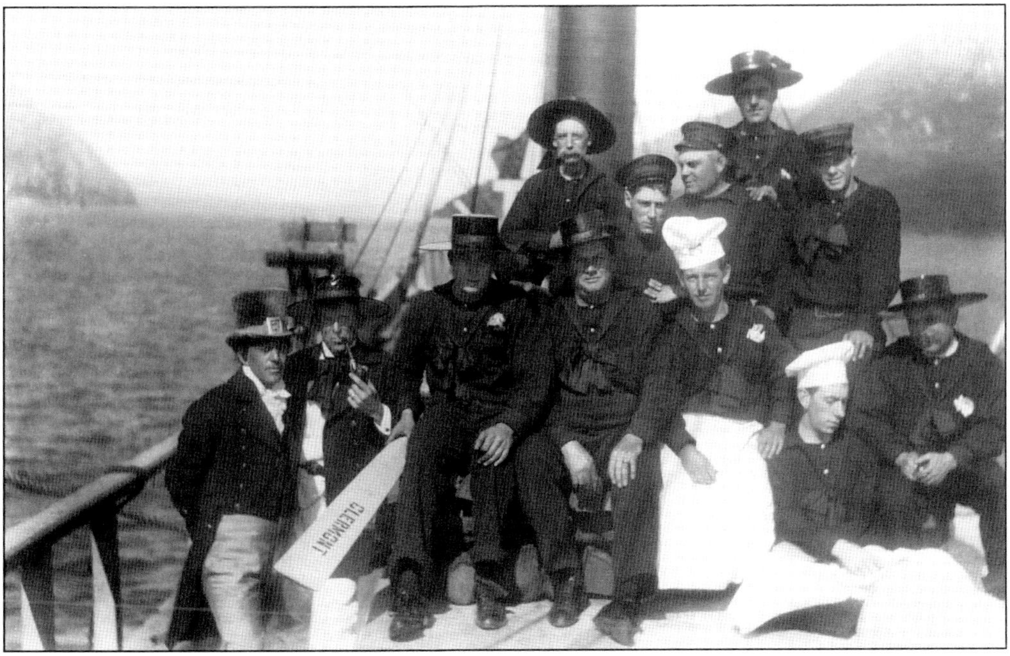

The crew of the *Clermont* poses for a photograph onboard during the ship's unscheduled stop at Cold Spring. A prominent Cold Spring resident, Mary Haldane, who was involved in the local organization of the Hudson-Fulton Tercentenary Celebration, prevailed upon the captain to anchor there several days before Cold Spring had its parade. (Courtesy of Mark Forlow.)

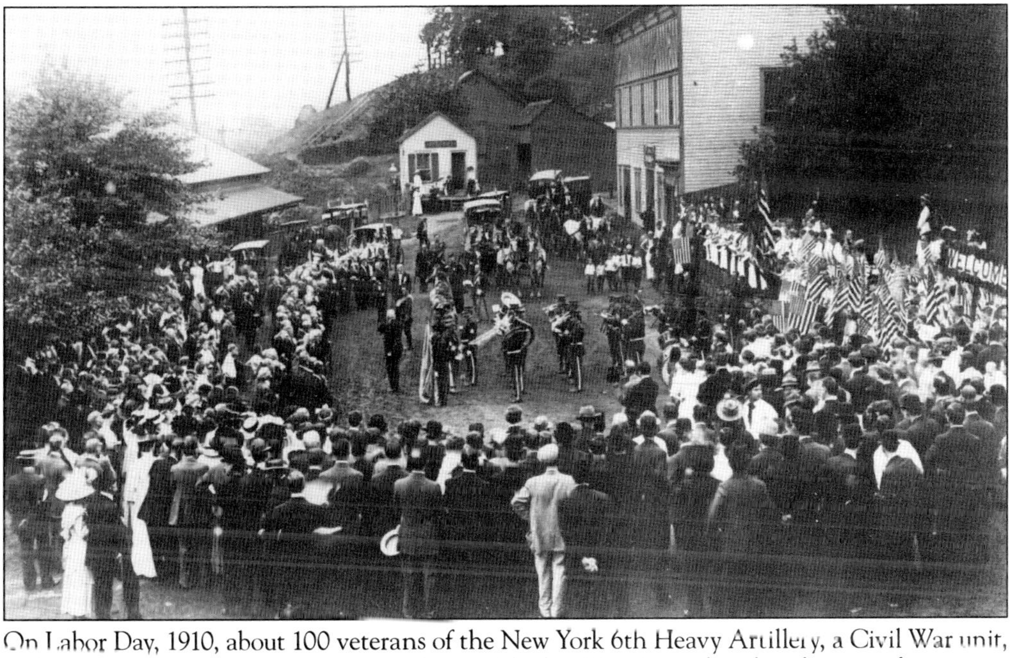

On Labor Day, 1910, about 100 veterans of the New York 6th Heavy Artillery, a Civil War unit, gathered for its 21st annual reunion, along with the West Point band and groups from every church and organization in town. Ceremonies began with a reception at Depot Square, followed by a march up Main Street, a visit to Gen. Daniel Butterfield's home, and a banquet at the Town Hall of Philipstown. (Courtesy of PCHS.)

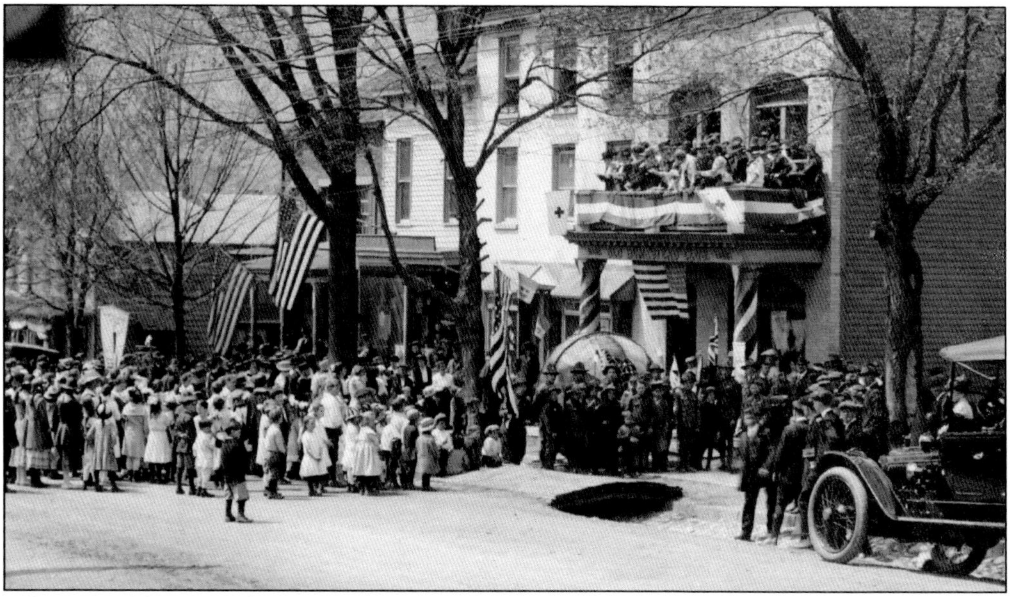

After a World War I Liberty Day parade, spectators, Boy Scouts, and dignitaries gather in 1918 at the Old Homestead Club Building on Main Street around a Liberty Ball, a popular patriotic symbol of the era. Sponsored throughout the country from 1917 to 1919, Liberty Day parades encouraged the purchase of Liberty and Victory bonds to raise money for the war and reconstruction in Europe. (Courtesy of Country Clocks.)

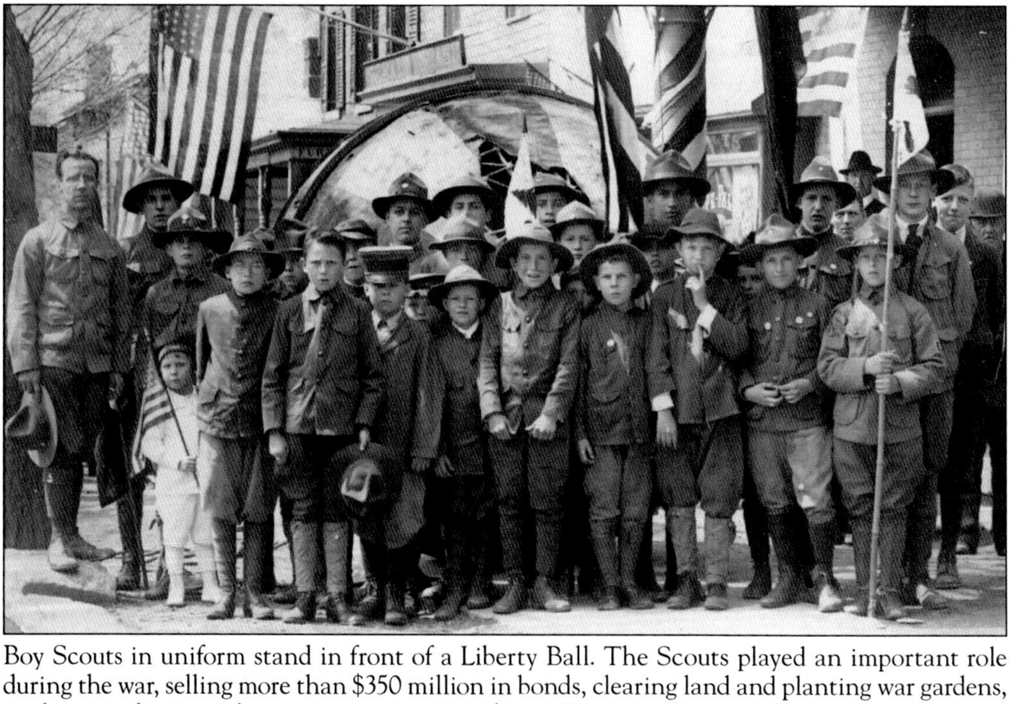

Boy Scouts in uniform stand in front of a Liberty Ball. The Scouts played an important role during the war, selling more than $350 million in bonds, clearing land and planting war gardens, working on farms, and participating in scrap drives. Famous posters of the day featured them, including *U*S*A Bonds: Third Liberty Loan Campaign* (1918) by J.C. Leyendecker, a well-known illustrator. (Courtesy of PCHS.)

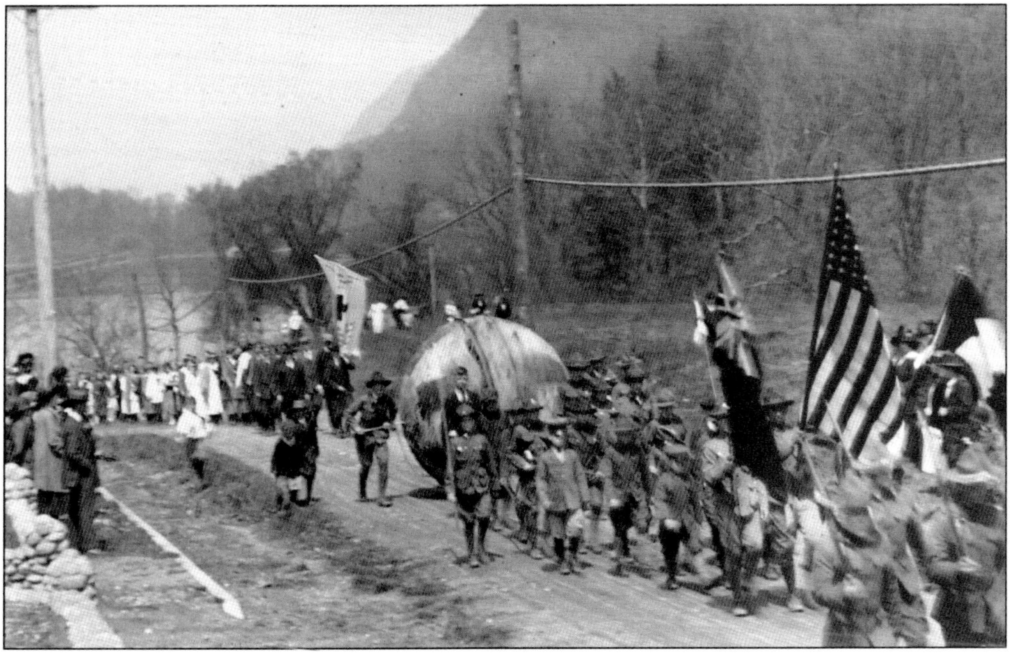

Liberty Balls were designed to be rolled by hand in parades. Here, Boy Scouts are doing the job as they follow their troop up Fair Street on the way to the Old Homestead Club. Bull Hill, at the right, and Little Stony Point, at the left, lie behind them. Breakneck can be seen in the far distance. (Courtesy of PCHS.)

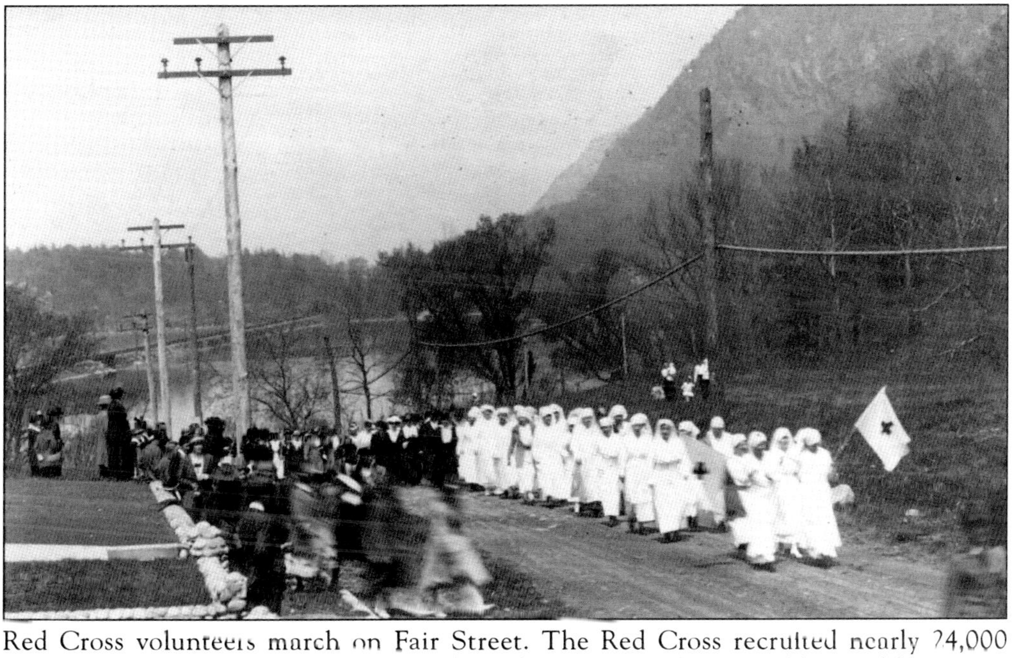

Red Cross volunteers march on Fair Street. The Red Cross recruited nearly 24,000 nurses during World War I to serve in the military and in the US Public Health Service, where they staffed hospitals and combated the 1918 influenza pandemic. Influenza killed 675,000 civilians in the United States, half the US soldiers who died in the war, and more than 50 million people worldwide. (Courtesy of PCHS.)

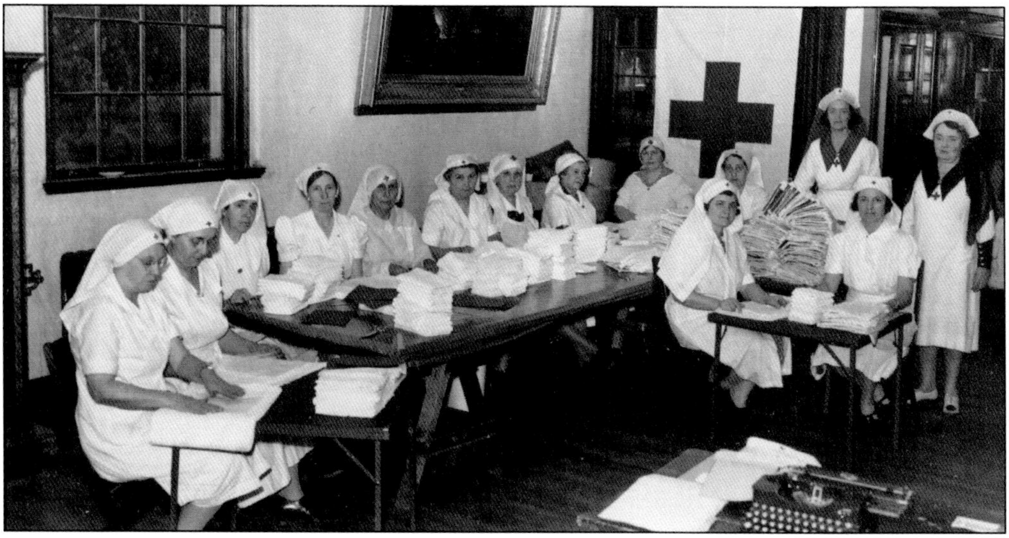

Red Cross volunteers from World War II fold bandages in a room at the Julia L. Butterfield Library on Morris Avenue near Main Street. In 1945, the Red Cross numbered 7.5 million volunteers. On the wall is *The Gun Foundry* (1866) by John Ferguson Weir, considered a major work reflecting early industrial America and now in the collection of the PCHS. (Courtesy of PCHS.)

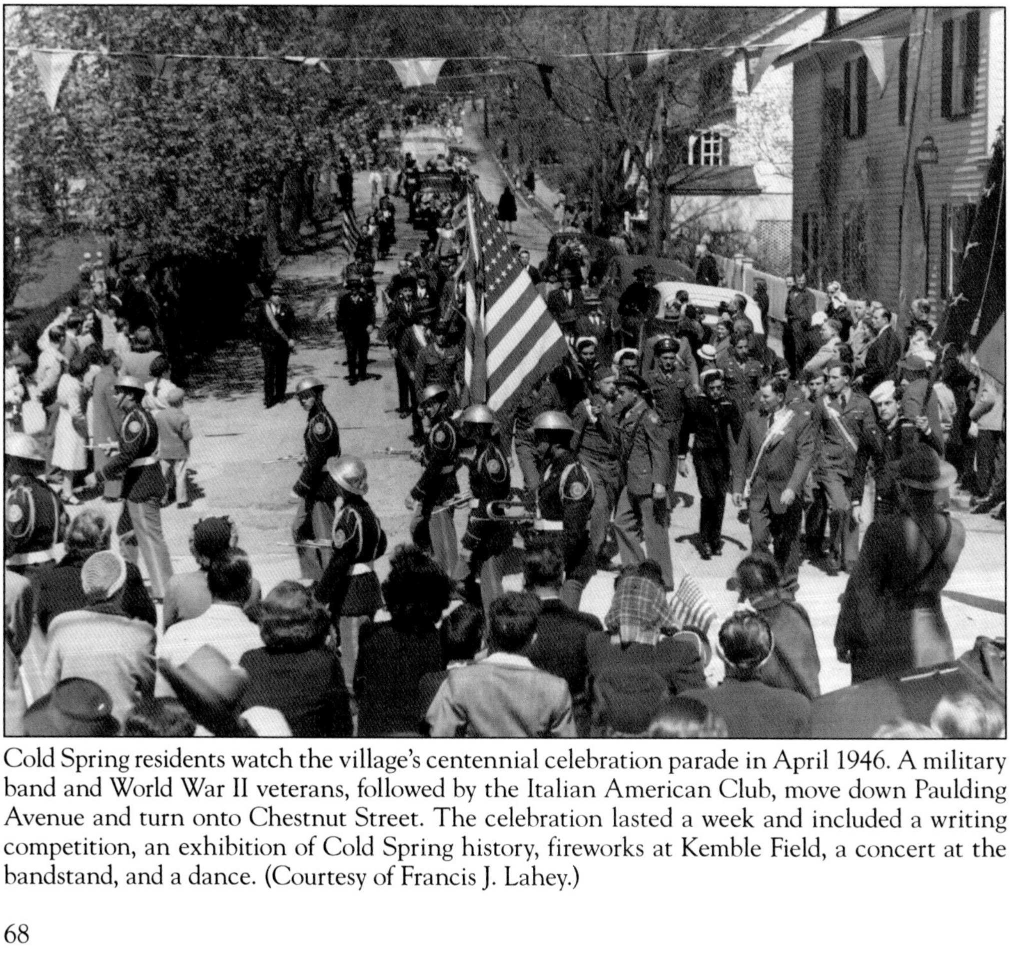

Cold Spring residents watch the village's centennial celebration parade in April 1946. A military band and World War II veterans, followed by the Italian American Club, move down Paulding Avenue and turn onto Chestnut Street. The celebration lasted a week and included a writing competition, an exhibition of Cold Spring history, fireworks at Kemble Field, a concert at the bandstand, and a dance. (Courtesy of Francis J. Lahey.)

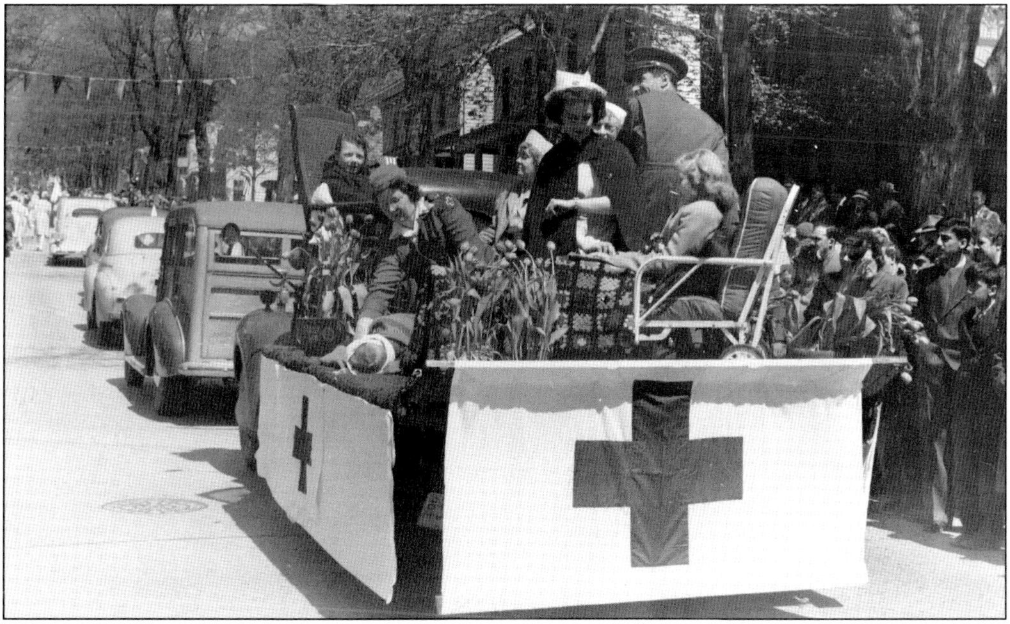

The Red Cross float heads up Main Street toward Nelsonville. A girl under an afghan has her temperature and pulse taken while a military nurse attends to a soldier with a bandaged head. Potted tulips decorate the float. In addition to military duty, Red Cross nurses filled in at hospitals with wartime staff shortages. (Courtesy of Francis J. Lahey.)

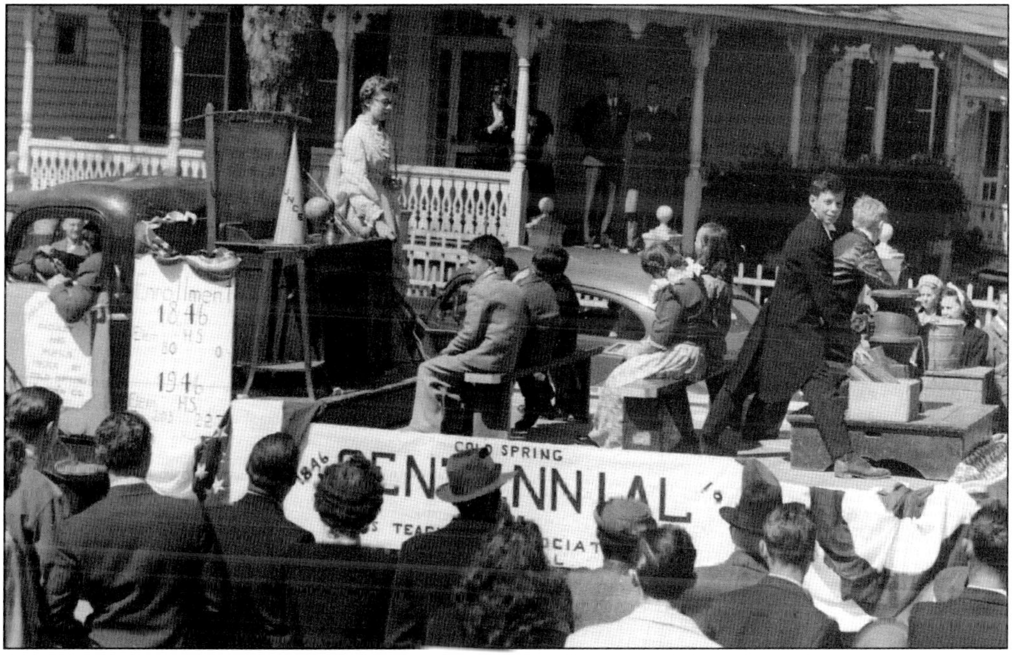

On the Teachers' Association float, a teacher and students in 19th-century dress recreate a one-room schoolhouse, complete with water bucket, wood stove, and dunce's cap. The boys at the back put wood into the stove. The float has turned onto Chestnut Street from Paulding Avenue. The porch ornamentation on the corner house is typical of the Carpenter Gothic style. (Courtesy of Francis J. Lahey.)

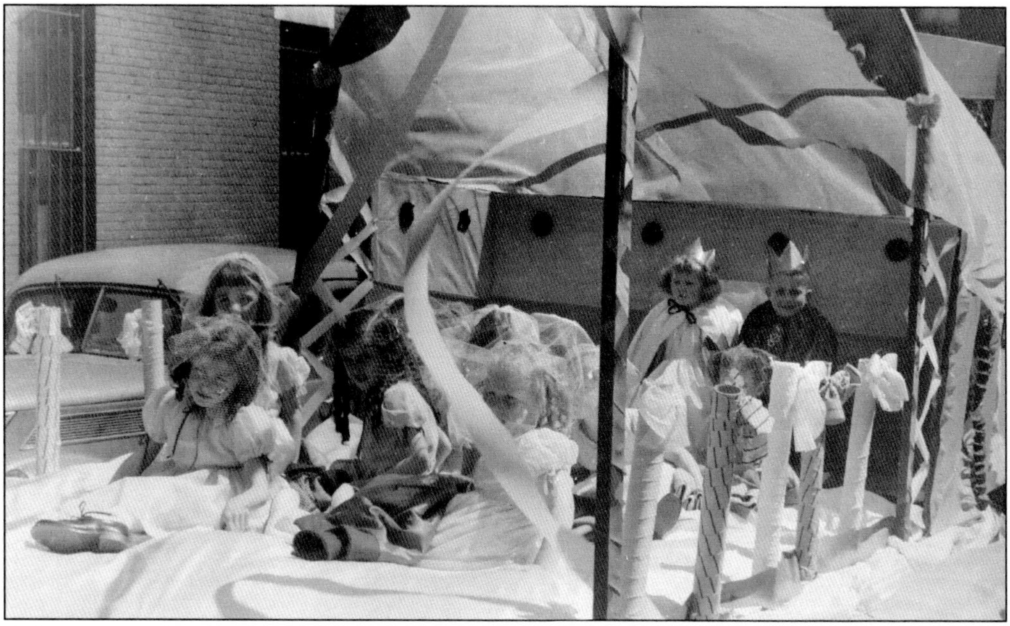

A float carries the parade king, six-year-old Anthony Phillips, and queen down Stone Street from Cold Spring's Italian American Club, a parade sponsor, toward Main Street. The old post office, at left with barred windows, is now a place of business. Phillips went on to be Cold Spring's mayor for 16 years, first elected in 1993. (Courtesy of Francis J. Lahey.)

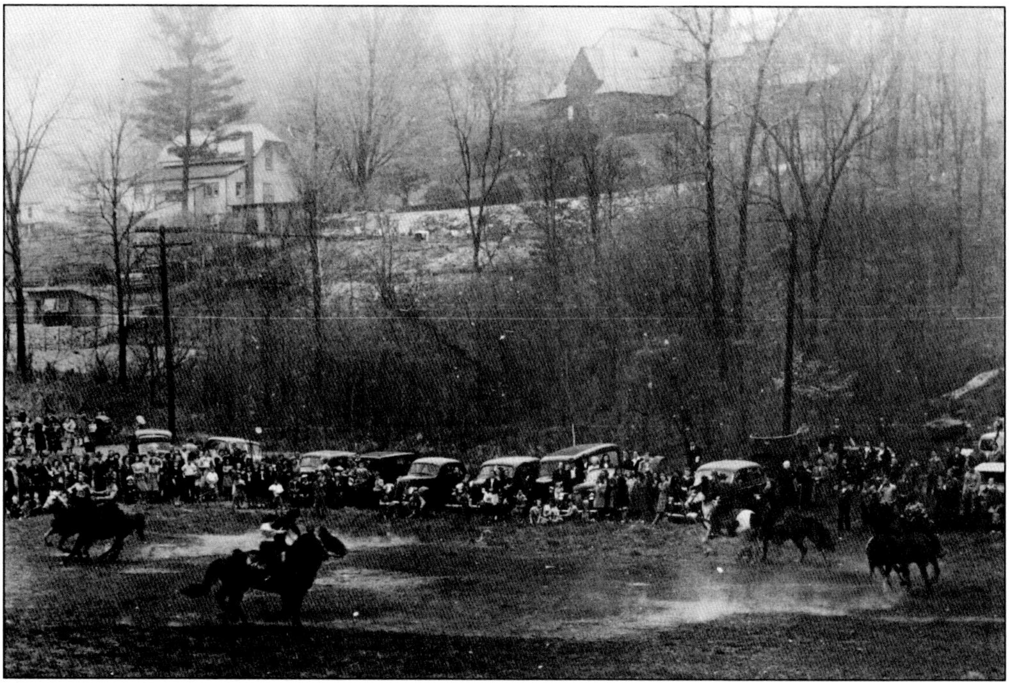

Not all centennial events took place on Main Street. At the Cinnabar Ranch rodeo at Kemble Field, on Kemble Avenue, four pairs of men and women circle at a gallop while spectators near a line of parked cars take in the competition. The Cinnabar was a dude ranch in Putnam Valley. (Courtesy of Francis J. Lahey.)

Five

IN COMFORT AND STYLE
HOUSES, ESTATES, AND RESIDENTS

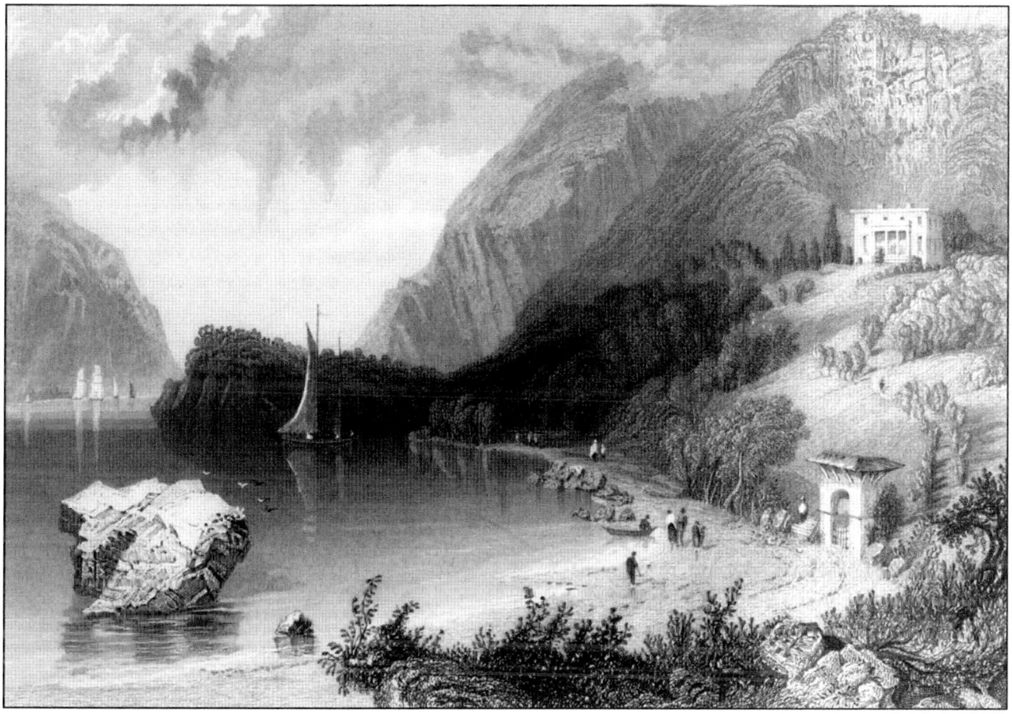

Famed for its setting and as a gathering place for literary and artistic figures of the era, Undercliff (1833), the Greek Revival home of George Pope Morris, was a landmark for steamboat travelers passing Cold Spring. Morris's influential periodicals, including the *New-York Mirror*, promoted the work of the Hudson River School and painters of scenes of American life. This engraving is from Nathaniel P. Willis's *American Scenery* (1840). (Courtesy of PCHS.)

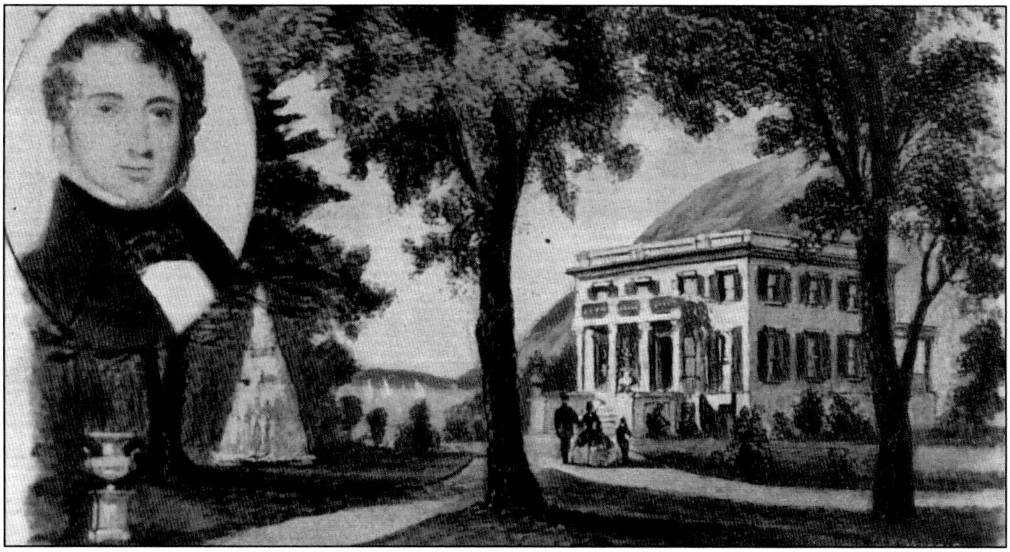

Committed to the development of an American cultural identity, Morris and his literary collaborator Willis commissioned and published the works of American writers on American themes. Morris also promoted the scenery, history, and mythology of the Hudson River and Highlands. Undercliff figured in many contemporary articles. After Morris's death, the house and estate joined the Butterfield property. The home was razed in 1938. (Courtesy of Larry Demers.)

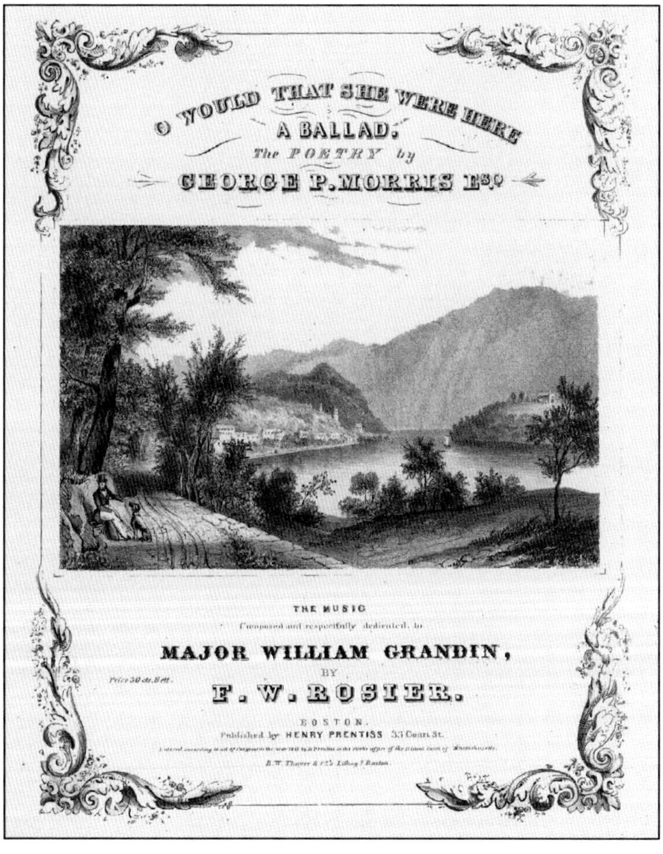

Although acclaimed as a publisher, poet, and writer, only Morris's reputation as "the Song-Writer of America" outlived him. He wrote "Woodman, Spare That Tree!" Among his other popular lyrics were songs that related to the Hudson River or had sheet music covers illustrated with idyllic views of the river or the Hudson Highlands, such as "O Would That She Were Here." The lithographic cover of that song is shown at left. (Courtesy of PCHS.)

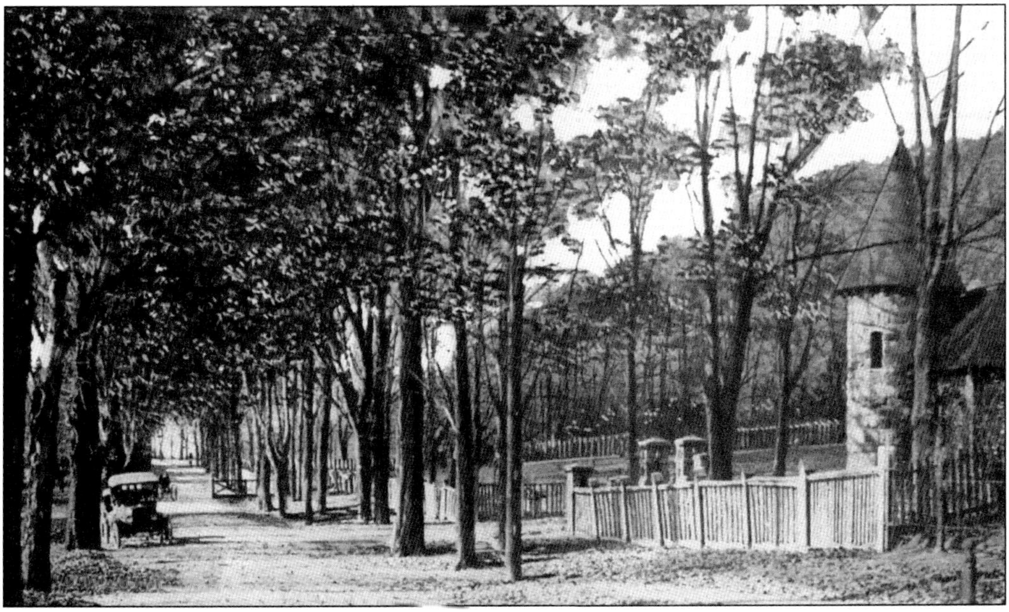

Morris Avenue, shown about 1904 at the intersection of Cragside Avenue, originally ran from Main Street to the gates of Undercliff. The road now continues north as Route 9D. At right is the gatehouse of Cragside, the 175-acre estate of Julia and Civil War general Daniel Butterfield. Julia Butterfield's first husband, financier Frederick P. James, purchased the property in 1852. (Courtesy of PCHS.)

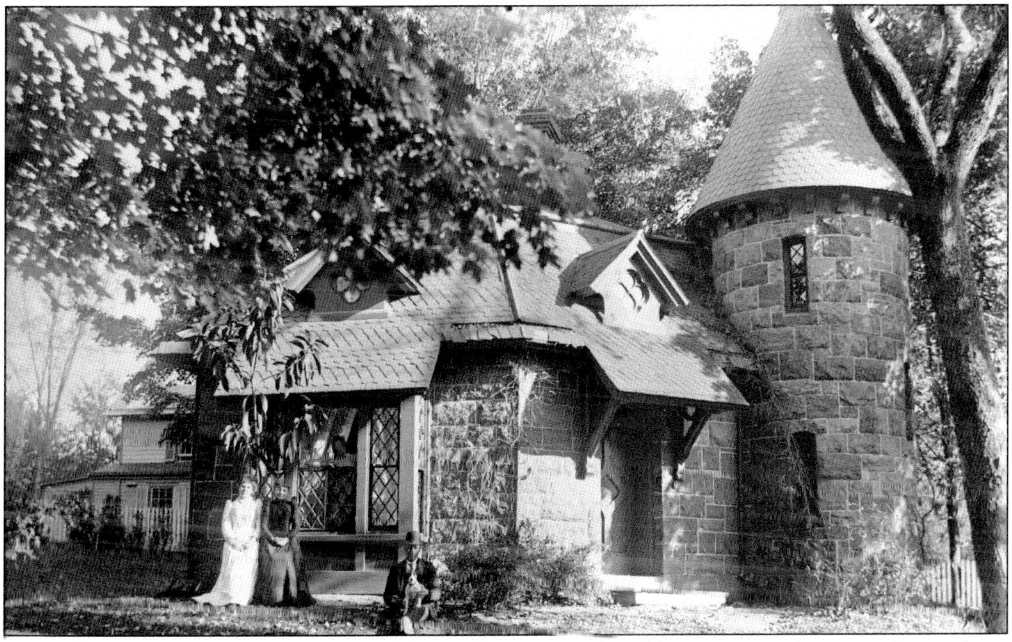

Several people, perhaps the Butterfields' staff, pose comfortably at the gatehouse to Cragside in 1892. With its rough-hewn stone and medieval tower, the gatehouse, still extant, is typical of the Gothic Revival style. After a remarkable Civil War record, Butterfield commanded forces in New York Harbor from 1865 to 1869. His father, John Butterfield, helped to found American Express. (Courtesy of PCHS.)

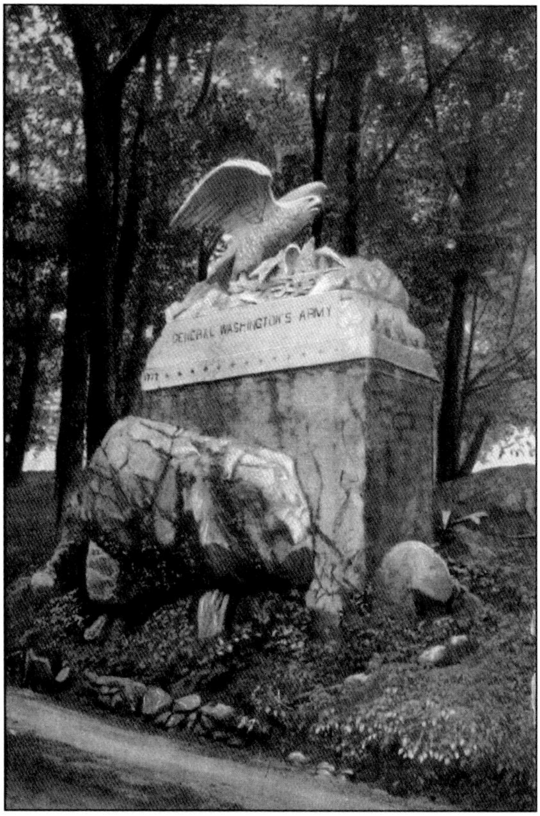

This carved eagle commemorates the "suffering and patriotism" of Continental Army soldiers protecting the Hudson Highlands while the West Point fortifications were built. Three regiments camped on Butterfield's property, his maternal grandfather, a soldier in the 7th Connecticut Regiment, with them. "Hence," Butterfield wrote, he erected "this memorial . . . of marble weighing ten tons on a solid rock and likely to remain a few years." (Courtesy of Janet Selleck Rust.)

Cragside (1852), the Italianate Butterfield mansion built by Frederick James, was surrounded by grounds that sloped down to the river with elaborate formal gardens, lawns, footpaths, orchards, fields, drives, fountains, statuary, a greenhouse, carriage house, and stables. The furnishings were opulent, eclectic, and arranged for the Butterfields' frequent and lavish entertaining of fashionable society, including presidents and royalty. (Courtesy of PCHS.)

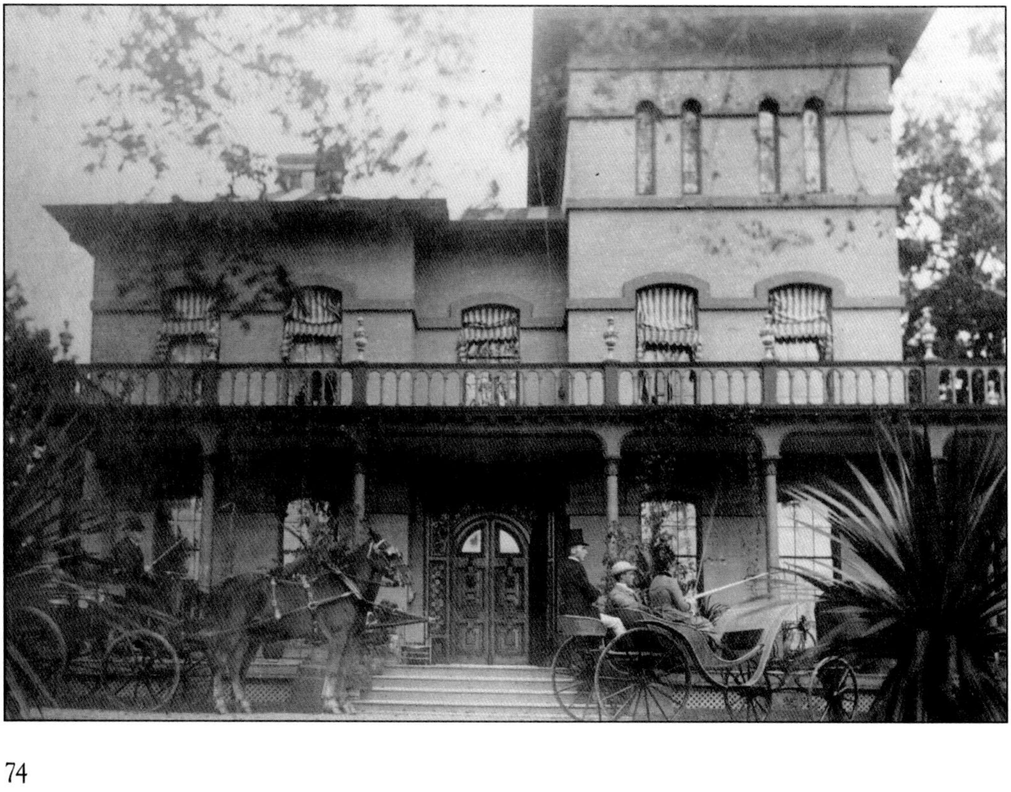

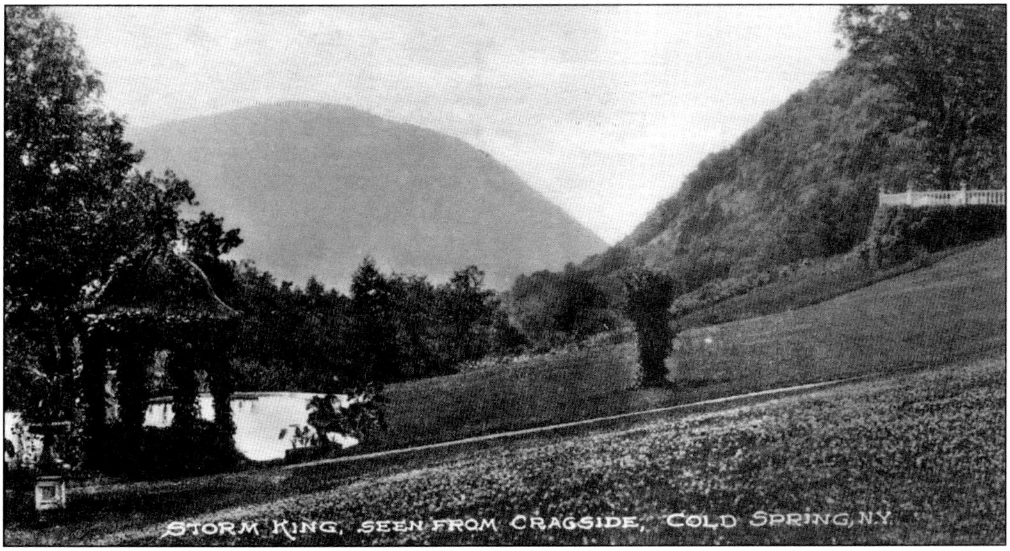

Storm King was visible from one of the lawns below the belvedere, which can be seen at far right. The mountain contour at right is that of Bull Hill. Cragside contained many remarkable objects acquired during the Butterfields' world travels and as gifts from guests. As a thank-you for the grand duke's party described below, the Russian government sent a sleigh in the form of a wild boar. (Courtesy of Janet Selleck Rust.)

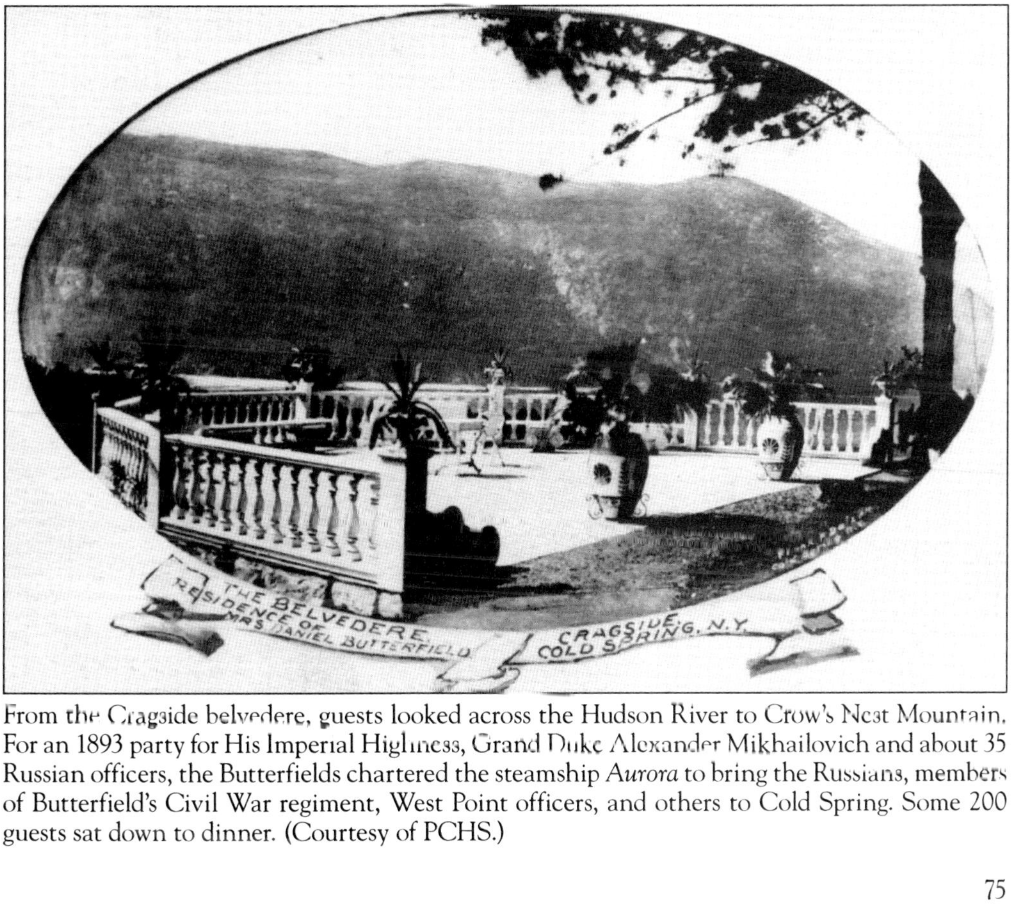

From the Cragside belvedere, guests looked across the Hudson River to Crow's Nest Mountain. For an 1893 party for His Imperial Highness, Grand Duke Alexander Mikhailovich and about 35 Russian officers, the Butterfields chartered the steamship *Aurora* to bring the Russians, members of Butterfield's Civil War regiment, West Point officers, and others to Cold Spring. Some 200 guests sat down to dinner. (Courtesy of PCHS.)

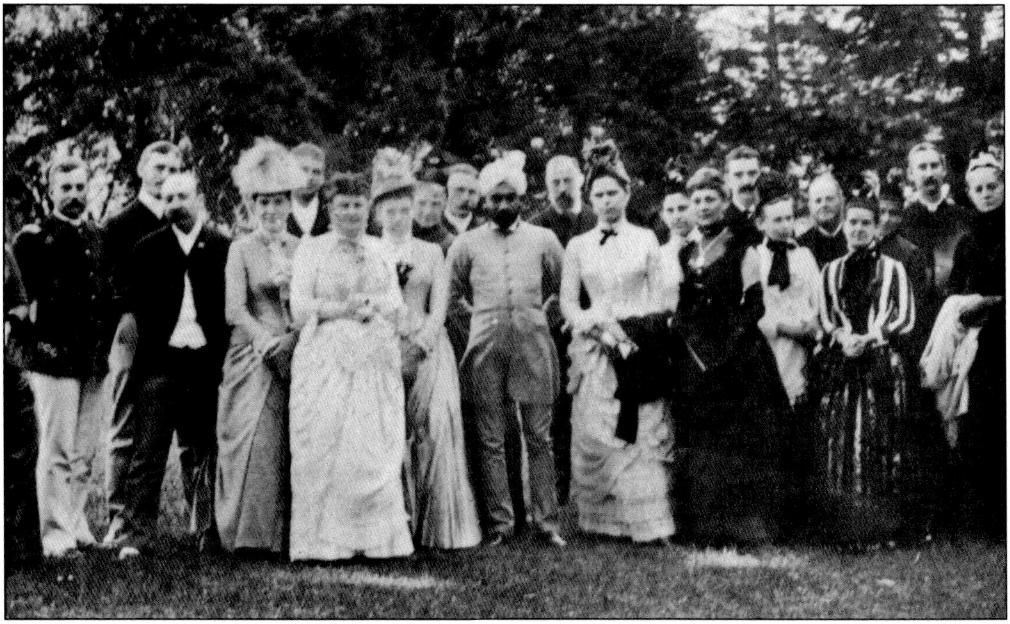

Among other guests entertained at Cragside was Tharah Sahib, an Indian prince on a world tour. The Butterfields gave a party for him in 1888. Julia Butterfield stands to the prince's right with hands folded at her waist. Tharah Sahib arrived in Cold Spring on Butterfield's privately hired steamer, escorted by a British naval officer assigned to him by Queen Victoria. The women wear morning promenade dresses. (Courtesy of PCHS.)

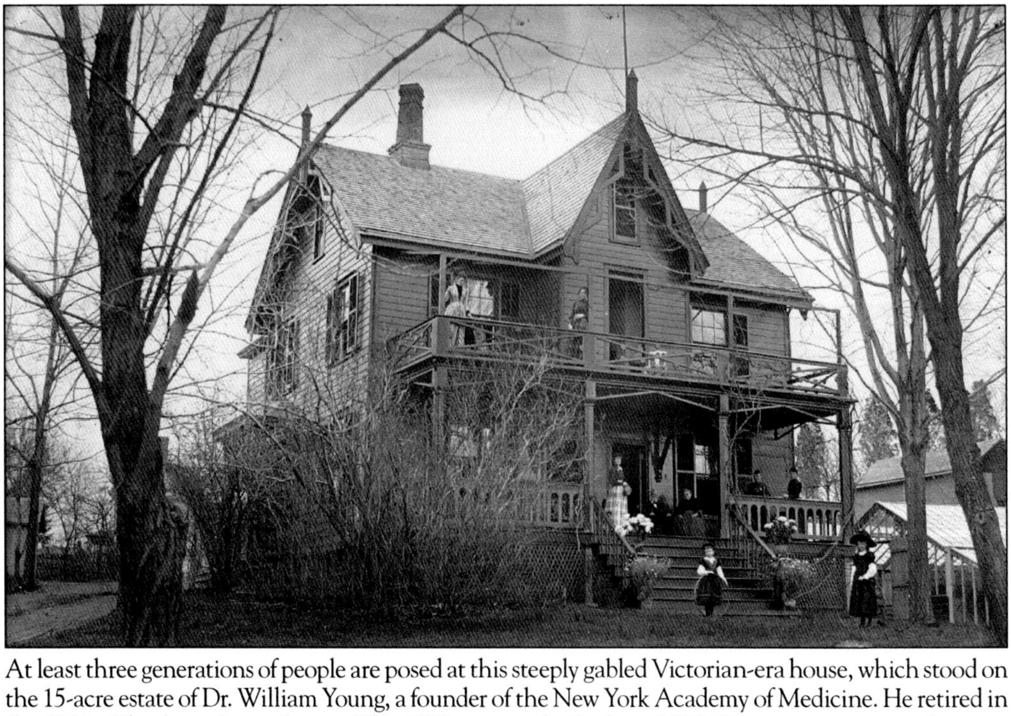

At least three generations of people are posed at this steeply gabled Victorian-era house, which stood on the 15-acre estate of Dr. William Young, a founder of the New York Academy of Medicine. He retired in the 1860s. The doctor's own home, Glen William, was built about 1828. The apartment complex near the train platform in Cold Spring was built about where his estate lay. (Courtesy of PCHS.)

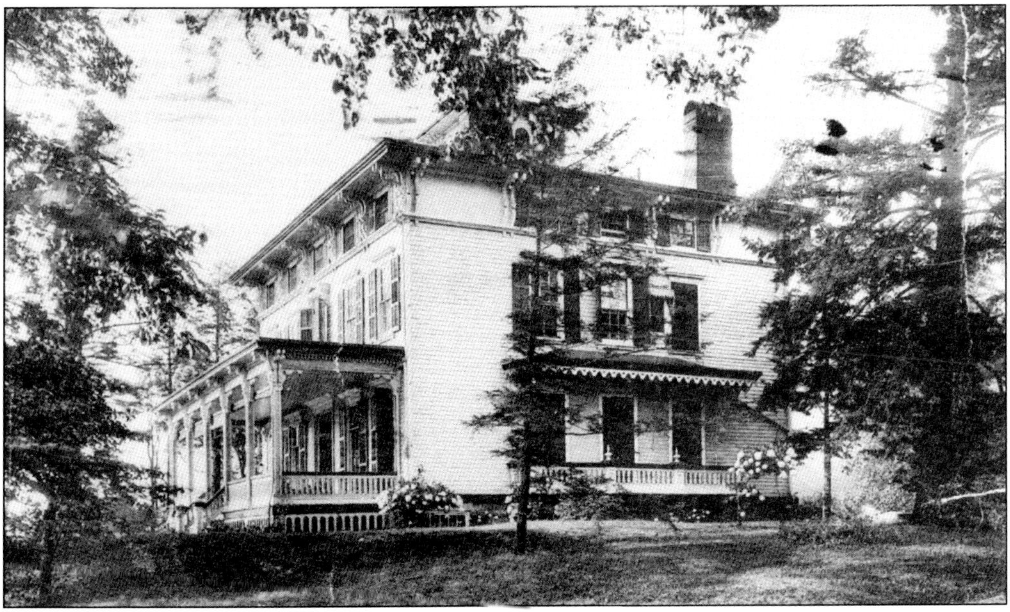

Roroyare (purchased 1888) was the vernacular Italianate home of Gen. John Campbell, who served in the Mexican War and the Indian campaigns and as a Civil War surgeon; later, he directed the National Bank of Cold Spring. Campbell died in 1905, and his wife, Mary, died in 1938. The house, which burned in 1940, stood on a rise to the north of Cold Spring's Depot Square. (Courtesy of Mark Forlow.)

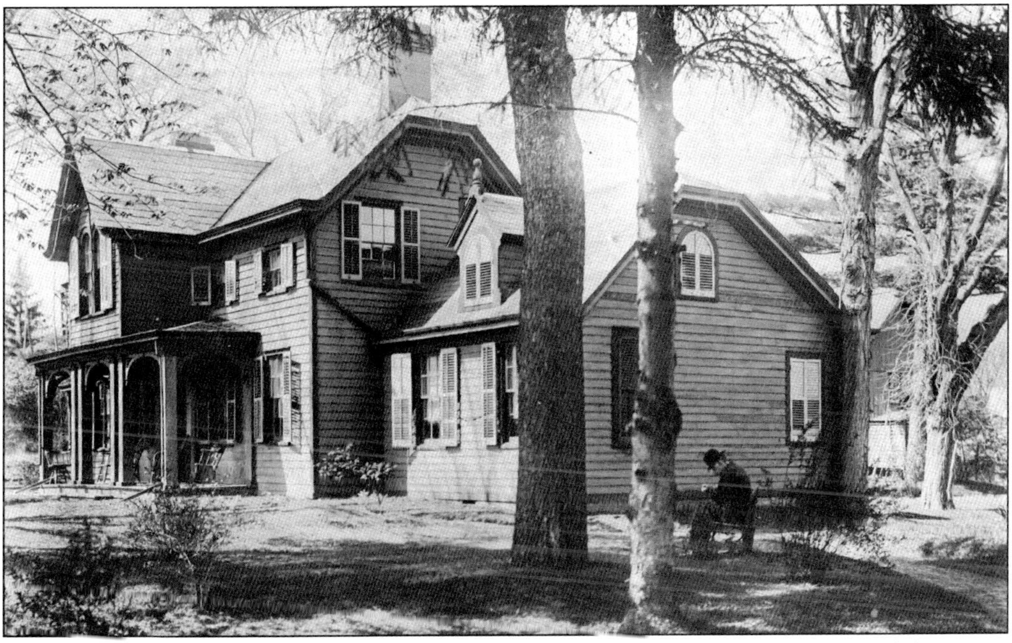

Seated outside his home on Paulding Avenue about 1880, Colin Tolmie Sr. has a peaceful moment reading. He came to Cold Spring when the West Point Foundry was established and worked there for many years, for a time in charge of the forging department. Tolmie died in 1882. Dating about 1850, his Gothic Revival home has Hudson River bracketing at the arches and a clipped gable roof. (Courtesy of PCHS.)

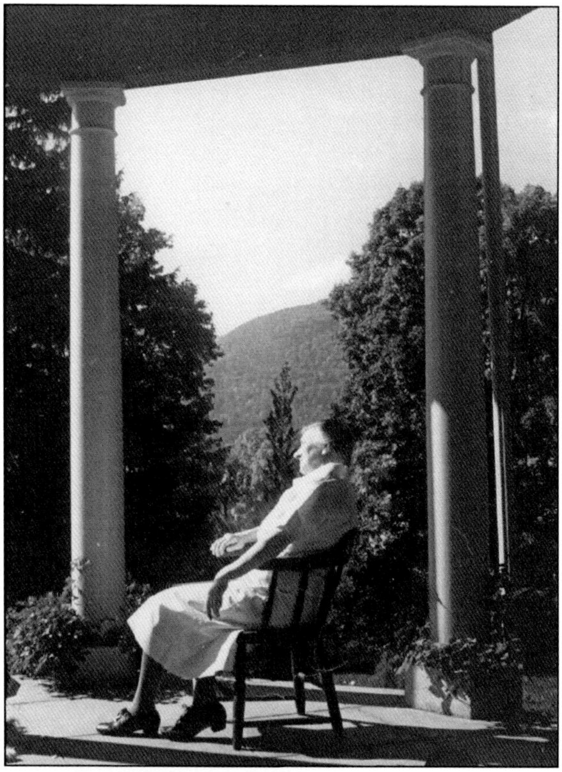

Dorothy Giles enjoys the sun and a view of the Highlands from the portico of her home on Paulding Avenue, probably in the 1940s. She was a ghostwriter for Gypsy Rose Lee, among others, and played an active role in community affairs. Giles was a local historian and an influential member of the Putnam County Historical Society. (Courtesy of PCHS.)

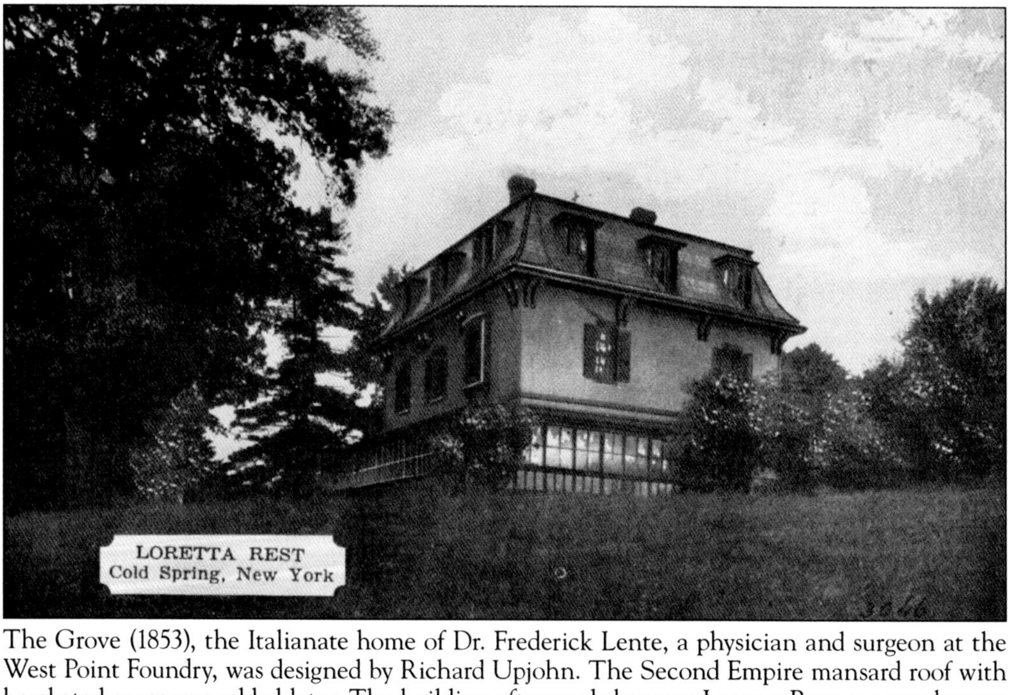

The Grove (1853), the Italianate home of Dr. Frederick Lente, a physician and surgeon at the West Point Foundry, was designed by Richard Upjohn. The Second Empire mansard roof with bracketed eaves was added later. The building afterwards became Loretto Rest, a convalescent home for priests, and then a convent for nuns teaching at Our Lady of Loretto School. It is now abandoned. (Courtesy of Janet Selleck Rust.)

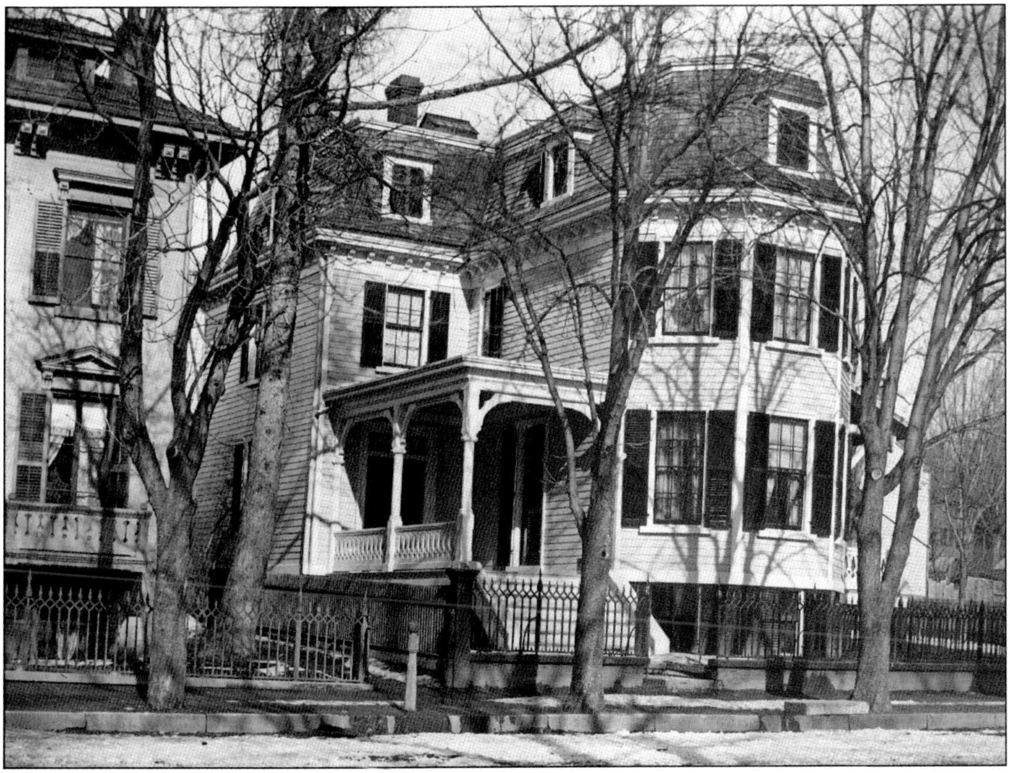

This white clapboard house standing on Chestnut Street was built in 1881 and is an example of Second Empire style, with a bulging tower and a mansard roof. The view of its right side is along Cherry Street. The neighboring home is in the Italianate style, with double corbels under the eaves. Both houses are separated from the sidewalk by iron fences. (Courtesy of PCHS.)

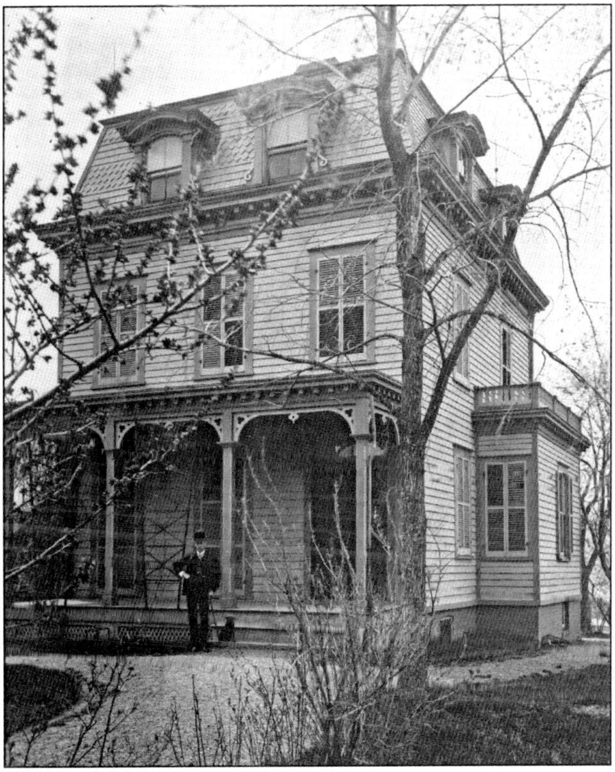

In 1897, a man with his dog strikes a pose in front of his 1880 Second Empire home with its rounded arch dormers, full-story windows, and a mansard roof. William Humphreys Jr., head draftsman at the West Point Foundry, designed the house. The porch roof was later removed. The residence stands on Morris Avenue between Main and Haldane Streets. (Courtesy of PCHS.)

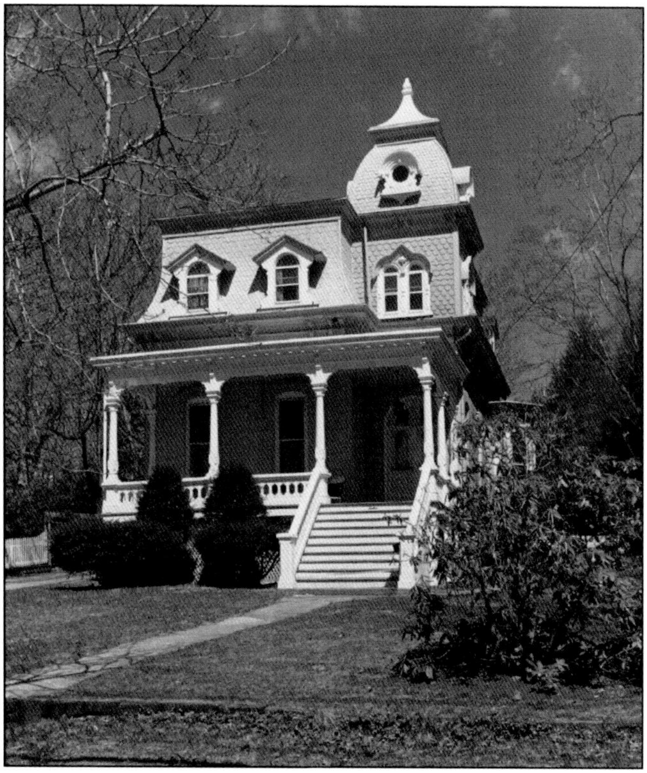

This Victorian house is another well-preserved and striking example of the Second Empire style, with a tower and many horizontal and other elements with ornate details. The mansard roof has decorative slate tiles. The home is located on Morris Avenue next to the Butterfield Library. Gene Kelly dances on its steps in the 1969 film *Hello, Dolly!* (Courtesy of PCHS.)

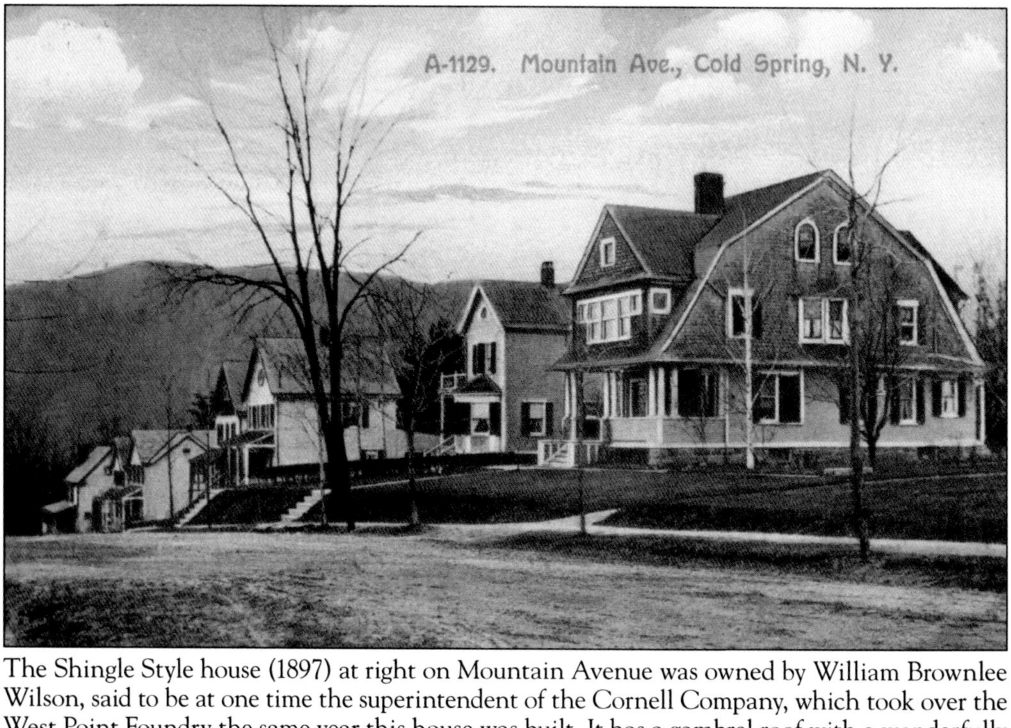

The Shingle Style house (1897) at right on Mountain Avenue was owned by William Brownlee Wilson, said to be at one time the superintendent of the Cornell Company, which took over the West Point Foundry the same year this house was built. It has a gambrel roof with a wonderfully mountain-like shape. (Courtesy of Janet Selleck Rust.)

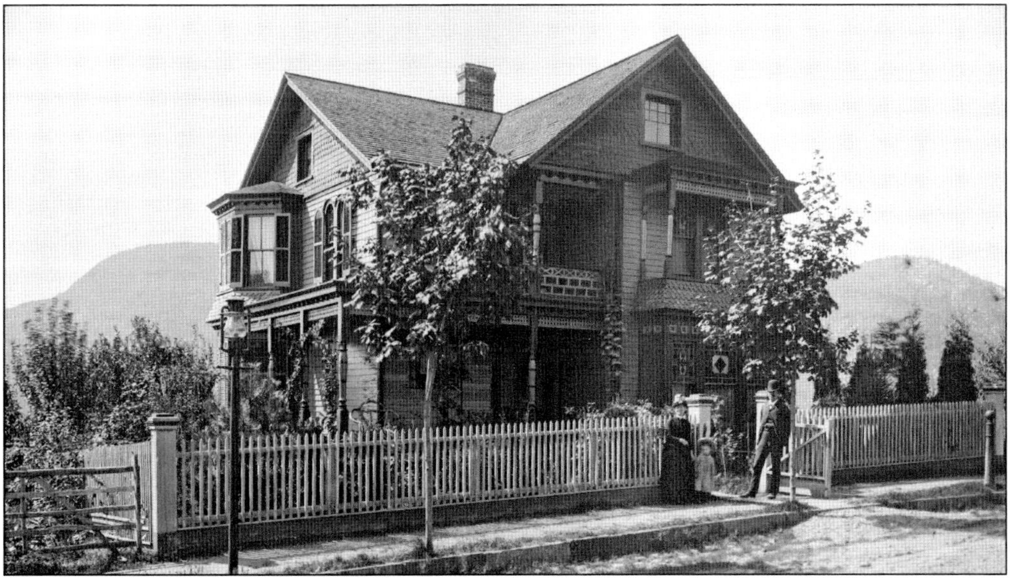

This colorful Queen Anne house on High Street, still privately owned, but now with close neighbors, has a varied roofline, projecting multiple bays, porches, balconies, and ornamental woodwork. The man wears a high-domed bowler, popular in the 1880s, and a high-buttoned suit jacket. The woman is corseted and wears a bustle, and the child sports a broad-brimmed hat and long coat. (Courtesy of PCHS.)

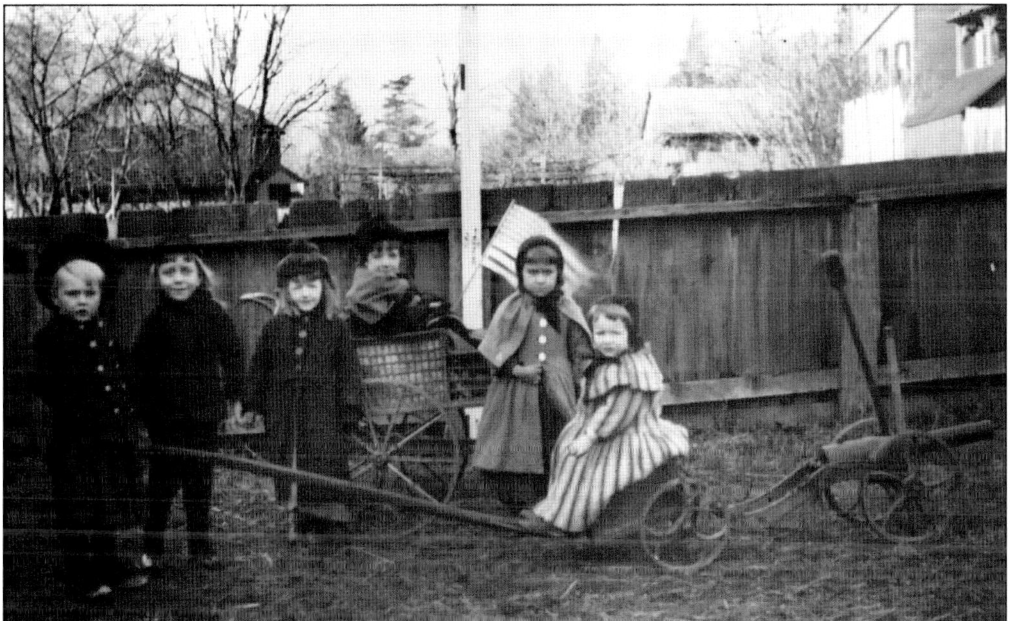

These children photographed about 1895 are in a backyard in Cold Spring. One of them is on a seat of what probably is a toy cannon or a small signal gun. West Point Foundry employees made small cannons for children, sometimes specifically with attached seats. Storm King Mountain looms in the distance. (Courtesy of PCHS.)

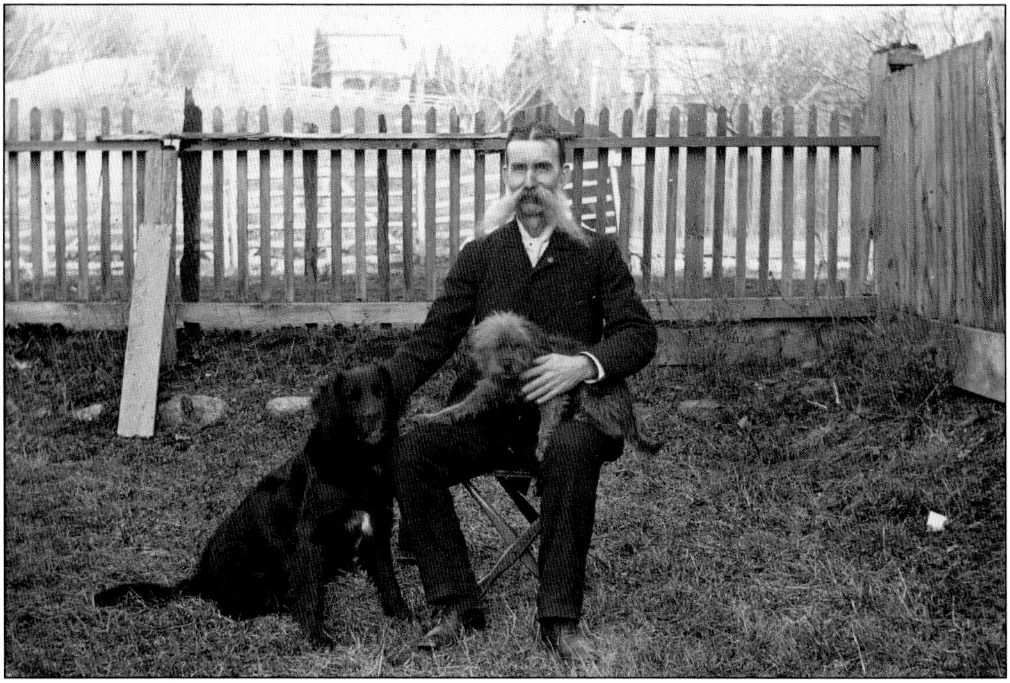

Ellis H. Timm was postmaster of Cold Spring when this picture was taken in 1901. He was also a village trustee, a Mason, and a member of the board of education. His suit jacket is tailored to hang open from the top button. The center parting of hair was popular at the time, but Timm's impressive mustache was unusual. The view is toward Morris Avenue. (Courtesy of PCHS.)

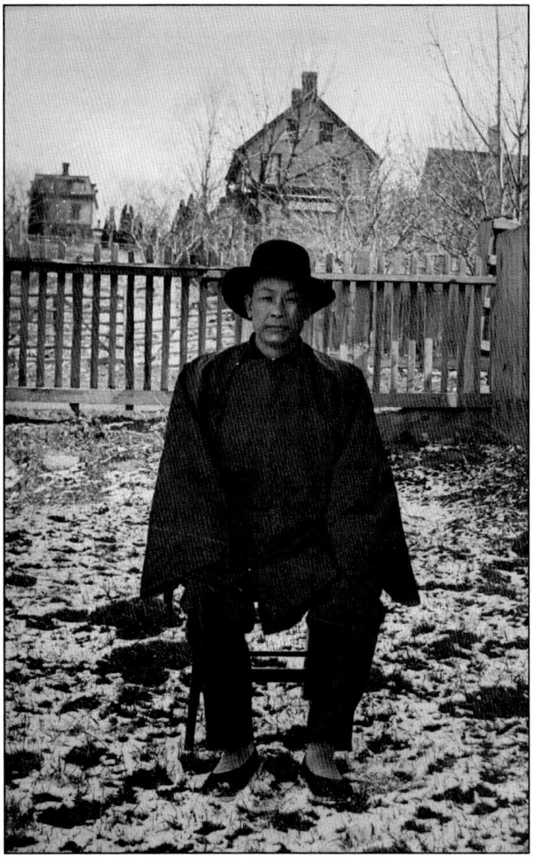

Ling Tsui sits in the same backyard as Ellis Timm (above). Tsui operated a laundry early in the 1920s, or earlier, on Main Street between Garden and Fair Streets. An older resident remembered him as kind to children, often giving them Chinese bracelets, and that he traveled to New York City on Sundays. He was murdered there during one visit. (Courtesy of PCHS.)

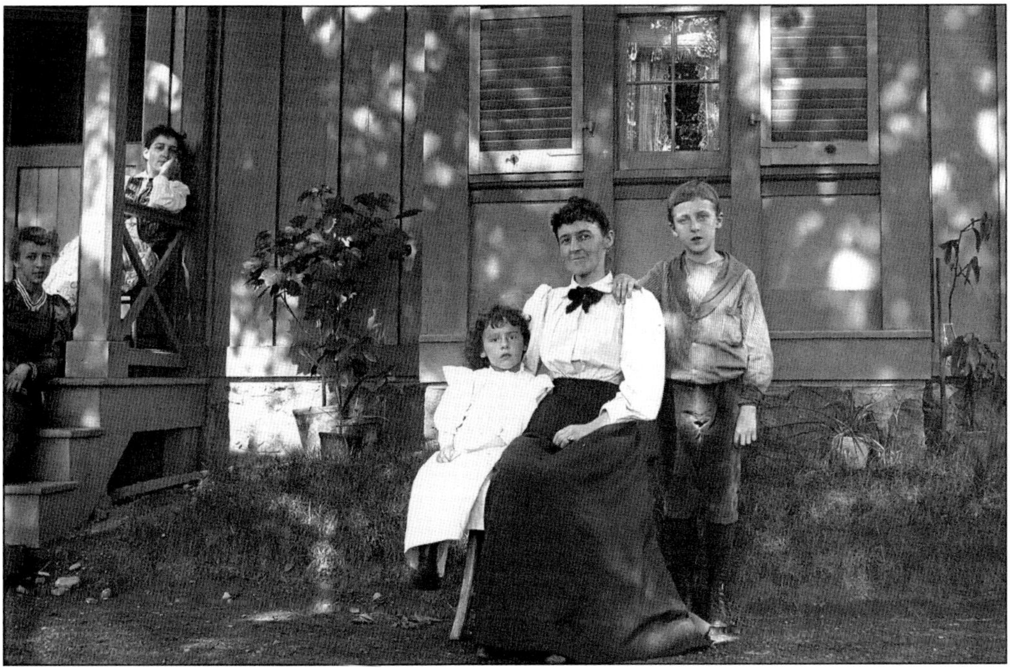

A smiling mother and two children pose in the shade in front of a house with board-and-batten siding while two young women look on from the steps at left. The mother's outfit of white blouse with puffed sleeves, closed at the neck with a bow, and a full, dark skirt, is a good example of daytime wear around 1900. (Courtesy of PCHS.)

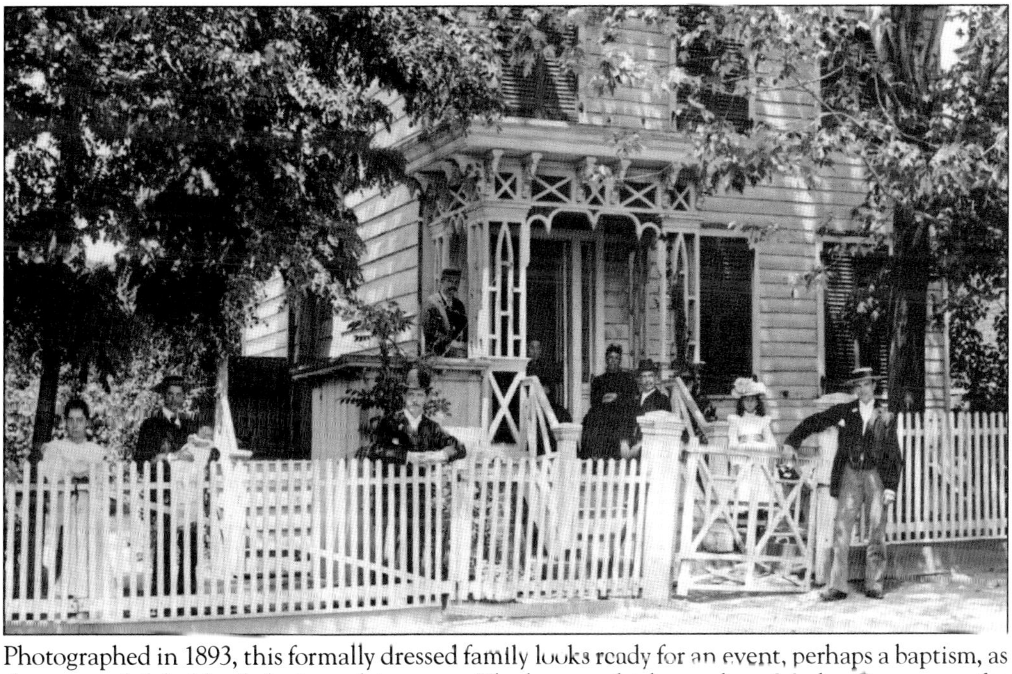

Photographed in 1893, this formally dressed family looks ready for an event, perhaps a baptism, as the man at left holds a baby in a white gown. The house, which stands on Market Street, was the birthplace in 1830 and childhood home of Maj. Gen. Gouverneur Kemble Warren, who served in the Civil War. The house was updated with an ornately bracketed porch. (Courtesy of PCHS.)

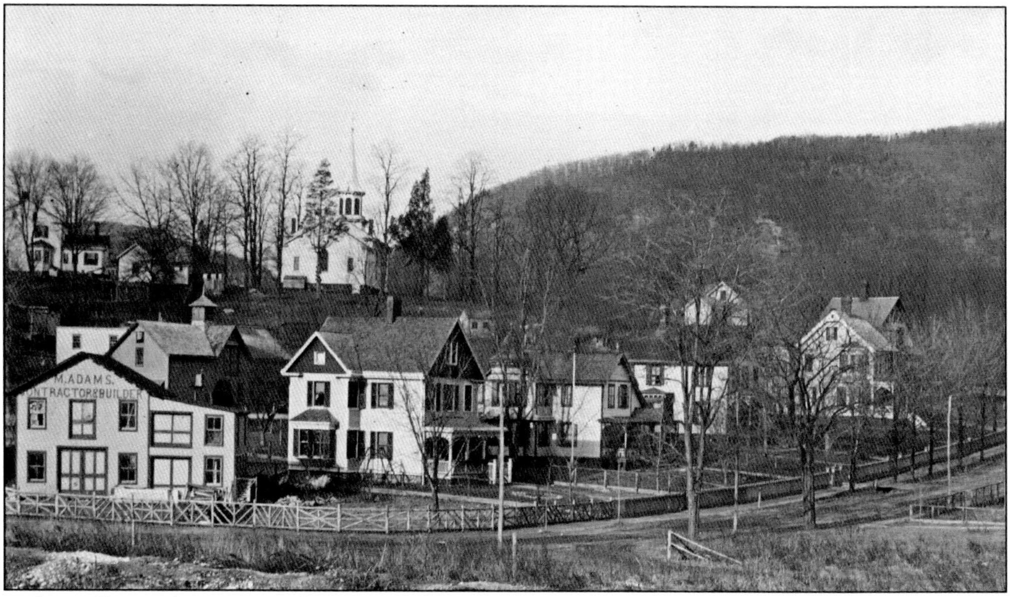

Nelsonville residences near the intersection of Bank and Division Streets are in the foreground. In the distance is the back of the Baptist church on Main Street, near the boundary between Cold Spring and Nelsonville. The houses are relatively modest examples of the vernacular Queen Anne style, with high gables, projecting bays, and porches. One has a tower. The date is 1901. (Photograph by Albert Terwilliger, courtesy of PCHS.)

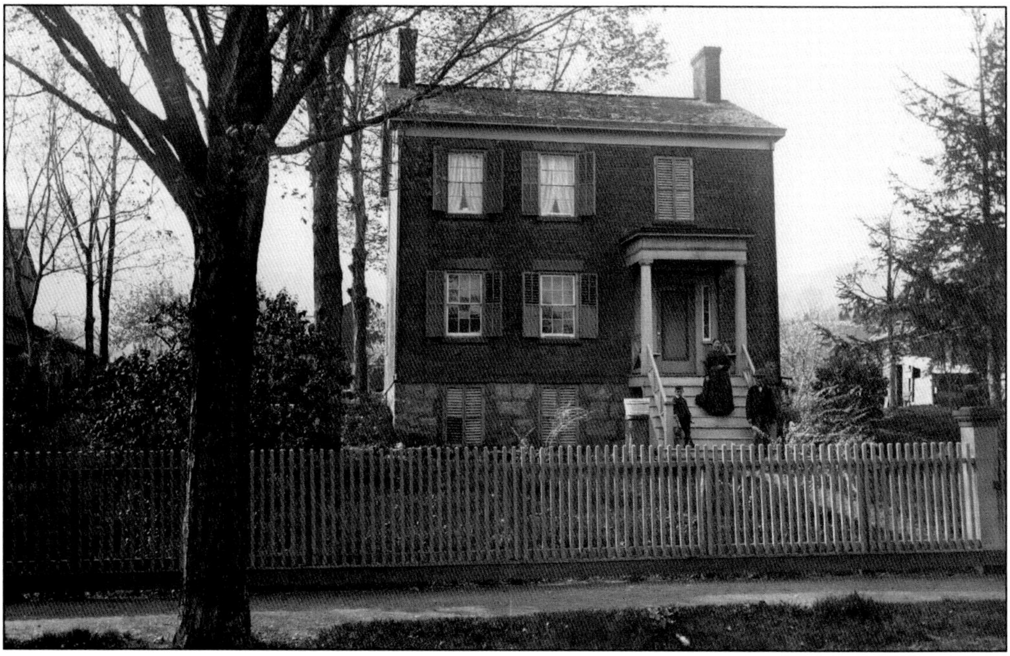

This elegant brick house at the corner of Main Street and Wood Avenue in Nelsonville rests on a heavy stone foundation. It has an entry porch with a vernacular Greek Revival entablature on columns, popular between 1820 and 1860. The boy, his languid attitude a contrast to the adults' formality, holds a broad-brimmed hat. The woman is corseted; her full skirt with broad ruffle trails on the ground. (Courtesy of PCHS.)

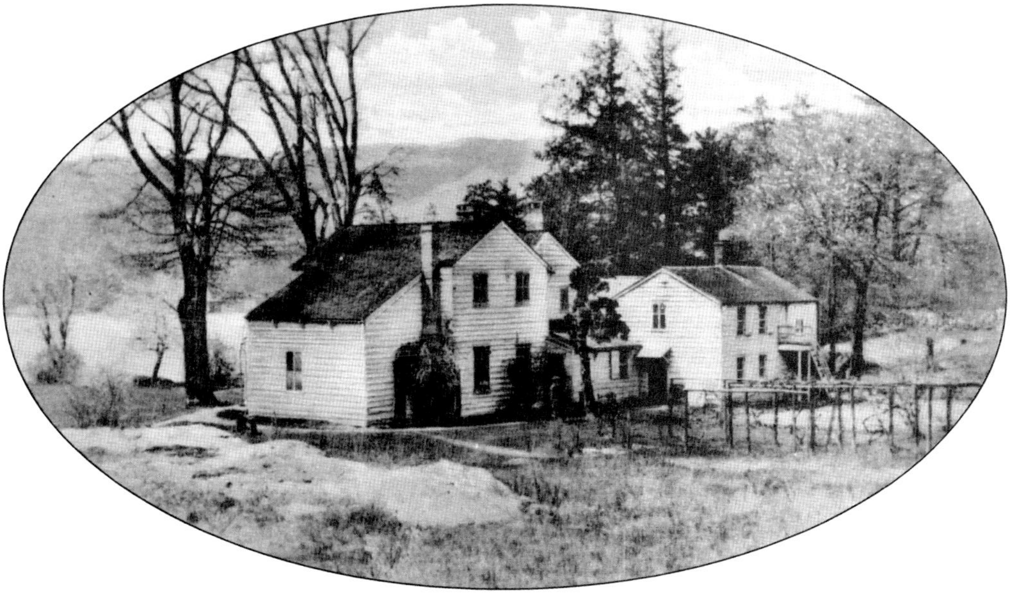

Wood Crag (pre-Revolutionary) on Constitution Island was purchased and enlarged by New York City attorney Henry W. Warner in 1836, initially as a summer home. His daughters, Susan and Anna, became successful writers. Susan Warner's *The Wide, Wide World* (1851) was eclipsed in popularity at the time only by *Uncle Tom's Cabin*. Constitution Island eventually became the property of West Point Military Academy. The Constitution Island Association preserves the house. (Courtesy of PCHS.)

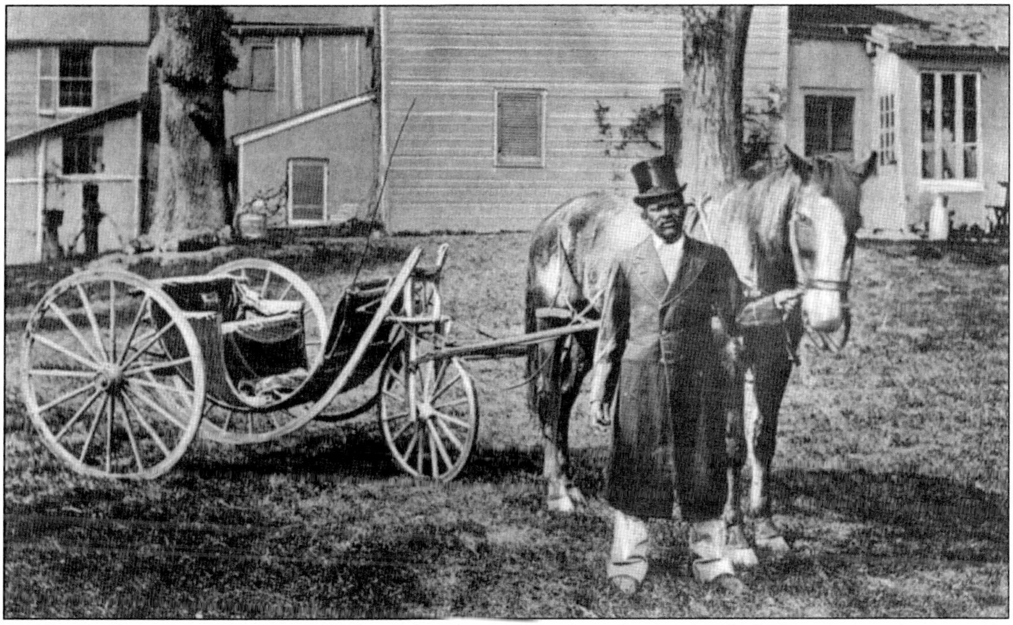

Willis Buckner, in uniform, stands with a horse beside a three-wheeled chaise in a photograph taken after 1868 and later made into a postcard. Buckner was the Warner sisters' driver and groom and taught Sunday school at the Methodist Episcopal Church in Cold Spring. His wife, Bertha, was the women's maid and companion. A former slave in the South, Buckner was said to have lash scars on his back. (Courtesy of PCHS.)

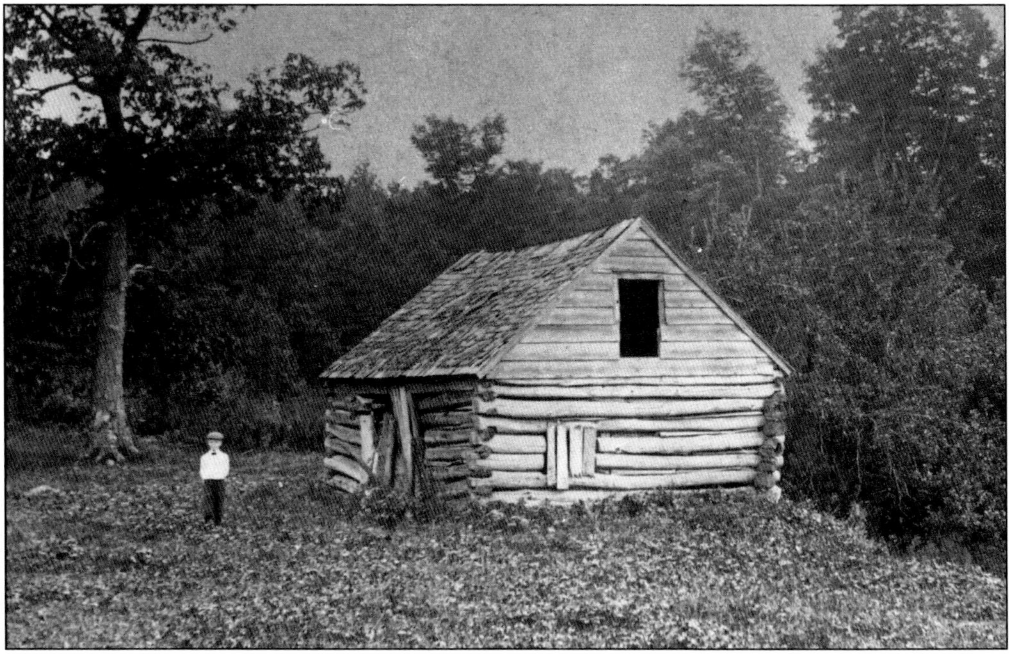

The David Hustis House (1732) stood on property in northern Philipstown, near Budd Mill Pond. Writer and history teacher Nelson DeLanoy noted that Hustis "settled among the Indians and procured his first corn planting from them." In 1928, the cabin was described as being in "fairly good condition." The photograph is from 1906. (Courtesy of PCHS.)

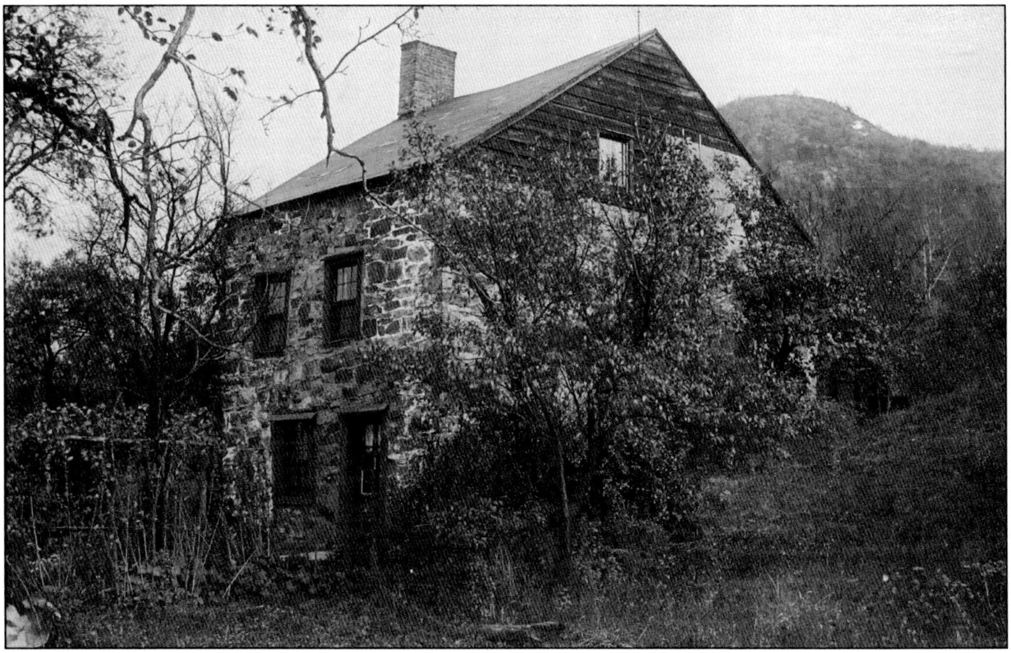

Although no facts are available about this house, other than that it stood in Philipstown, it has been included here because of its picturesque quality and early construction. It probably dates from the late 18th or early 19th century. This photograph was taken about 1900. (Photograph by Albert Terwilliger, courtesy of PCHS.)

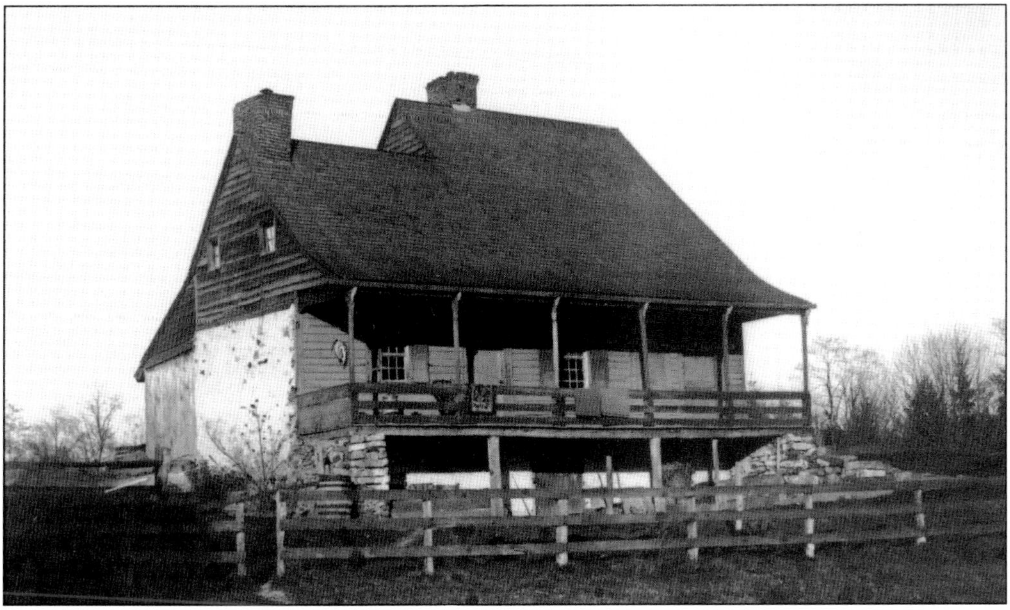

Known as the Red House (1756), this farmhouse was built by Jacob Mandeville on Frederick Philipse's property. The projecting roof slope creates an arcaded porch. The house, on the property of the Highlands Country Club in Garrison, has been restored and is currently a residence. A pre–Revolutionary War gristmill, Dutch barn, and a partially preserved cottage survive nearby. (Courtesy of PCHS.)

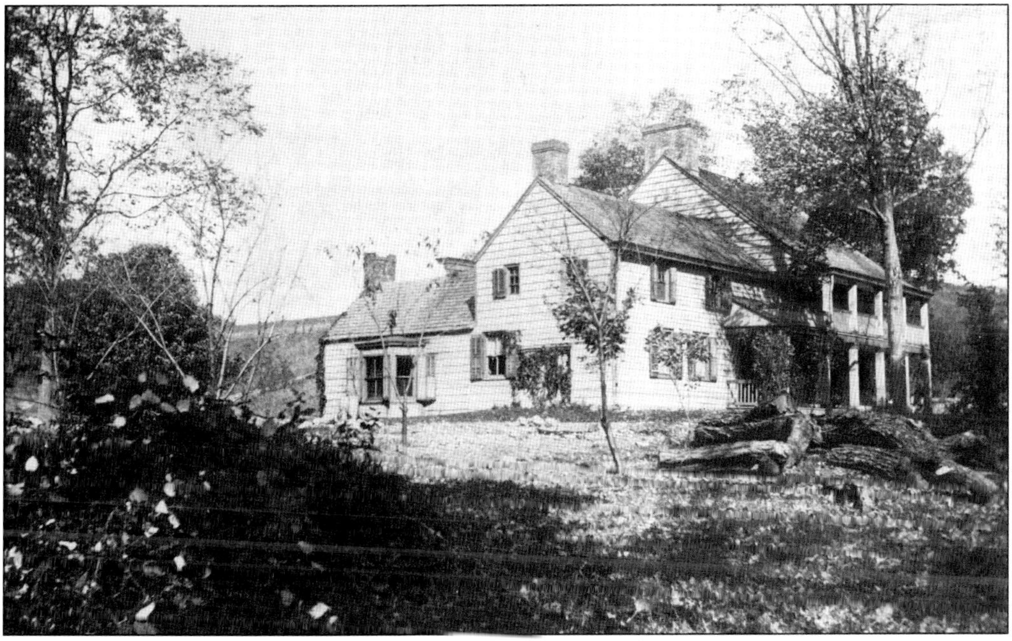

The Warren House (1761), a stagecoach stop and tavern on the Old Albany Post Road, was used as a headquarters by the Continental Army during the Revolution. In 1832, steamboat traffic on the Hudson River helped put the tavern out of business, and a farm took over the property until 1916. In the 1940s, the building was restored to its 18th-century appearance and opened as the Bird and Bottle Inn. (Courtesy of PCHS.)

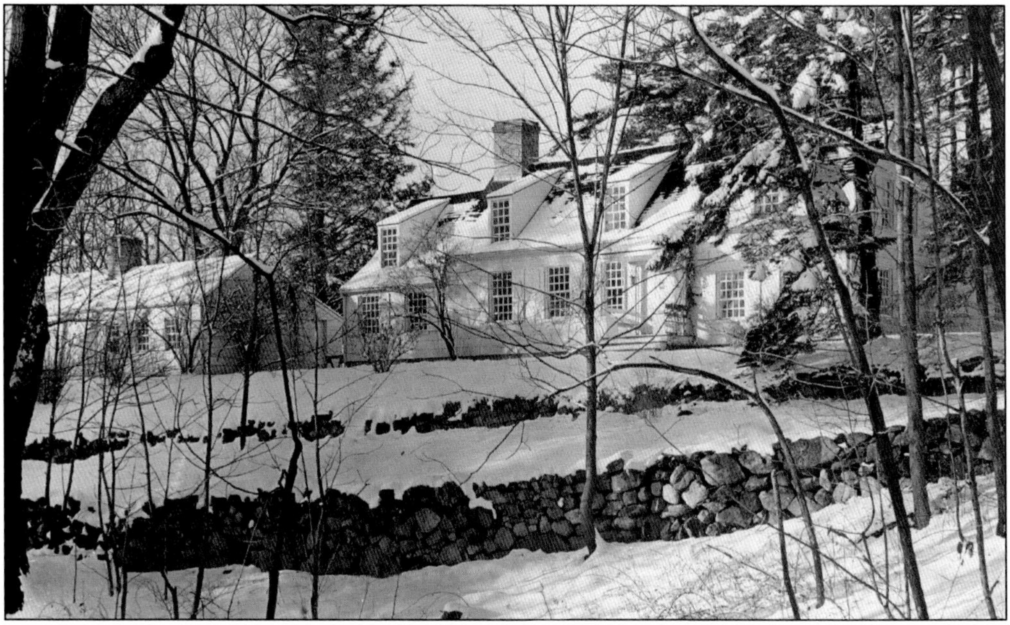

The Mandeville House, located in Garrison and photographed in 1941, was leased to Jacob Mandeville in 1735. A kitchen wing and upstairs rooms were added later. Gen. Israel Putnam headquartered here during the Revolution. Architect Richard Upjohn bought the house in 1852, expanded it, and redid its exterior in the Gothic Revival style. A 1920s restoration brought the house closer to its colonial appearance. (Courtesy of PCHS.)

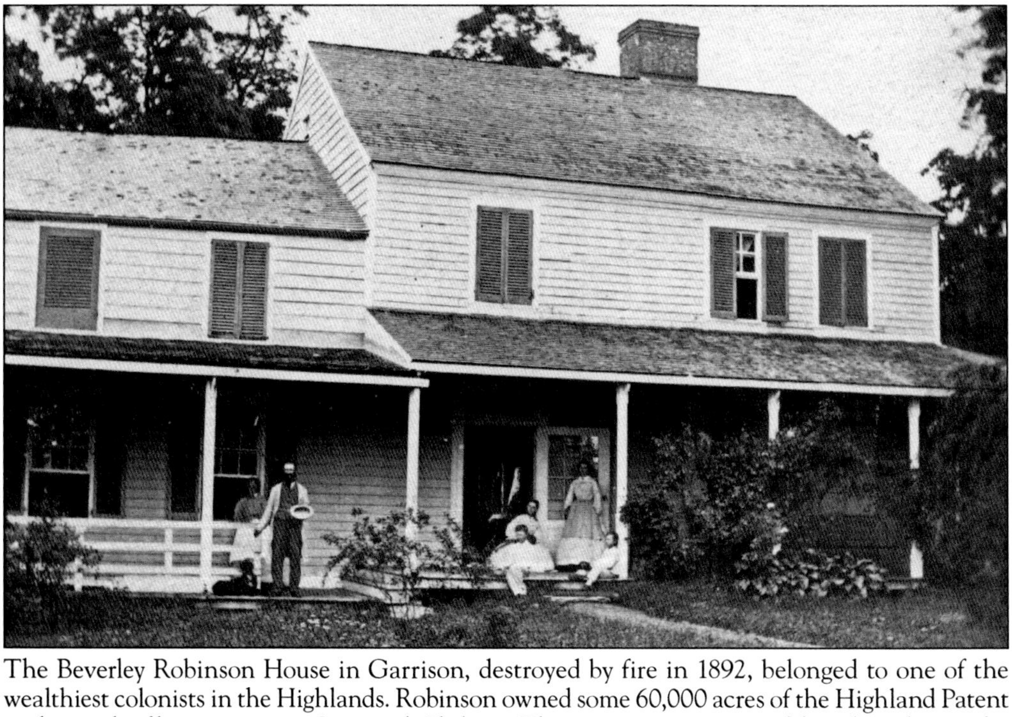

The Beverley Robinson House in Garrison, destroyed by fire in 1892, belonged to one of the wealthiest colonists in the Highlands. Robinson owned some 60,000 acres of the Highland Patent as the result of his marriage to Susannah Philipse. The property was stripped from him during the Revolution because of his royalist activities. (Courtesy of Antipodean Books, Maps & Prints.)

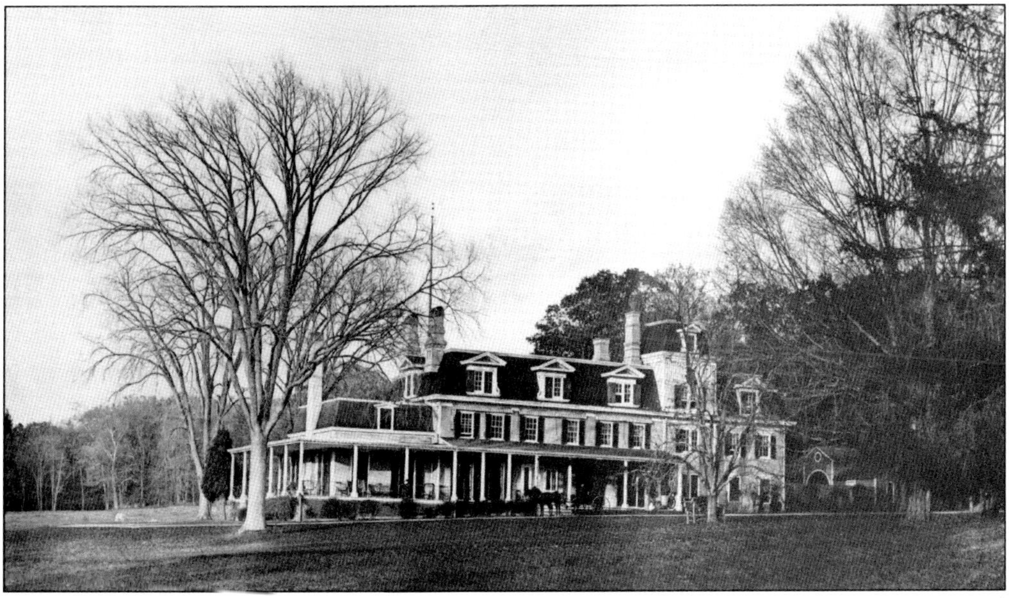

Henry Casimir de Rham, a prominent banker and merchant, purchased his Garrison property and an 1802 Federal-style house in 1834. De Rham enlarged the house and named it Giez, after his Swiss birthplace. The de Rhams were among the first New Yorkers to summer in Garrison. The house remained in the family until 1949, undergoing three renovations with additions, including a large wraparound porch. (Courtesy of the Nice family.)

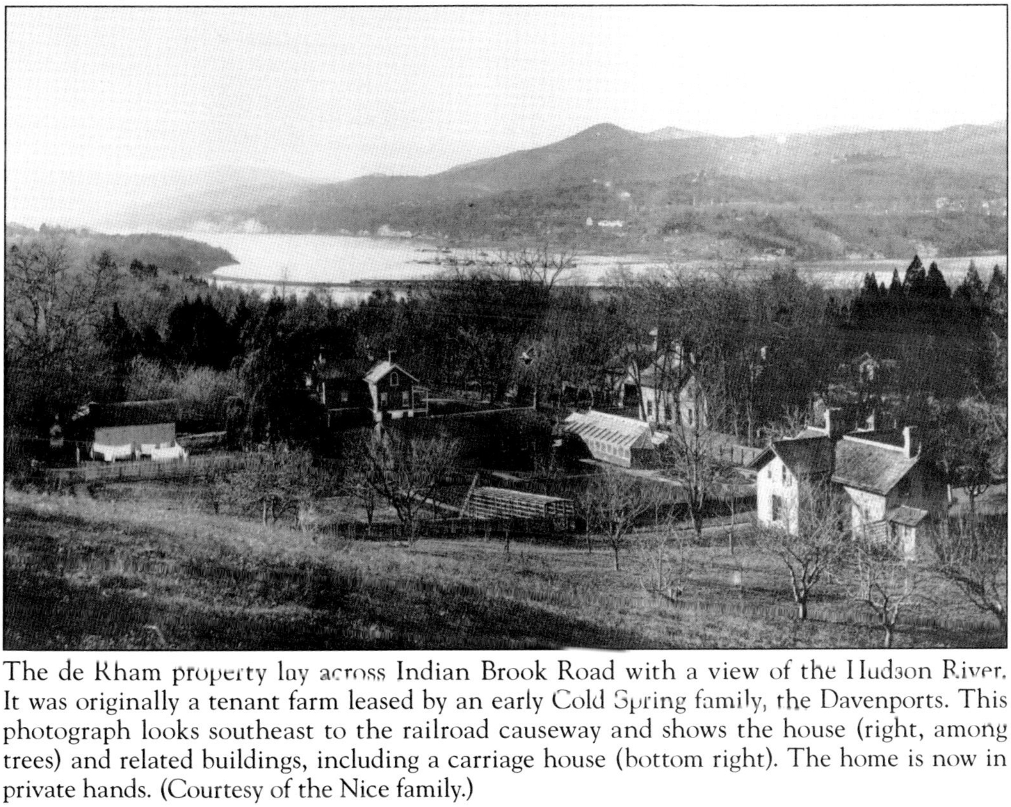

The de Rham property lay across Indian Brook Road with a view of the Hudson River. It was originally a tenant farm leased by an early Cold Spring family, the Davenports. This photograph looks southeast to the railroad causeway and shows the house (right, among trees) and related buildings, including a carriage house (bottom right). The home is now in private hands. (Courtesy of the Nice family.)

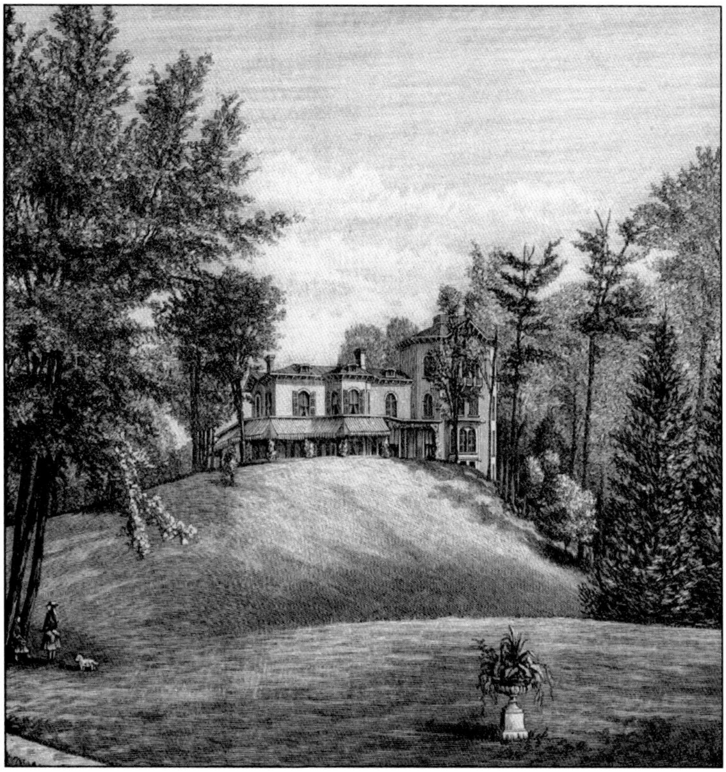

Glenclyffe (about 1858) was the home of Hamilton Fish, 16th governor of New York State and secretary of state under Ulysses S. Grant. Fish bought the house, built near the river in Garrison from a design by Calvert Vaux, in 1861 and enlarged it. In 2001, the Open Space Institute acquired Fish's estate in order to preserve the land. The engraving predates 1887. (Courtesy of PCHS.)

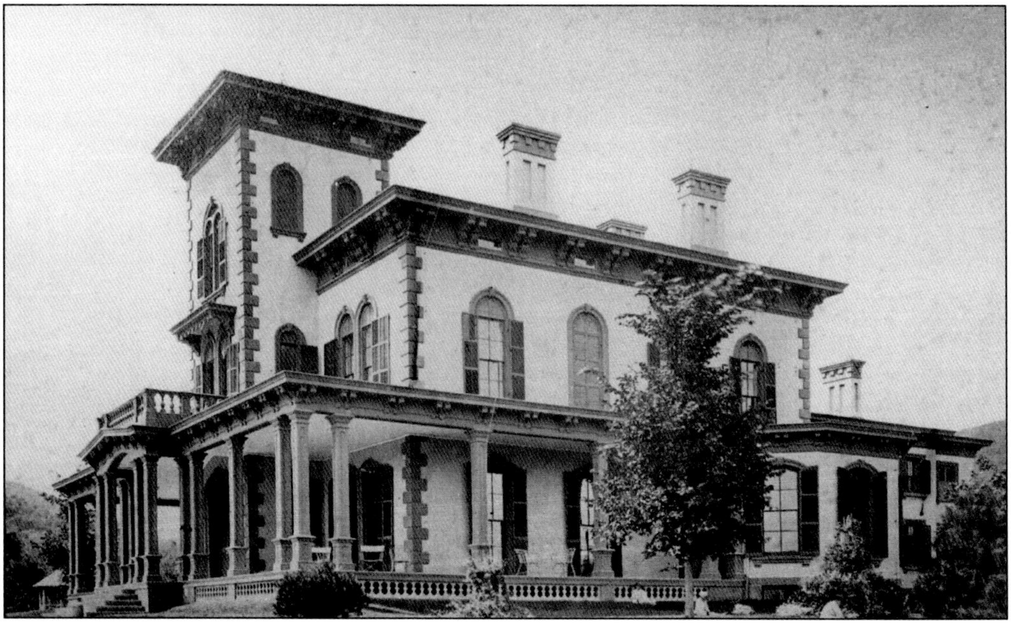

Oulagisket (1864), the home of Samuel Sloan, president of 17 railroads during his career, was a stuccoed brick house with Italianate elements. This view shows arched windows, porches, the tower, and a multicolumned projecting main entry. Sloan acquired and landscaped more land over the years. The Sloans were active socially, and their dinner parties involved many guests and fireworks. (Courtesy of PCHS.)

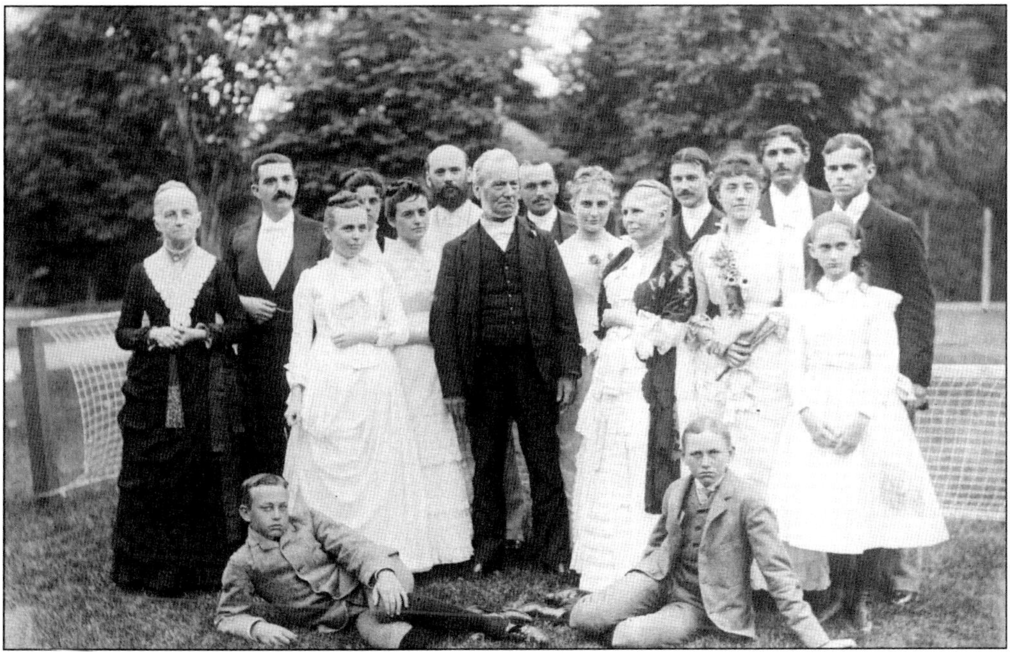

Samuel Sloan and his wife, Margaret, pose at center with some of their nine surviving children and other family members on a grass court on July 4, 1887. A collector of fine porcelains, Margaret Sloan had nearly 12 dozen sets of plates in her city and country homes. Many of the men are dressed for dinner in white tie and tails. The women wear bustles and corsets under frilly afternoon frocks. (Courtesy of PCHS.)

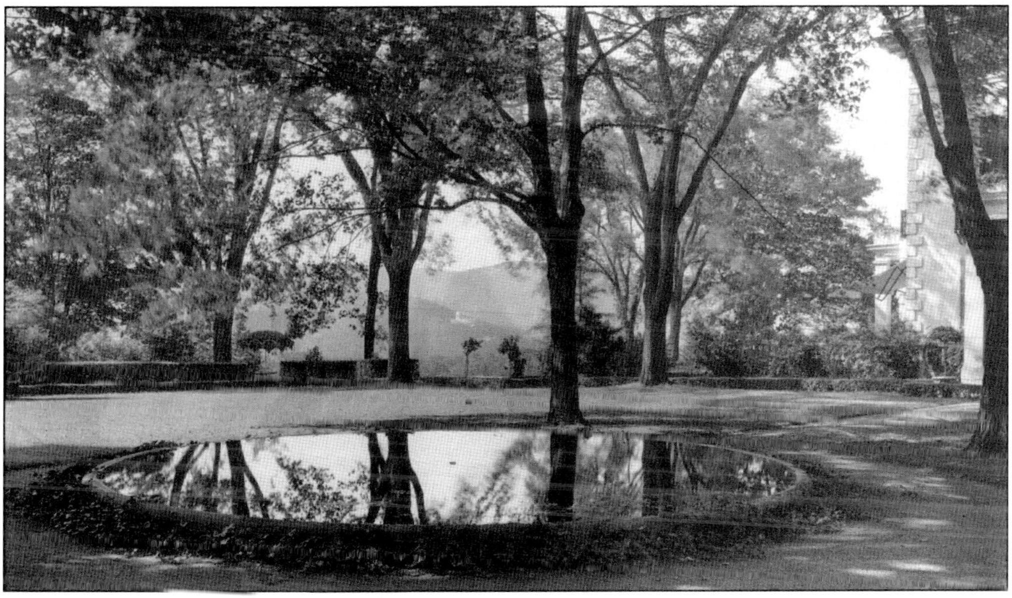

Sloan and his wife loved trees and planted many varieties of them. In the 1920s and 1930s, Samuel Sloan Jr. and his wife, Katherine, developed the estate further with the help of the famous landscape architect Fletcher Steele, who designed this reflection pool as well as elaborate terraces, stairways, and colonnades. (Courtesy of PCHS.)

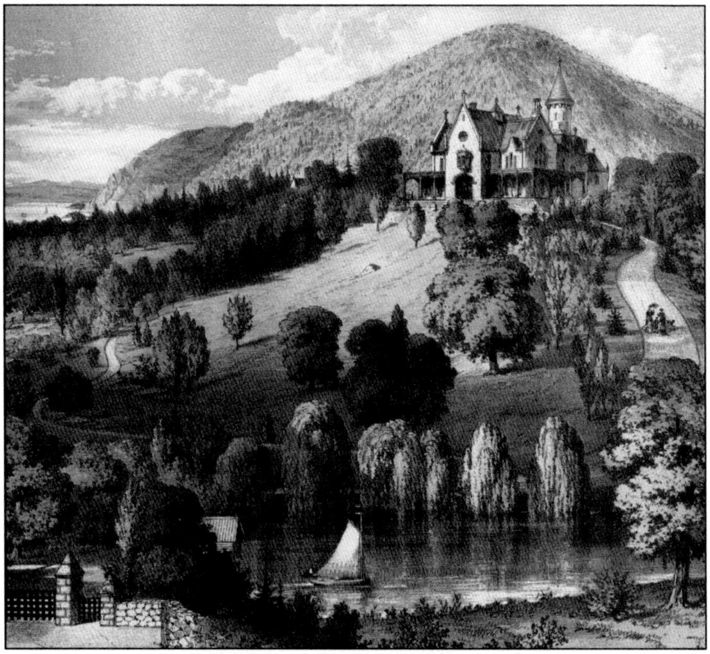

Pierrepont Terrace (1863–1867), the Gothic Revival home of Edwards Pierrepont, was built of stuccoed brick and later enlarged. The original design may have been by Alexander Jackson Davis, the leading American architect of Gothic Revival and Italianate country houses. Pierrepont was US attorney general in Grant's second term and later ambassador to the United Kingdom. The house, once called Hurst-Pierrepont (a hurst being a wooded hill), is privately owned. (Courtesy of PCHS.)

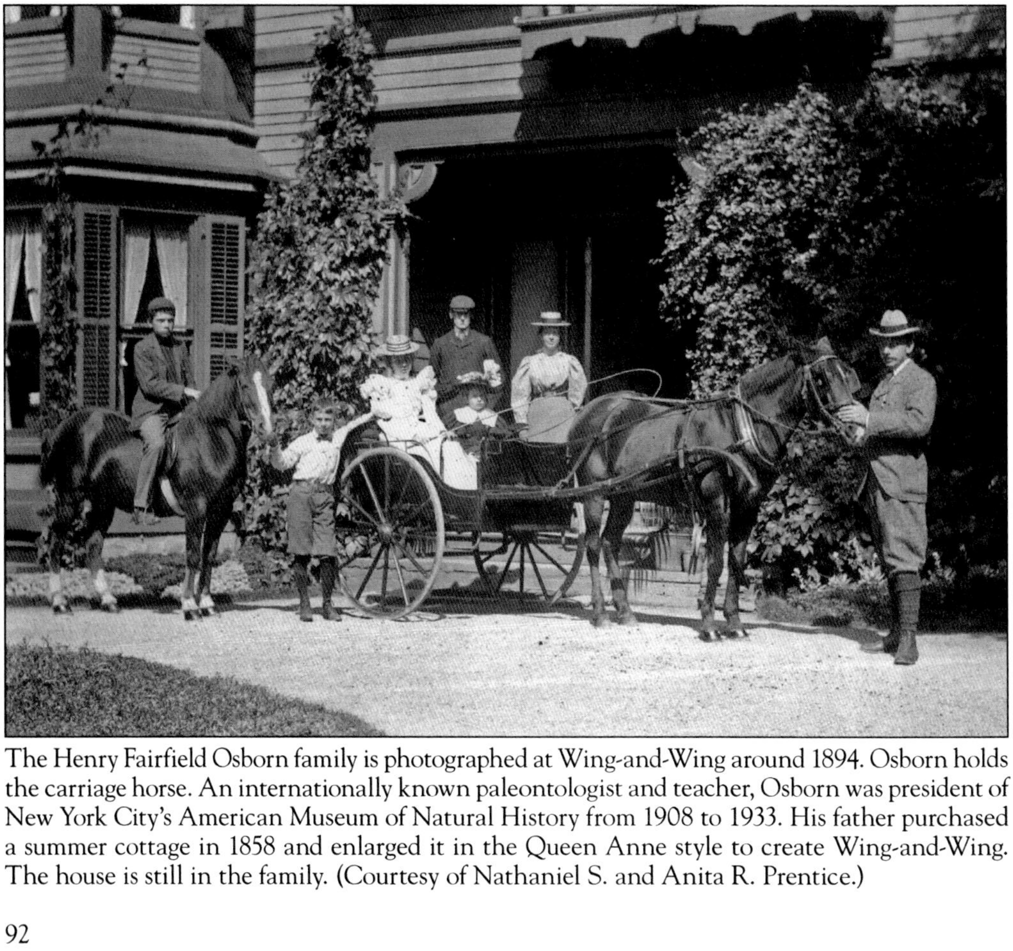

The Henry Fairfield Osborn family is photographed at Wing-and-Wing around 1894. Osborn holds the carriage horse. An internationally known paleontologist and teacher, Osborn was president of New York City's American Museum of Natural History from 1908 to 1933. His father purchased a summer cottage in 1858 and enlarged it in the Queen Anne style to create Wing-and-Wing. The house is still in the family. (Courtesy of Nathaniel S. and Anita R. Prentice.)

William Henry Osborn, head of the Illinois Central Railroad between 1855 and 1882, built Castle Rock (1881), located about 1.5 miles from Wing-and-Wing. Perched like a medieval castle on a 650-foot elevation suggested by the landscape painter Frederic E. Church, the house gives sweeping Hudson River views. Jarvis Morgan Slade designed this Gothic fantasy, which is now in private hands. (Courtesy of Janet Selleck Rust.)

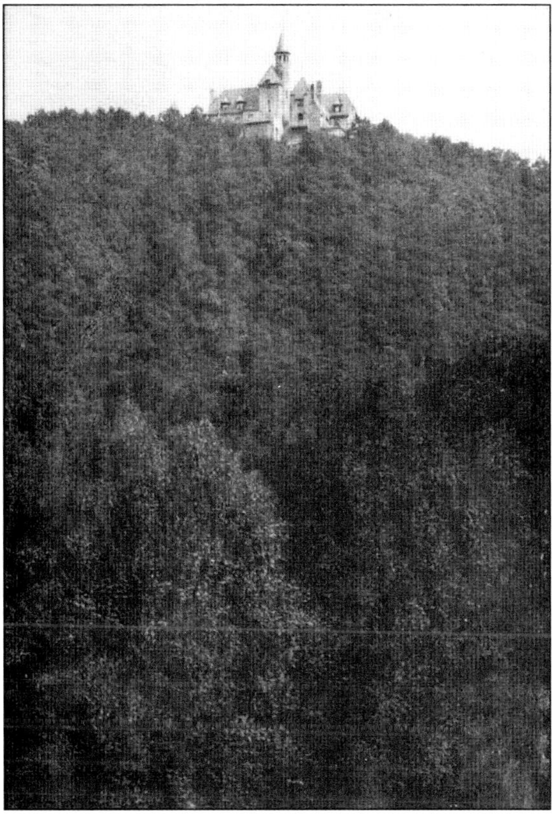

Henry Fairfield Osborn inherited Castle Rock in 1902 and added wings to house dining and music rooms and enlarged the library. A central tower nearly 100 feet high dominates the asymmetrical, 34-room building. Osborn built the stone entrance to the castle in 1906. Architect Edward Hamilton Bell, who designed the architectural decorations for Biltmore, George Washington Vanderbilt II's North Carolina estate, directed the additions. (Courtesy of PCHS.)

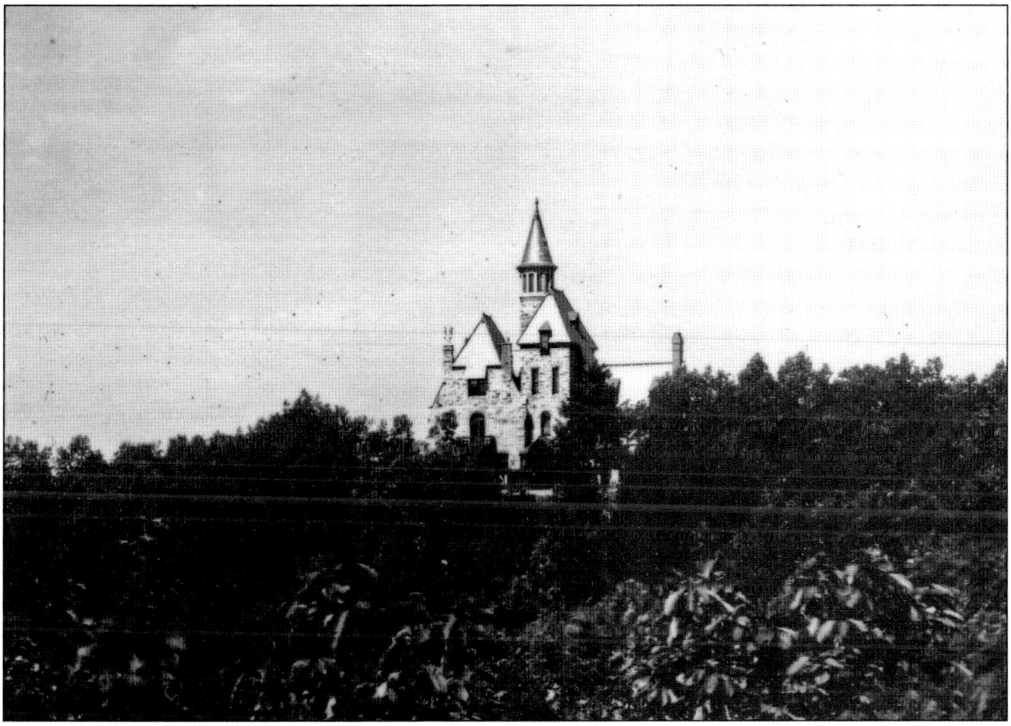

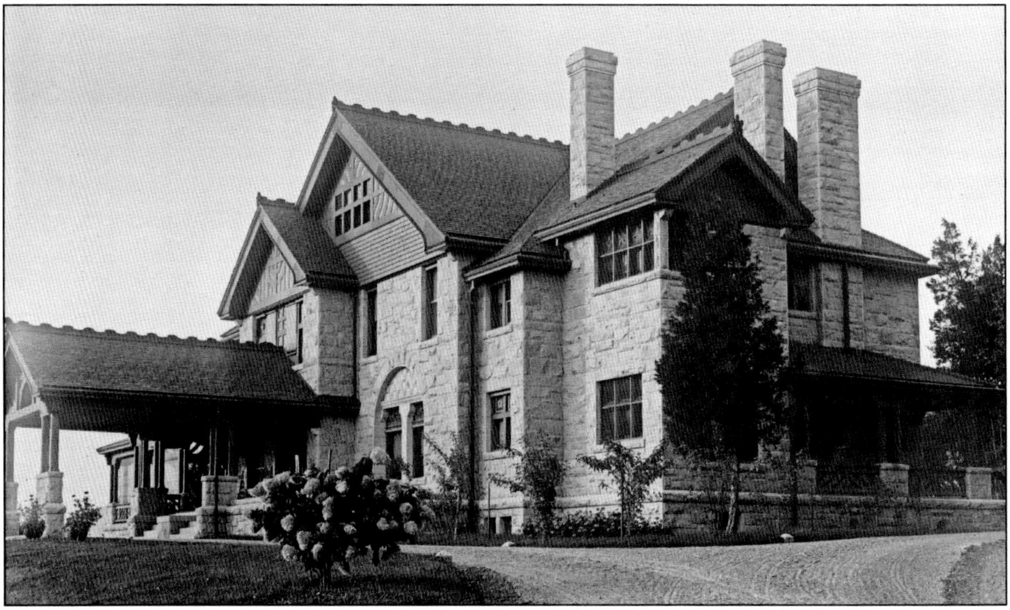

Cedar Crest, on Snake Hill Road in Garrison, was built by John M. Toucey, the general superintendent of the New York Central & Hudson River Railroad. In 1867, Cornelius Vanderbilt acquired the New York Central and merged it with his Hudson River Railroad. Toucey's late-Victorian stone house with decorative half-timbered gables and a large porte cochere now sits in the woods in altered form. (Courtesy of PCHS.)

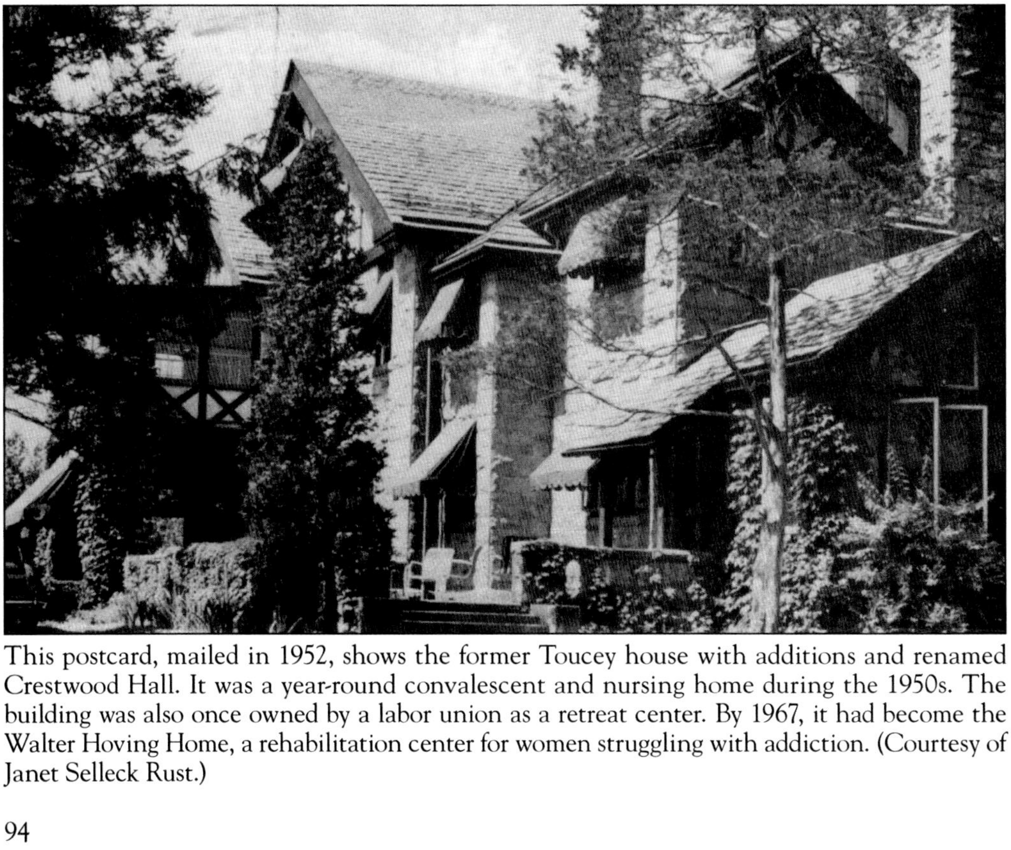

This postcard, mailed in 1952, shows the former Toucey house with additions and renamed Crestwood Hall. It was a year-round convalescent and nursing home during the 1950s. The building was also once owned by a labor union as a retreat center. By 1967, it had become the Walter Hoving Home, a rehabilitation center for women struggling with addiction. (Courtesy of Janet Selleck Rust.)

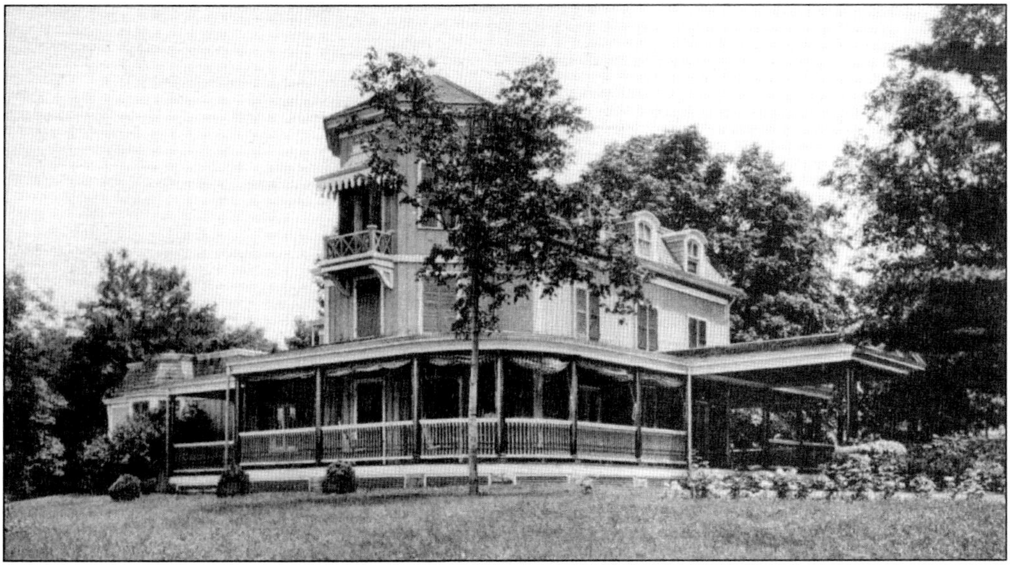

The James A. Glover house on Upper Station Road in Garrison faces the river, which could be seen from the wraparound porch. Glover was successful in real estate in New York City. In 1911, he was among several prominent individuals, including Stuyvesant Fish, Henry Fairfield Osborn, and the Reverend T. Charles Chorley, who sued a company constructing the Catskill Aqueduct for spoiling a road in Garrison. (Courtesy of PCHS.)

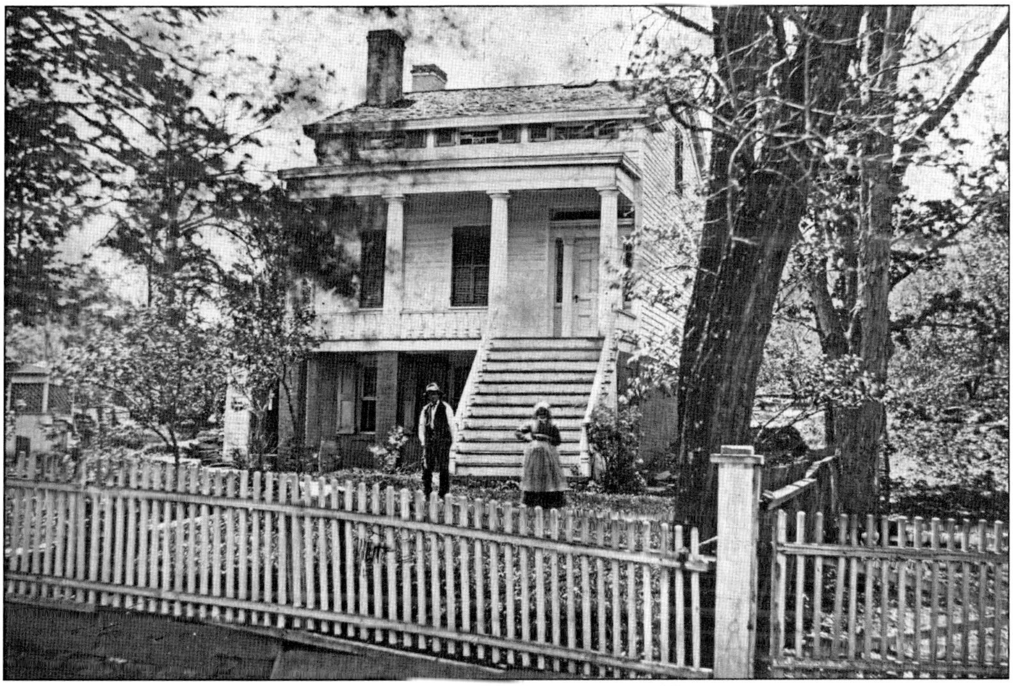

This house stands with an addition on the left at the corner of Steuben and Gallows Hill Roads in Continental Village in southern Philipstown. Elegantly proportioned columns hold up an extended entablature along the porch line, with eyebrow windows above, in this example of Greek Revival style of the early 1800s. As was customary, the kitchen would likely have been in the basement. (Courtesy of PCHS.)

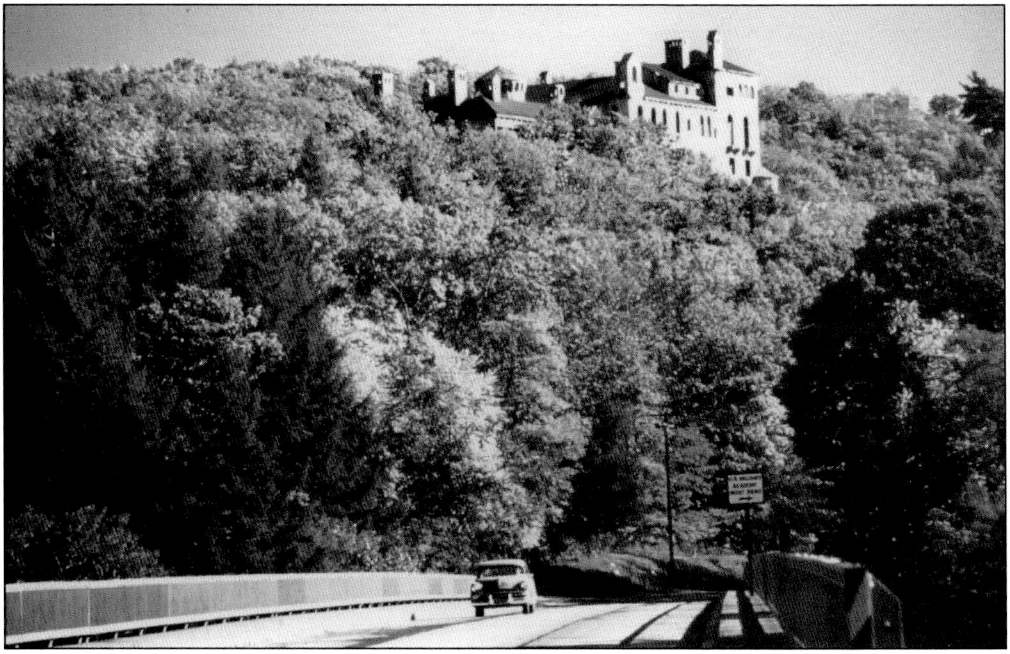

Dick's Castle (begun 1904), seen from Route 9D between Cold Spring and Garrison, was built by financier Evans R. Dick, who completed only its shell before abandoning the building in 1911. It was inspired by the Moorish architecture of the Alhambra in Granada, Spain. In 1944, an Austrian engineer purchased it. A new owner has converted it to condominiums. (Courtesy of PCHS.)

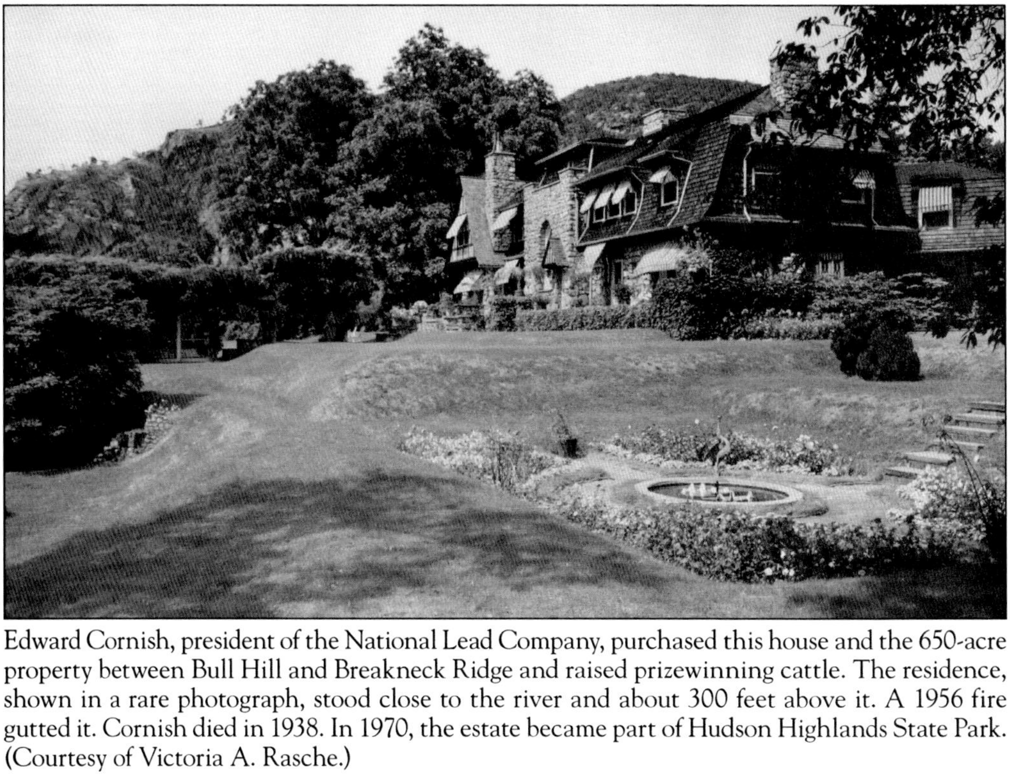

Edward Cornish, president of the National Lead Company, purchased this house and the 650-acre property between Bull Hill and Breakneck Ridge and raised prizewinning cattle. The residence, shown in a rare photograph, stood close to the river and about 300 feet above it. A 1956 fire gutted it. Cornish died in 1938. In 1970, the estate became part of Hudson Highlands State Park. (Courtesy of Victoria A. Rasche.)

Six

Serving a Growing Populace
Civic Structures, Schools, and Churches

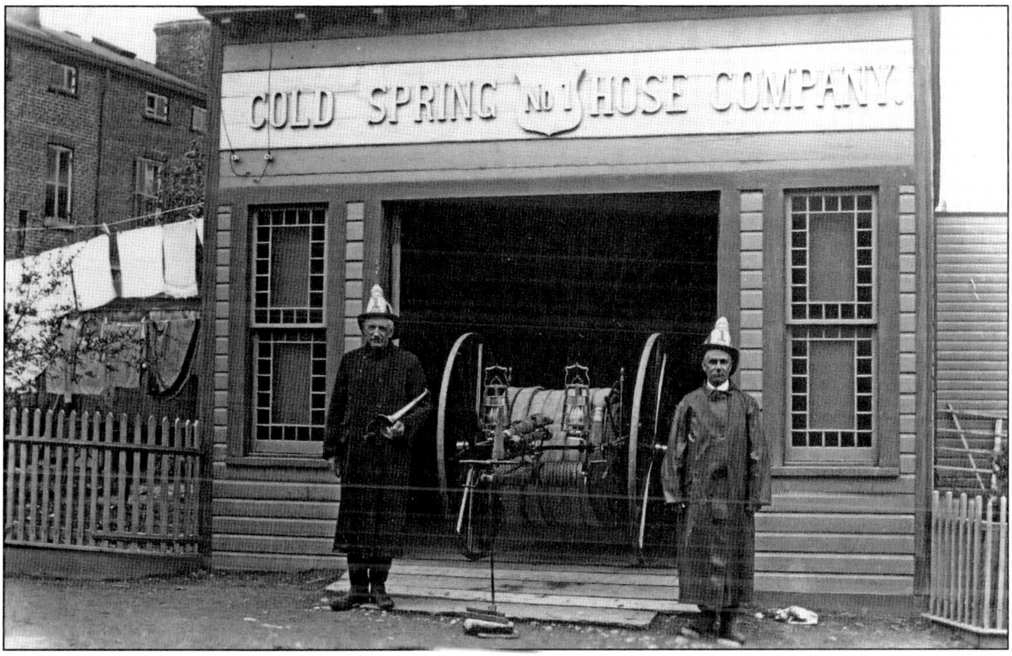

Two volunteer firemen in full gear—the foreman being the one with the horn—display their hose cart with lanterns. They would have pulled it to a fire. The Cold Spring Hose Company No. 1, organized in 1896, replaced the old bucket brigade and moved into this first firehouse, with belfry on top, in 1898. The building, used for 28 years, stood on Garden Street. A horse-drawn hook and ladder was donated in 1899. (Courtesy of PCHS.)

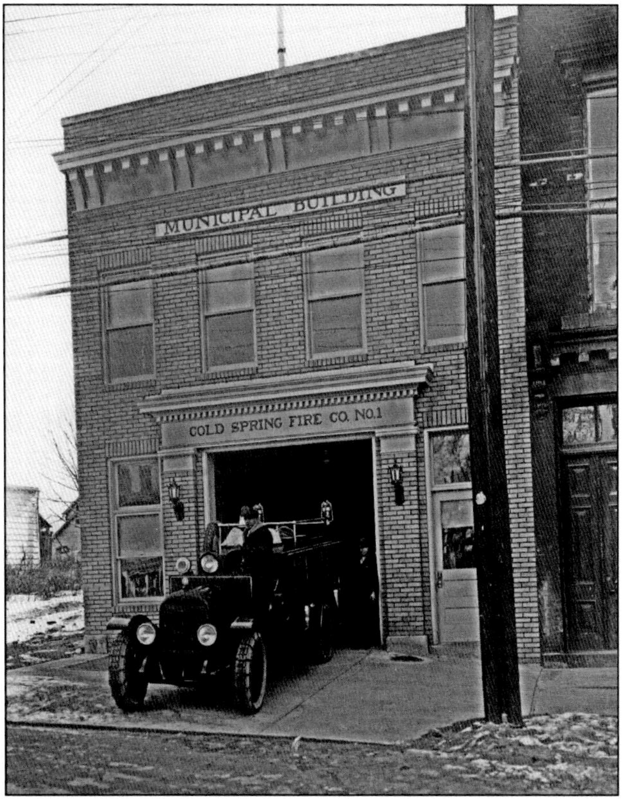

When the Cold Spring Fire Company purchased its first truck, this 1923 American LaFrance chemical truck, the firehouse was too small, so the company petitioned the village for a new one, resulting in the 1926 Municipal Building, a two-story brick structure on Main Street designed by local architect Louis Mekeel. The village's offices, located on the second floor, were moved to the adjacent building in 1958. The fire company still serves Cold Spring. (Courtesy of PCHS.)

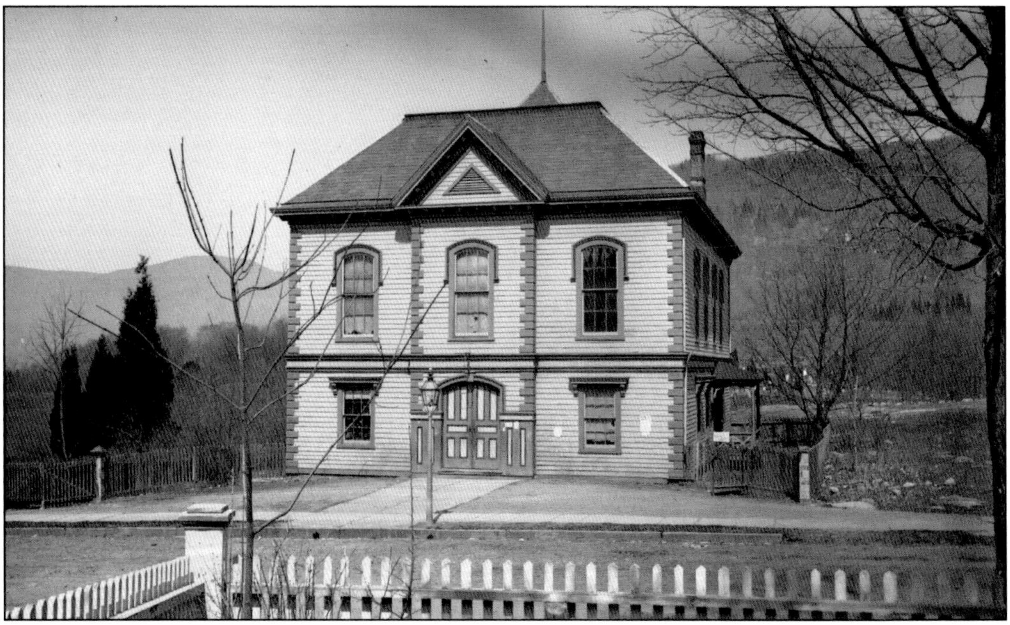

The Town Hall of Philipstown (1867) remains prominent on Main Street at the border of Cold Spring and Nelsonville. It was built to house a jail, court sessions, and town elections. Decorative wooden cornerstones imitate stone on this clapboard structure and define the central bay, which is topped by a gable and pediment. (Courtesy of PCHS.)

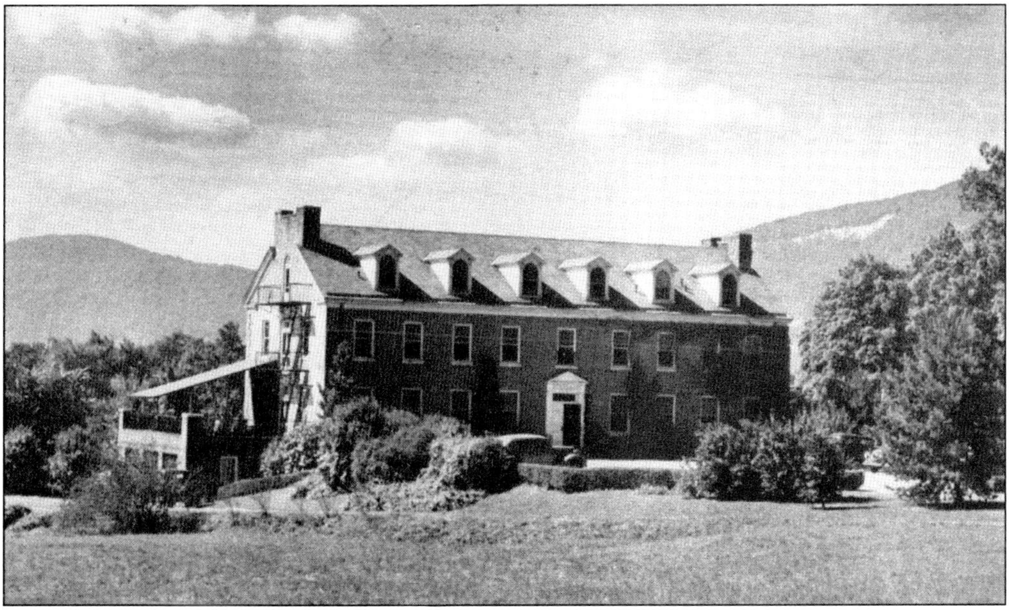

The Julia L. Butterfield Memorial Hospital (1925), facing Paulding Avenue, was built with funding from her estate. The building's Colonial Revival style is evidenced by the symmetry of the facade and gabled dormers. The mountains in the distance are on the opposite shore of the Hudson River. The hospital closed in 1995. The building was reconstructed in a modern style in 1963. (Courtesy of Janet Selleck Rust.)

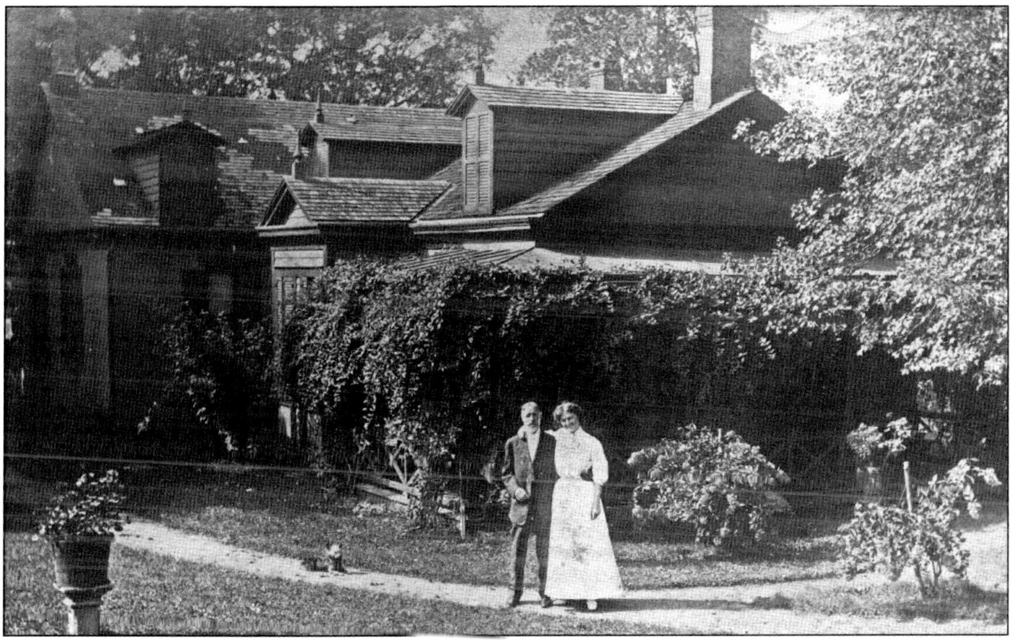

William H. Taylor Jr., former superintendent of the West Point Foundry, and his daughter Anna stand outside their home around 1914, after he purchased the property. The original building was a one-story schoolhouse (1830) for foundry apprentices. The school was incorporated into the public school system in 1867, and the structure was enlarged. In 1960, the PCHS purchased it, enlarged it in 1971, and restored its 1867 layout in 2005. (Courtesy of PCHS.)

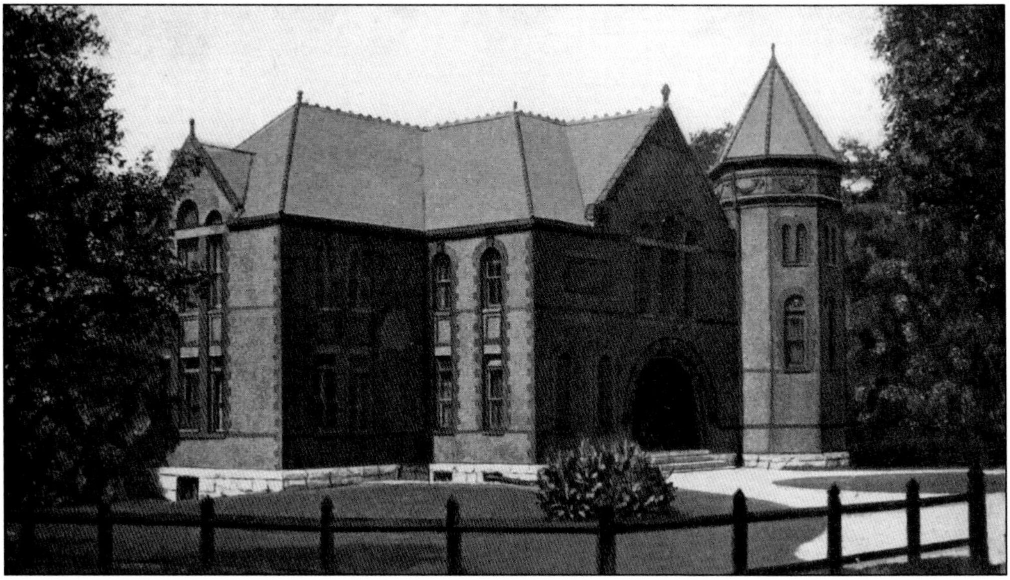

The Haldane Union Free School (1889) served Cold Spring children of all ages between 1891 and 1936. The redbrick Romanesque Revival building with mansard roof and tower stood on Morris Avenue on the former Butterfield estate. It was named for the iron merchant James H. Haldane, whose bequest funded it. Children from the Foundry and Rock Street Schools were transferred here. (Courtesy of Mark Forlow.)

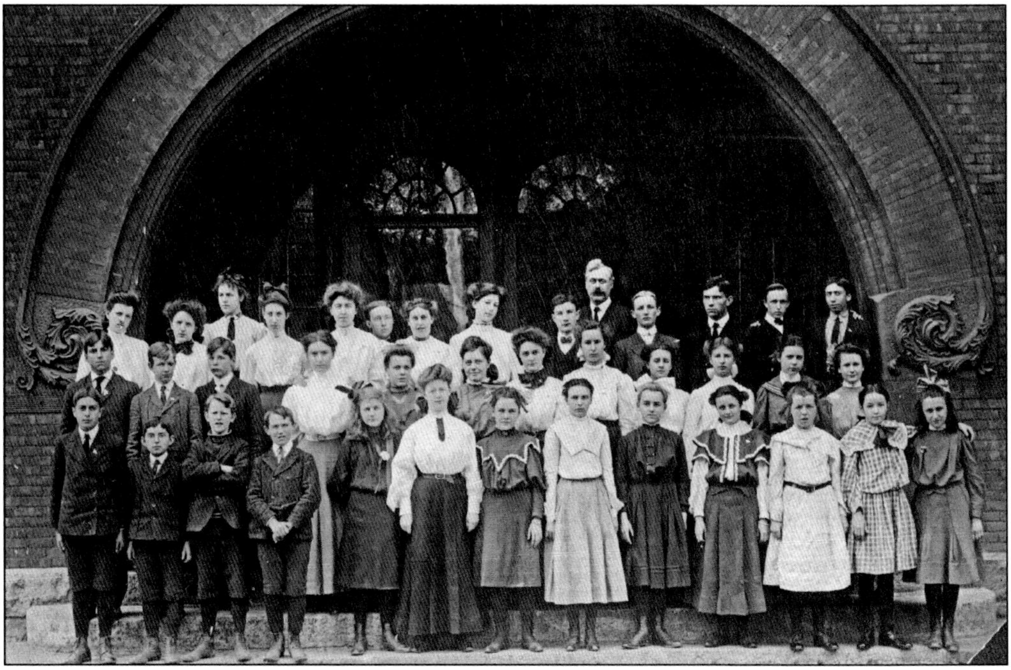

About 1900, Haldane students and teachers stand at the main door of the school, its arch decorated with stylized foliage. The young women wear high collars, some elaborately ruffled, and Gibson Girl hairstyles. Many of the girls have cape-like collars on their dresses and large bows around the neck or in their hair. The boys wear short pants. Boots are the common foot attire. (Courtesy of PCHS.)

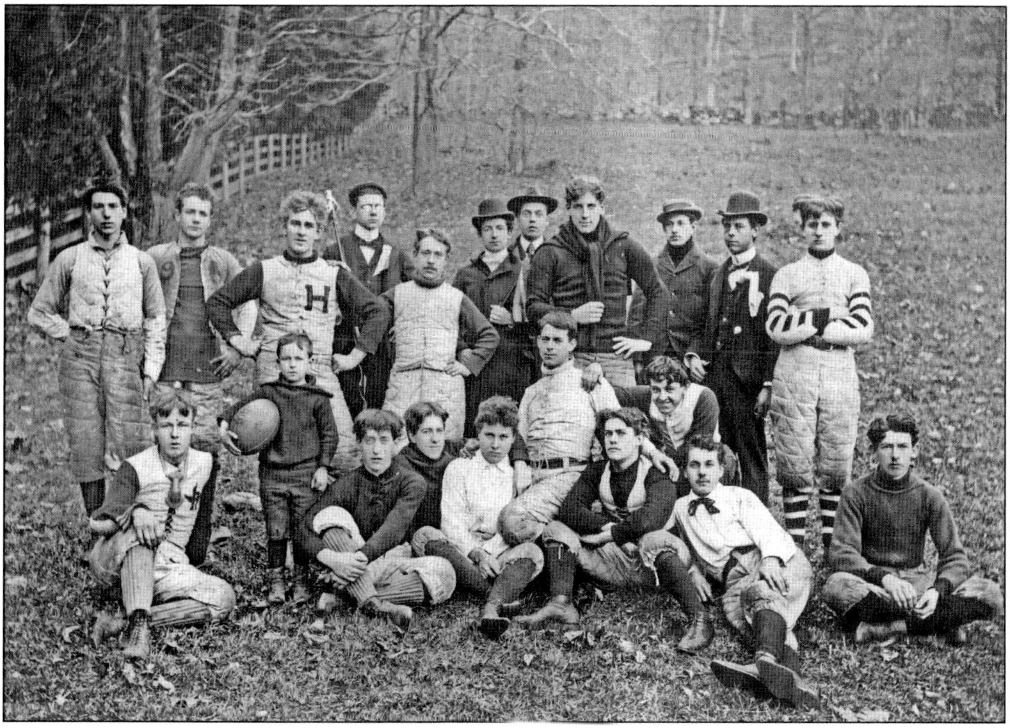

Haldane students, possibly with their coaches and referees, look ready for practice or a game, probably in the 1890s. The team wears an array of sportswear. Vests and padded, quilted knee-highs predominate. The little boy, perhaps the water boy, holds a football. The location may be Kemble Field, south of Main Street. (Courtesy of PCHS.)

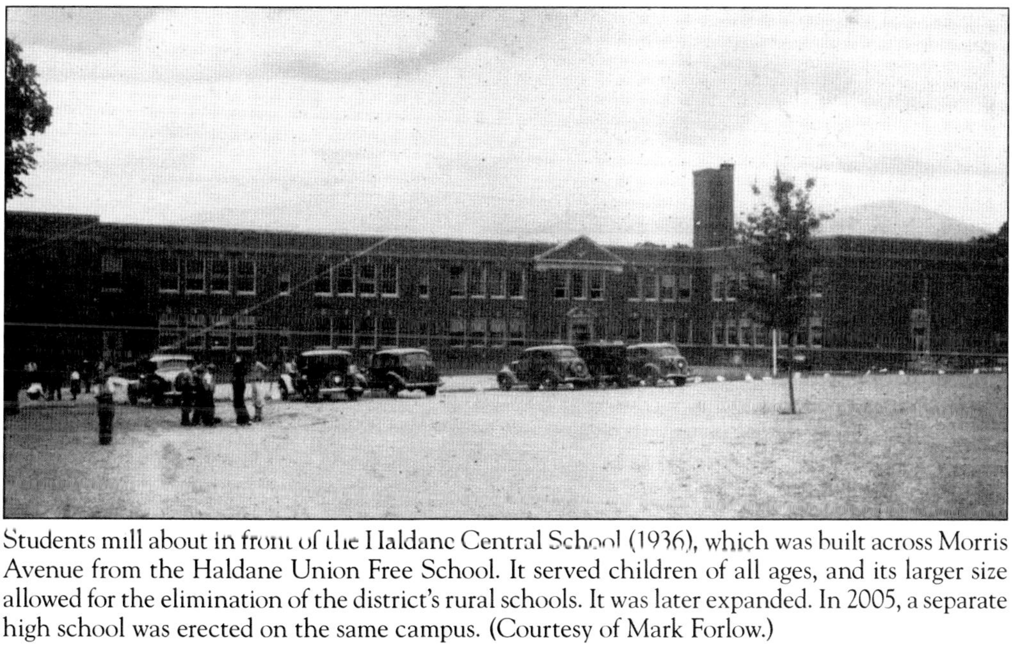

Students mill about in front of the Haldane Central School (1936), which was built across Morris Avenue from the Haldane Union Free School. It served children of all ages, and its larger size allowed for the elimination of the district's rural schools. It was later expanded. In 2005, a separate high school was erected on the same campus. (Courtesy of Mark Forlow.)

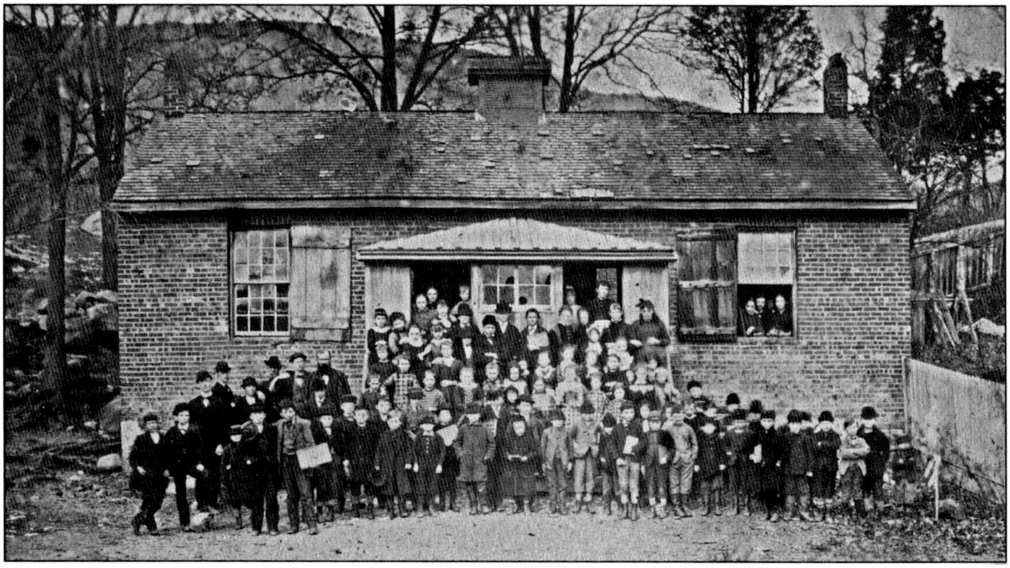

More than 100 children stand on the steps and grounds and at a window of Nelsonville's Pear Tree Hill School (about 1830), shown in 1879. The four-room, redbrick building had a wood-shingled gable roof with a belfry and was in use until 1881. Older and younger children had separate entrances. The building, now a residence, stands on Secor Street behind Champlin's blacksmith shop. (Courtesy of Josephine Doherty.)

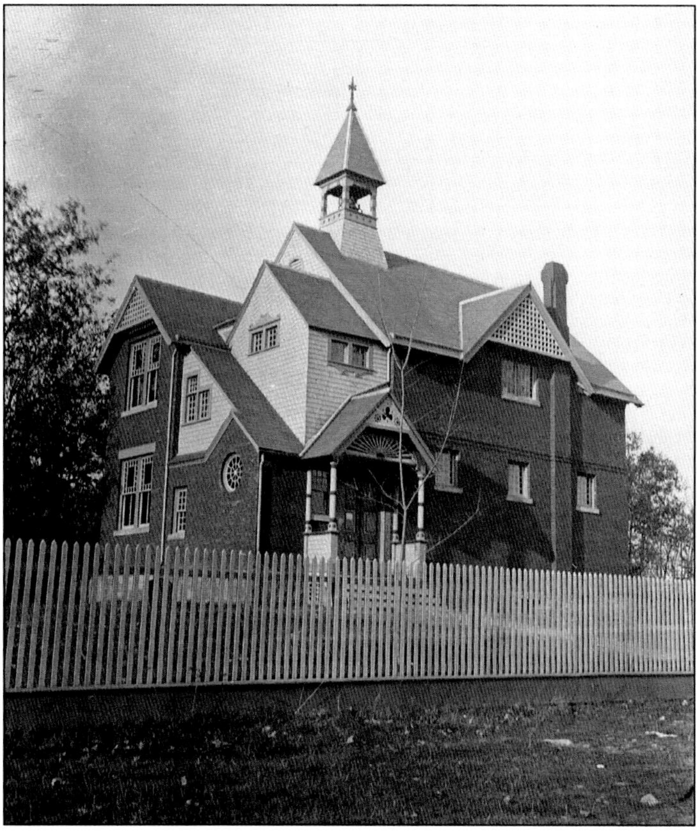

The Nelsonville Union Free School (1881) on Secor Street served its district until 1933. The Queen Anne building has changing rooflines, varying materials and window types, and a Stick-style porch. Its bell could be heard throughout Nelsonville and in parts of Cold Spring. The building has been a Masonic temple since 1937. Because of a change in the street, the building today appears to sit lower. (Courtesy of PCHS.)

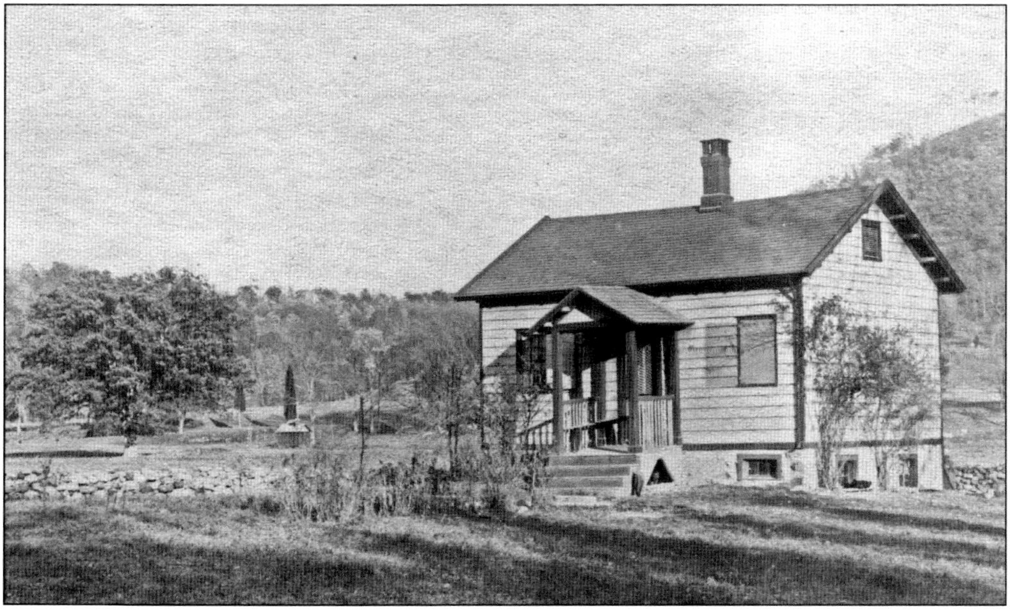

Identified by a longtime resident as the first schoolhouse in Garrison, this building is typical of one-room schoolhouses built before 1850. Each schoolhouse and the families within walking distance constituted a separate school district before 1853. That year, the state authorized the creation of union free districts, formed from the merger of smaller, common school districts. (Courtesy of PCHS.)

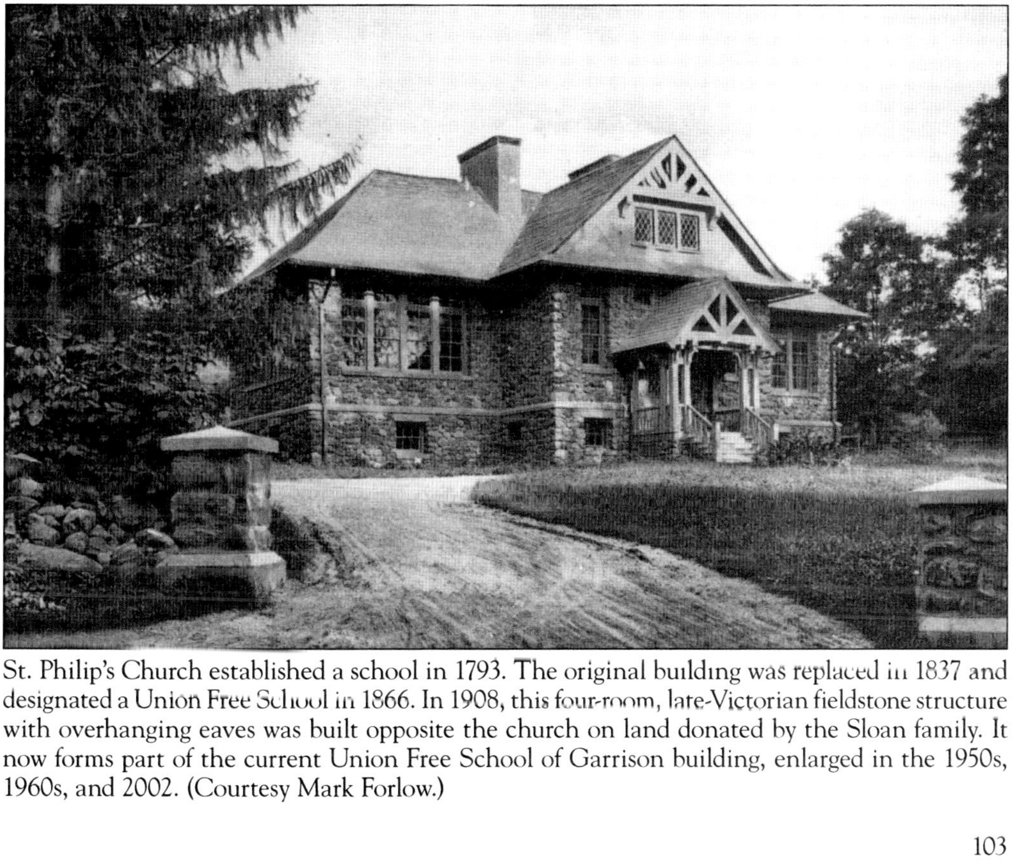

St. Philip's Church established a school in 1793. The original building was replaced in 1837 and designated a Union Free School in 1866. In 1908, this four-room, late-Victorian fieldstone structure with overhanging eaves was built opposite the church on land donated by the Sloan family. It now forms part of the current Union Free School of Garrison building, enlarged in the 1950s, 1960s, and 2002. (Courtesy Mark Forlow.)

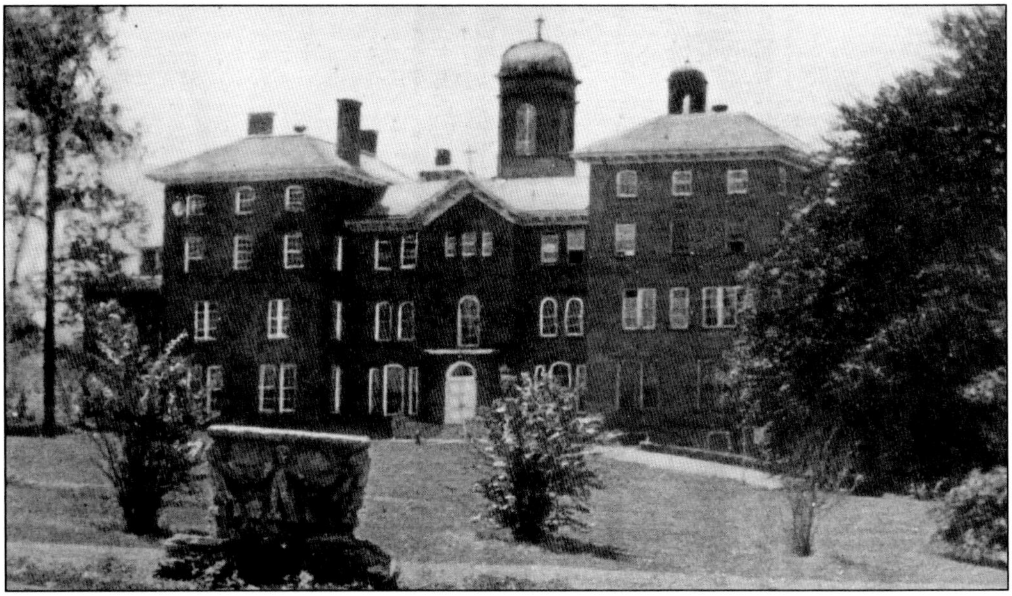

Glenclyffe High School, constructed from the former Stuyvesant Fish home and shown about 1958, is now abandoned. In 1923, the Capuchin Franciscan Province of St. Joseph purchased the Hamilton Fish estate, which included the Stuyvesant Fish home, and established a boys' high school about 1930. The high school closed long before 2001, when the Open Space Institute acquired the estate for preservation. (Courtesy of PCHS.)

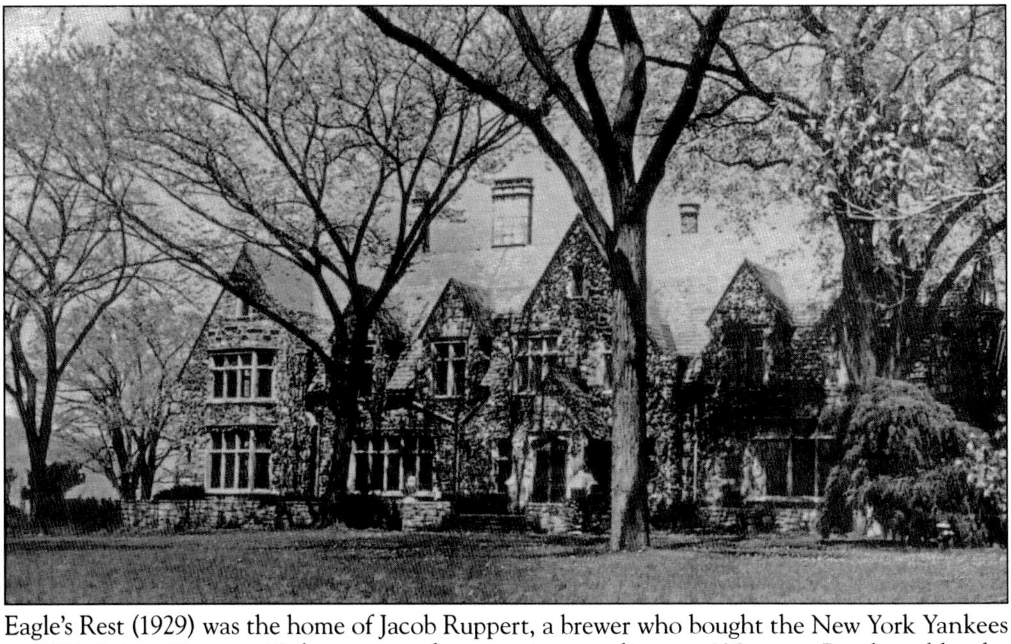

Eagle's Rest (1929) was the home of Jacob Ruppert, a brewer who bought the New York Yankees in 1914. It is a 40-room, Tudor manor of cut granite standing on 400 acres. Purchased by the Greek Orthodox Archdiocese of America Ladies Philoptochos Society in 1944, it is now St. Basil Academy, which provides care for children in need. (Courtesy of St. Basil Academy.)

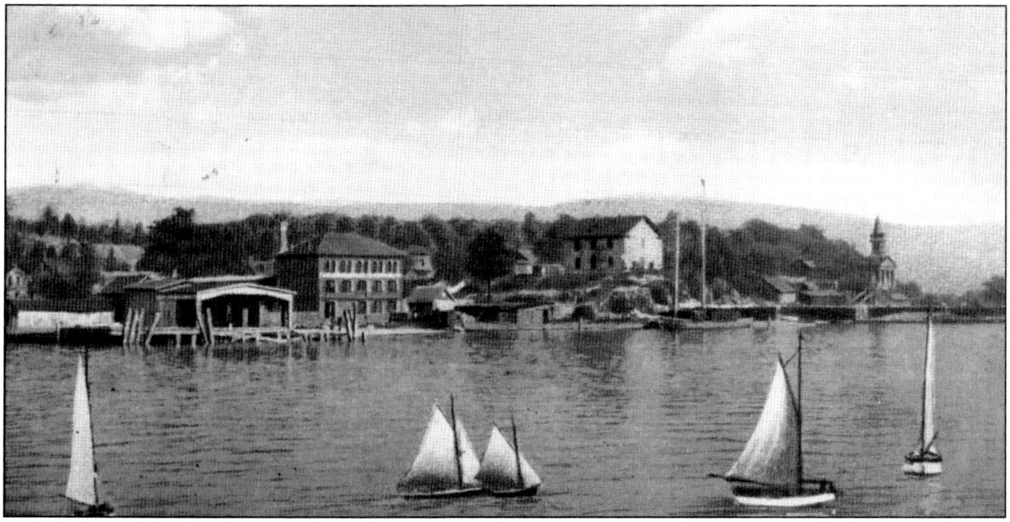

Union Church, Protestant (1827), the two-story building near center right, was the first church in Cold Spring. The stone, cedar-roof building stood near the river on Market Street and served several denominations. Presbyterians used it in the morning, other denominations in the afternoon. The Methodists were the first to build their own church; all other denominations eventually followed. In the 1890s, Titus Truesdell used the building as a pickle factory. (Courtesy of PCHS.)

The Chapel of Our Lady, Catholic (1834), constructed for workers of the nearby West Point Foundry, was designed by Thomas Wharton, then 16, in the austere Tuscan style. It was built of brick covered and painted to look like stone. Gouverneur Kemble, a foundry backer, donated the land and some funds. The engraving by Hudson River artist Robert Weir appeared in 1834 in the *New-York Mirror*. (Courtesy of PCHS.)

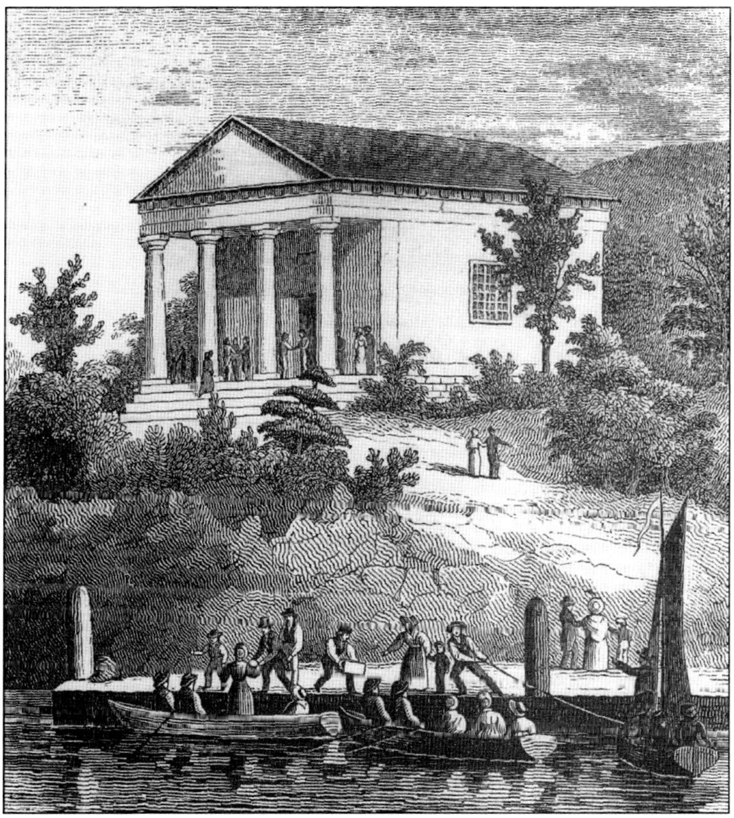

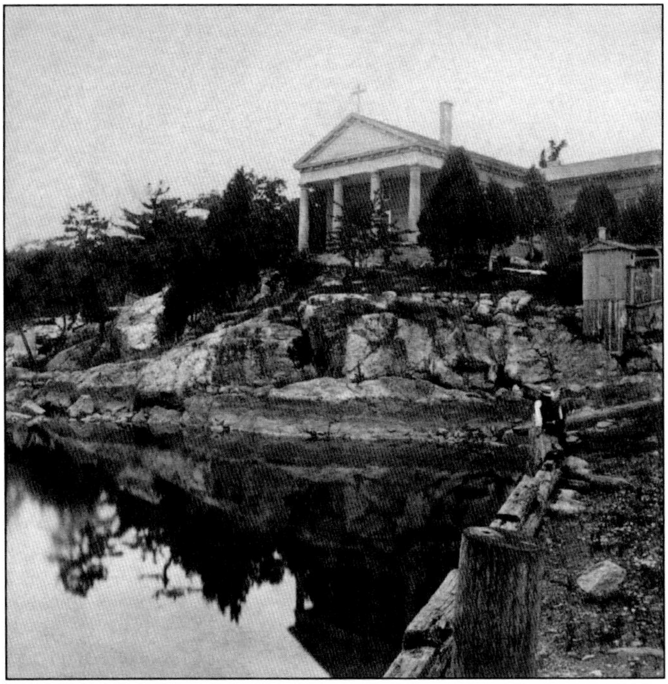

A rare early photograph shows the Chapel of Our Lady during reconstruction and renovation, begun about 1867. A hall has been added to the back. The church was damaged during the Civil War by shocks produced by the frequent testing of the Parrott guns at the West Point Foundry. Robert Parrott, the foundry superintendent, paid the cost of rebuilding the church. (Courtesy of the Highland Studio Inc.)

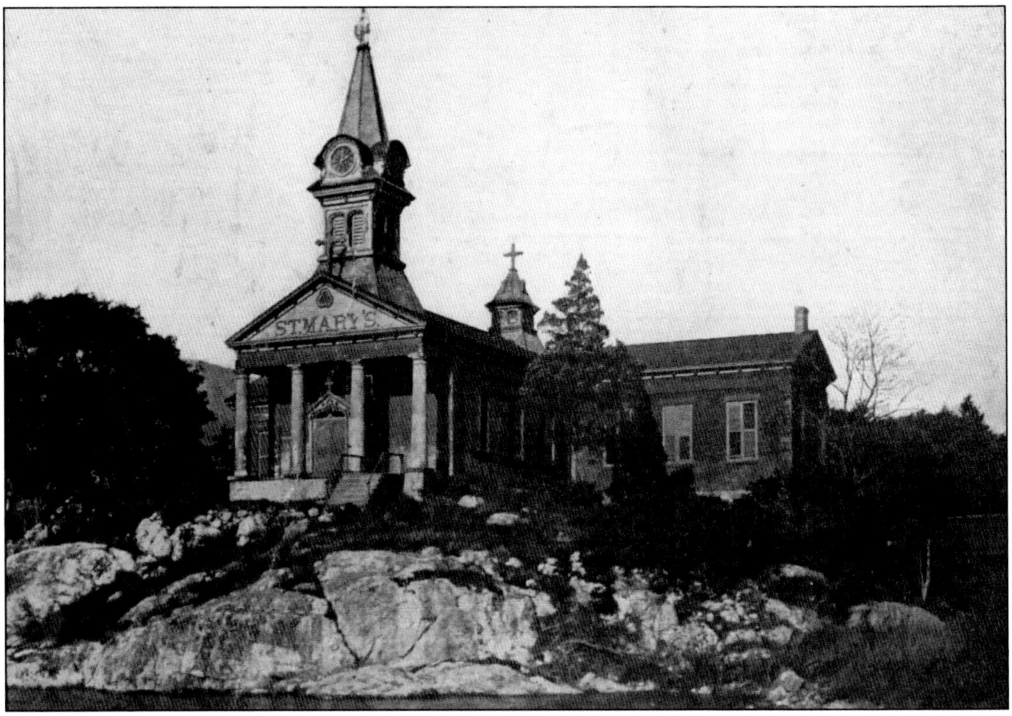

The appearance of the chapel, renamed St. Mary's, was substantially altered once its Victorian renovation was complete. The church's name was emblazoned across its pediment, and a cupola and disproportionately large steeple were added, creating an incongruous mix of architectural elements. The church closed and was abandoned in 1906 when the congregation outgrew it. (Courtesy of PCHS.)

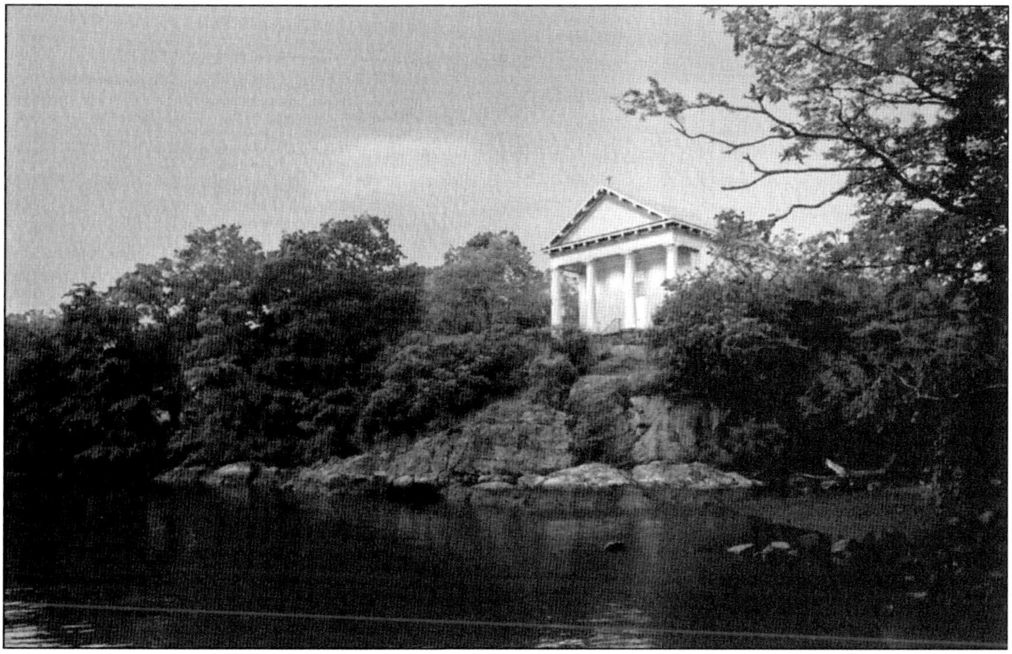

The Chapel of Our Lady Restoration, ecumenical (1977), closely resembles the original church. It was restored by a coalition of groups and is used for both private and public functions. The chapel, photographed in 1990, stands on a high promontory on the bank of the Hudson River behind the railroad platform in Cold Spring. Photographers and artists have reproduced it many times over its history. (Photograph by Jan Thacher, courtesy of PCHS.)

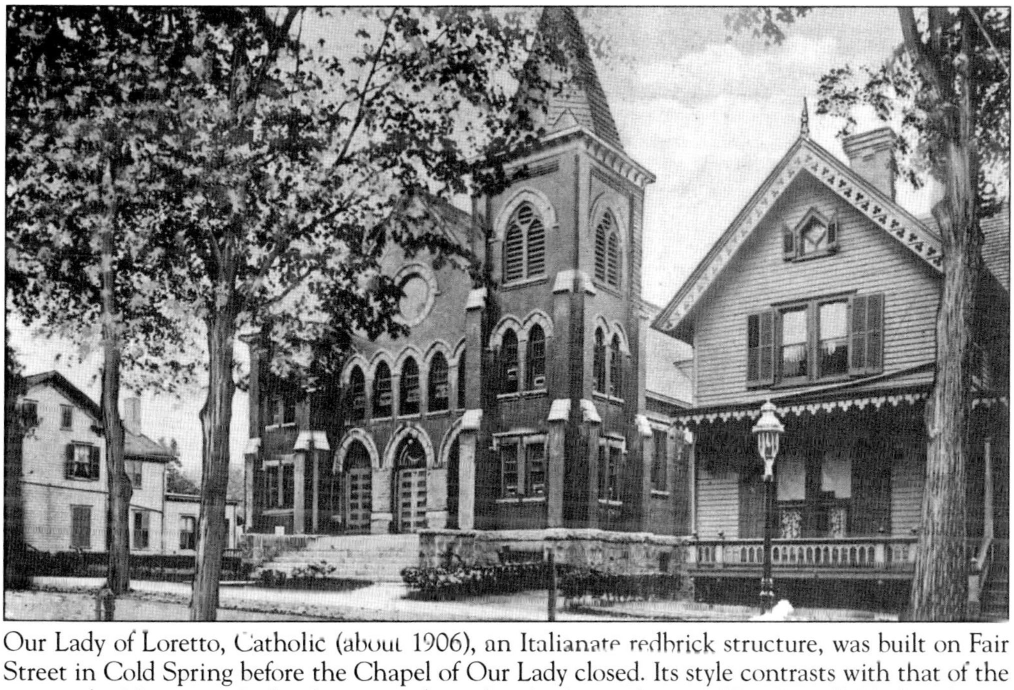

Our Lady of Loretto, Catholic (about 1906), an Italianate redbrick structure, was built on Fair Street in Cold Spring before the Chapel of Our Lady closed. Its style contrasts with that of the vernacular Victorian Gothic house on the right, the former home of Dr. Coryell Clark, a doctor in Cold Spring for more than 50 years. (Courtesy of Mark Forlow.)

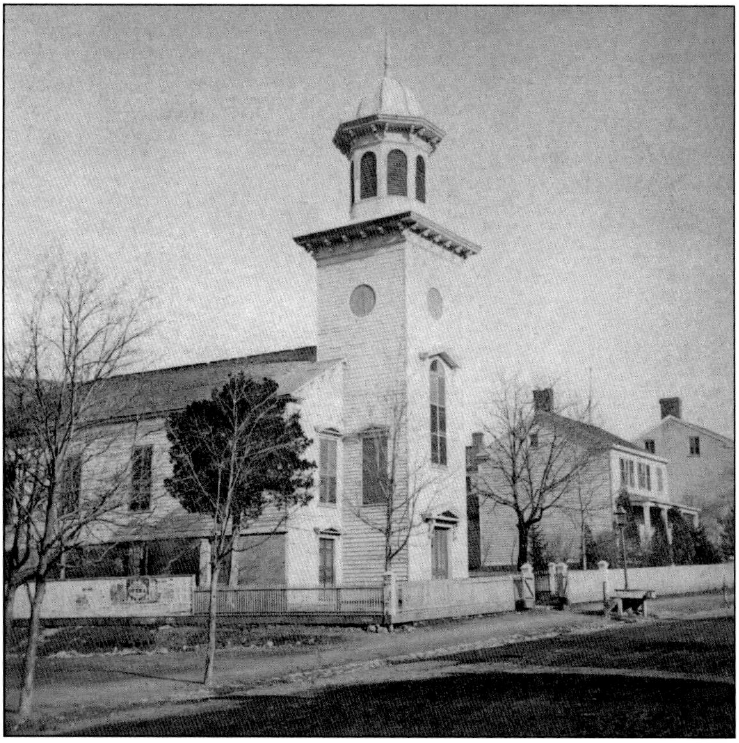

The old Methodist Episcopal Church in Cold Spring (1833), with square steeple and rounded cupola, stood on the corner of Main and Church Streets. Before then, Methodists shared the Union Church with other denominations. Since 1876, businesses have occupied the building, which was sold in 1870. Despite alterations, the church's core remains, in whole or part. Before Main Street was straightened in 1838, it passed behind the building. (Courtesy of Mark Forlow.)

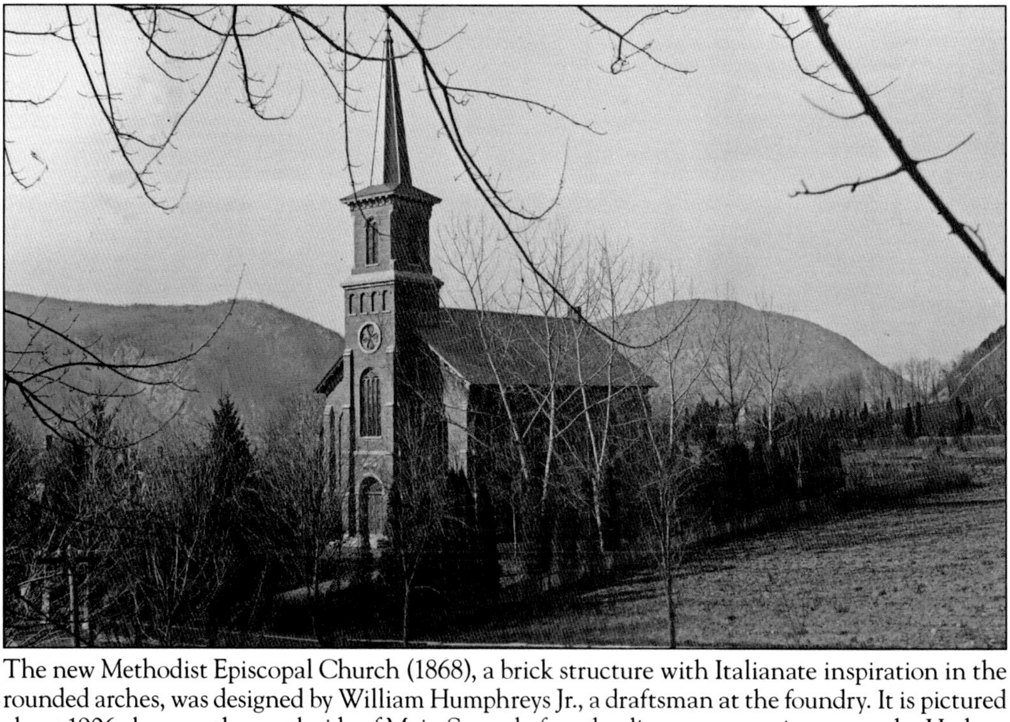

The new Methodist Episcopal Church (1868), a brick structure with Italianate inspiration in the rounded arches, was designed by William Humphreys Jr., a draftsman at the foundry. It is pictured about 1906 alone on the north side of Main Street before the distant mountains across the Hudson River, with Crow's Nest on the left and Storm King on the right. Today, other buildings stand close by. (Courtesy of PCHS.)

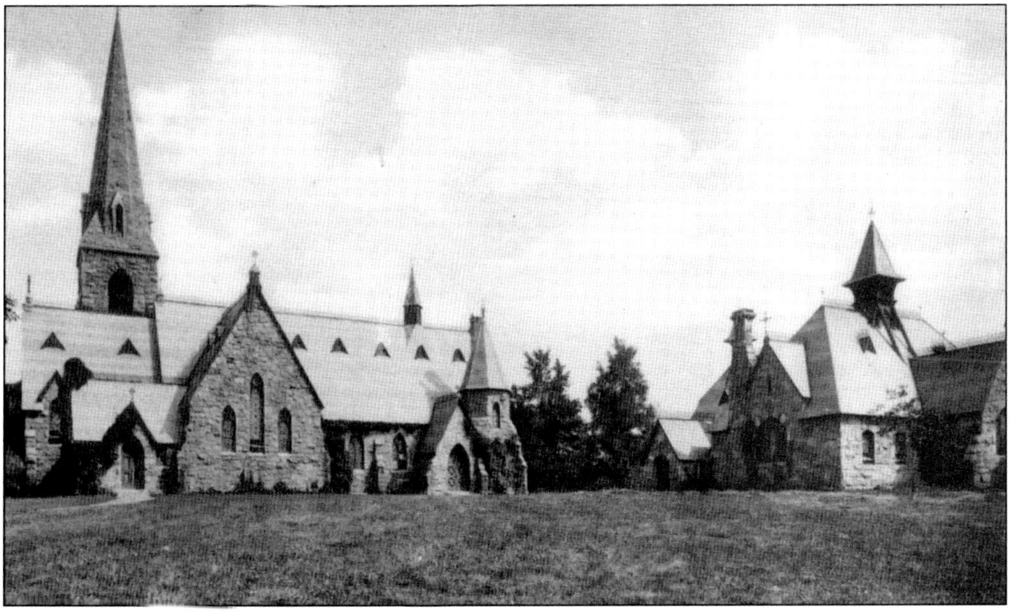

St. Mary-in-the-Highlands, Episcopal (1868), was designed by the distinguished architect George Edward Harney in the Victorian Gothic style. Constructed of gray granite from the estate of Frederick P. James on land donated by Robert Parrott, it is at the corner of Cold Spring's Main and Chestnut Streets. Many leading community members were parishioners. The Parish Hall (1874) was given by the James family. (Courtesy of Mark Forlow.)

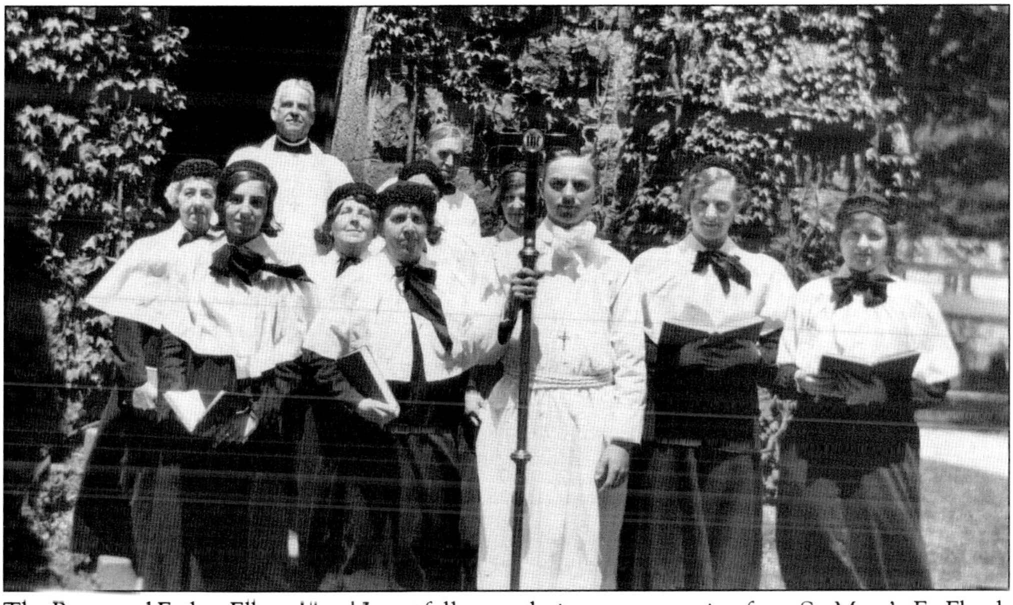

The Reverend Father Elbert Floyd Jones follows a choir group emerging from St. Mary's. Fr. Floyd-Jones, rector from 1895 to 1946, was an active figure in the community. Among his writings are a history of St. Mary's (1920) and a monograph on the establishment of milestones on the Albany Post Road. (Courtesy of St. Mary-in-the-Highlands.)

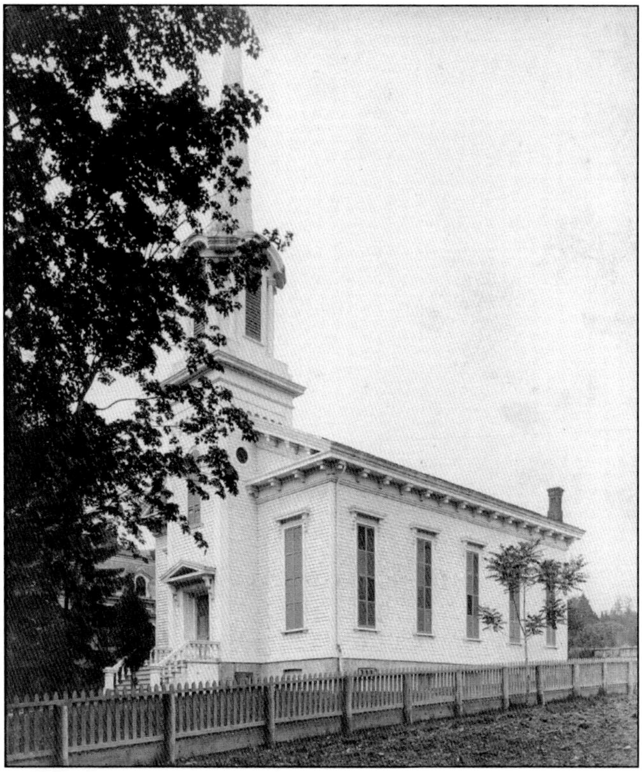

The First Dutch Reformed Church (about 1855) had elements in the Neoclassical style, including symmetry, a bracketed projecting cornice, and a large broken pediment. The church was replaced by the Julia L. Butterfield Library, a rectangular brick building erected in 1927 on Morris Avenue and still in use. (Courtesy of PCHS.)

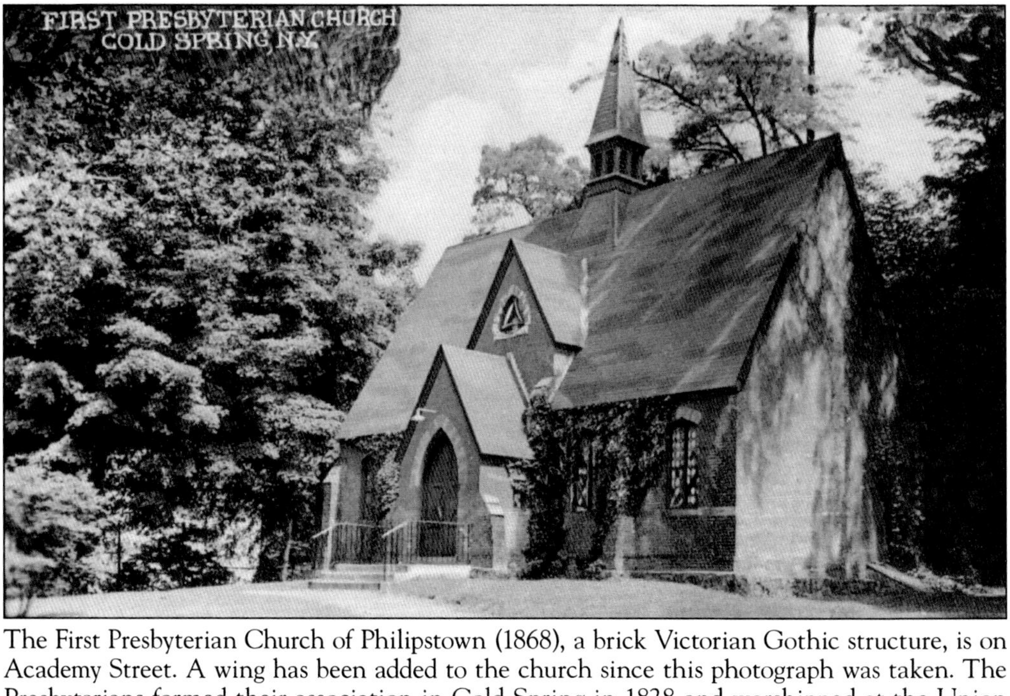

The First Presbyterian Church of Philipstown (1868), a brick Victorian Gothic structure, is on Academy Street. A wing has been added to the church since this photograph was taken. The Presbyterians formed their association in Cold Spring in 1828 and worshipped at the Union Church on Market Street for 40 years. The church grounds were once those of the West Point Foundry's stables. (Courtesy of Mark Forlow.)

The Cold Spring Baptist Church (1833) stands on a hill rising above Main Street in Nelsonville, just past the Cold Spring border. The frame clapboard building, photographed in 1930, has rounded, stained-glass windows and elements in the Neoclassical style. Neoclassical corner pilasters and a plain entablature frame the doorway of the projecting entrance bay. A bracketed cornice emphasizes the building's simple proportions. (Courtesy of PCHS.)

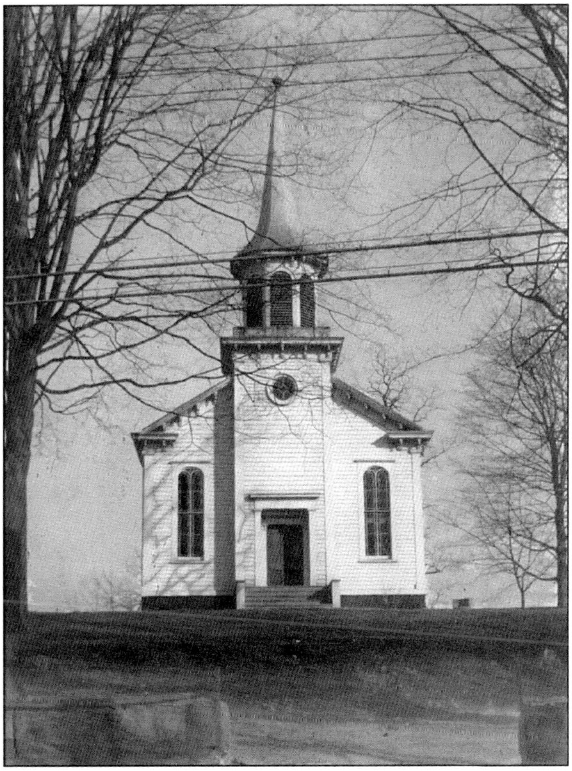

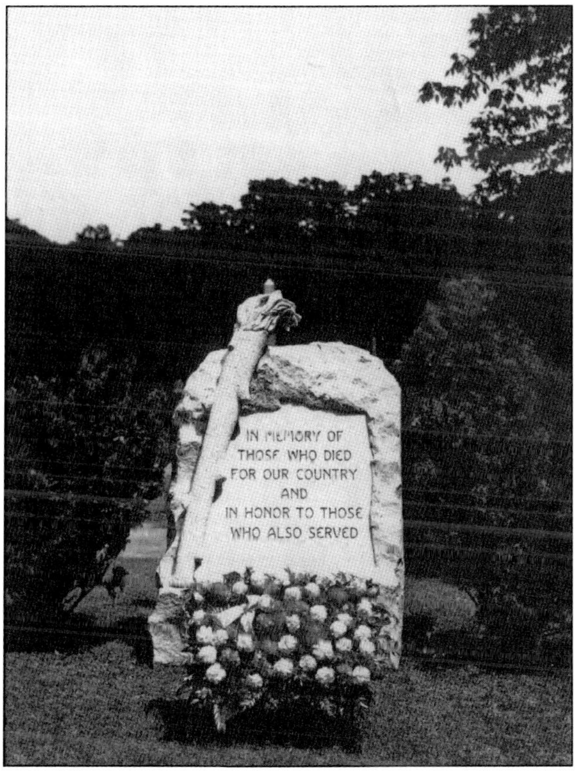

Photographed in 1952, this monument in Cold Spring Cemetery was commissioned soon after World War II and dedicated "in memory of those who died for our country and in honor to those who also served." Kenneth Logan of George A. Logan & Sons, which has made monuments and tombstones since 1889, carved the granite. (Courtesy of PCHS.)

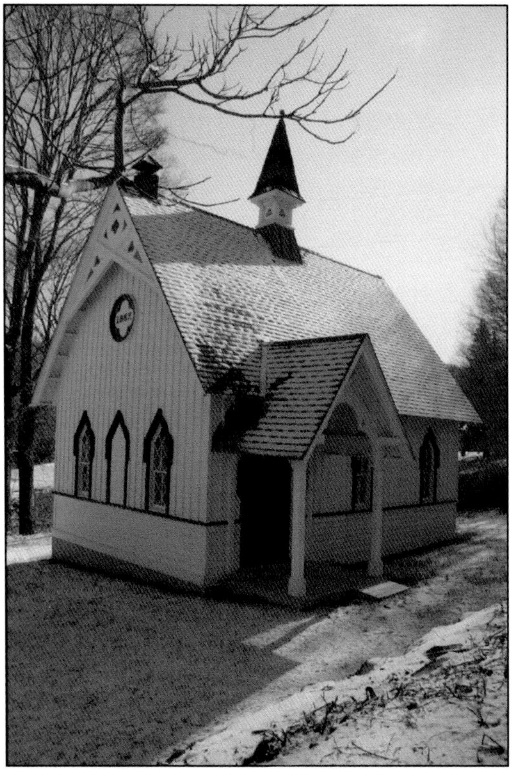

Mekeel's Corners Chapel, ecumenical (1867), at the corner of Route 9 and Route 301, was a Methodist church until the early 1900s, serving farmers and others. The vertical clapboard Carpenter Gothic building has a steeply sloped roof, high pointed window arches, and wooden tracery in the front. A nearby cemetery predates the church. The Mekeel family was one of the oldest in the area. (Photograph by Jan Thacher, courtesy of PCHS.)

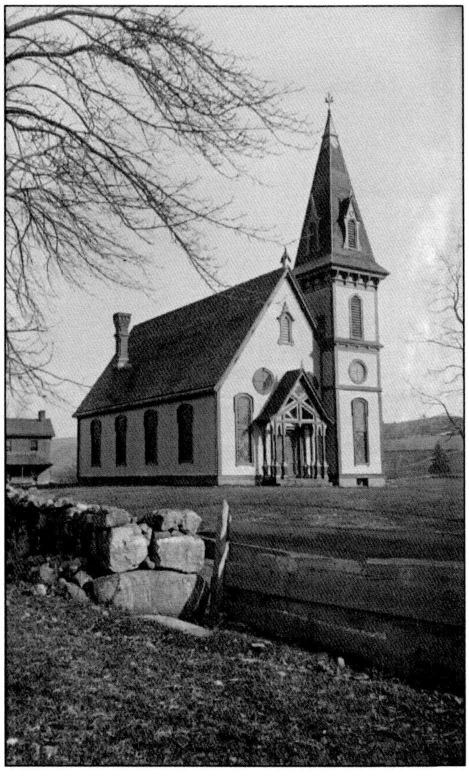

The North Highland Methodist Episcopal Church (1879), a Carpenter Gothic structure with a beautifully ornamented entryway, stood in northern Philipstown. The church was built by Cold Spring contractor William La Due. The Nelsonville and Cold Spring fire departments saved the church when lightning struck it in July 1938. The church closed in 1948. (Photograph by John Riggs, courtesy of PCHS.)

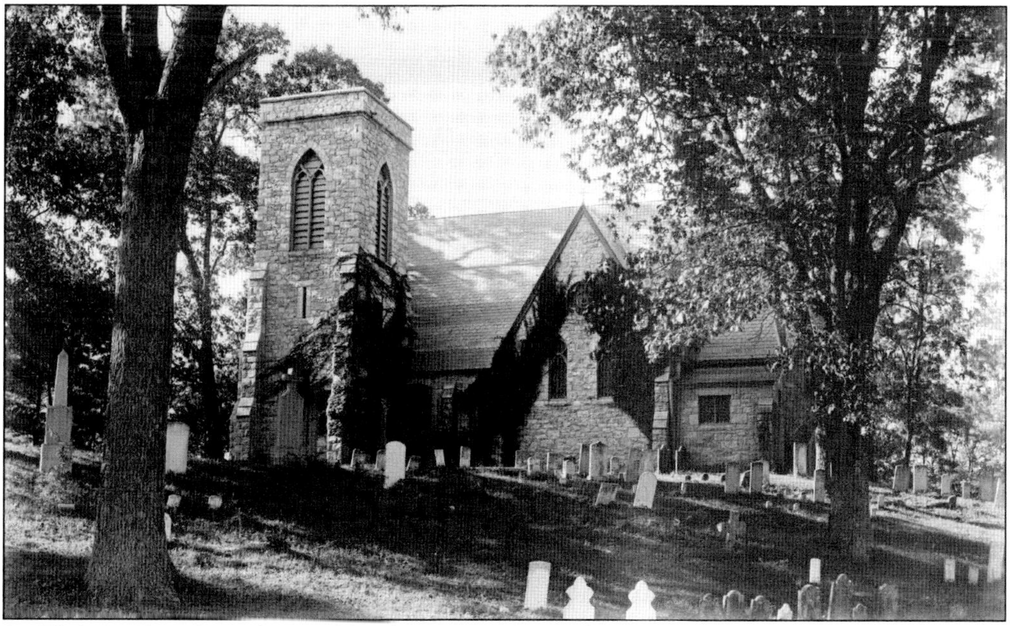

St. Philip's Church in the Highlands, Episcopal (1862), a granite Victorian Gothic structure designed by Richard Upjohn and located on Route 9D near Upper Station Road, replaced an earlier wooden building. Beverley Robinson, the church's first warden, donated land to build the first St. Philip's in 1771. Prominent Garrison residents have been parishioners, including the Osborns, Fishes, Sloans, and Pierreponts. (Courtesy of PCHS.)

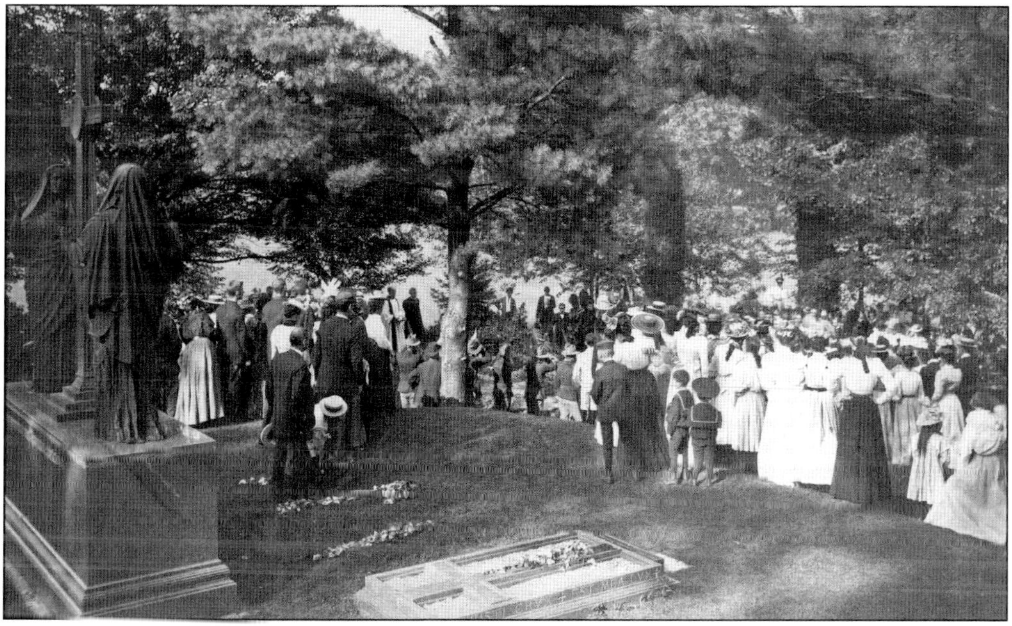

Mourners attend the funeral in 1898 of Sgt. Hamilton Fish, a Rough Rider said to be the first American killed in action in the Spanish-American War, at the Battle of Las Guasimas. He was a grandson of New York State governor and US secretary of state Hamilton Fish, who is also buried at St. Philip's, and a great-grandson of Revolutionary War general Nicholas Fish. (Courtesy of PCHS.)

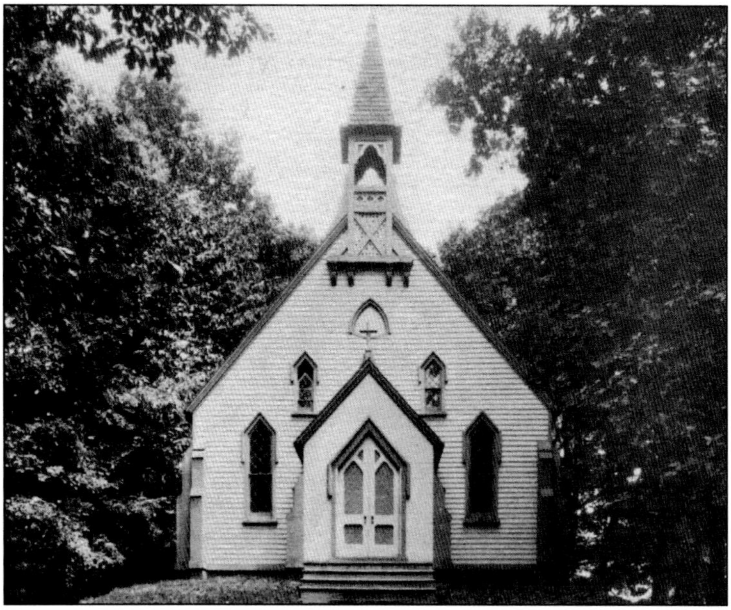

St. Joseph's Chapel, Catholic (early 1870s), in Garrison on Upper Station Road, was built in the vernacular Gothic Revival style on land purchased from Frederick Philipse, a descendant of Adolphe Philipse. A stained-glass window near the altar commemorates Edward Thornton, who helped establish the chapel. He was the superintendent and gardener of Samuel Sloan's estate for many years. (Courtesy of PCHS.)

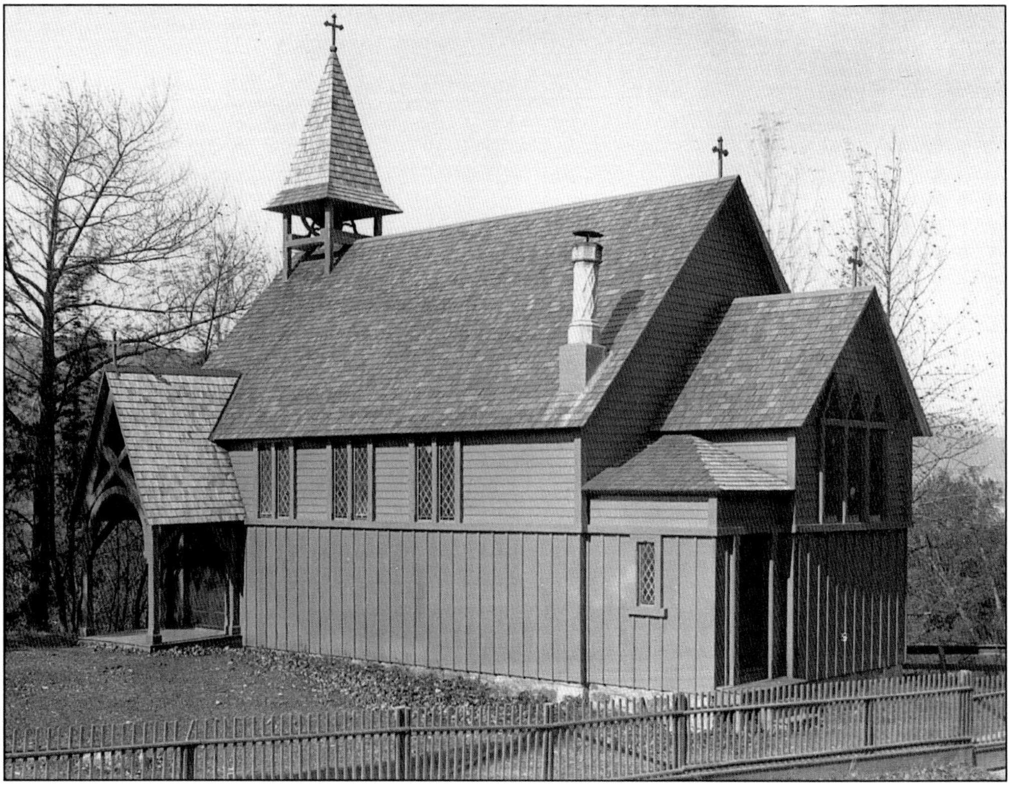

St. James Chapel, Episcopal (1837), stands on Route 9D, just north of the Bear Mountain Bridge in Manitou. Originally consecrated as St. Philip's Church in Garrison, it served the community until 1863, when the vernacular Early Gothic Revival structure was moved here and reconsecrated as the St. James Chapel of St. Philip's parish. Clergy from St. Philip's traveled between the church and the chapel for Sunday services. (Courtesy of PCHS.)

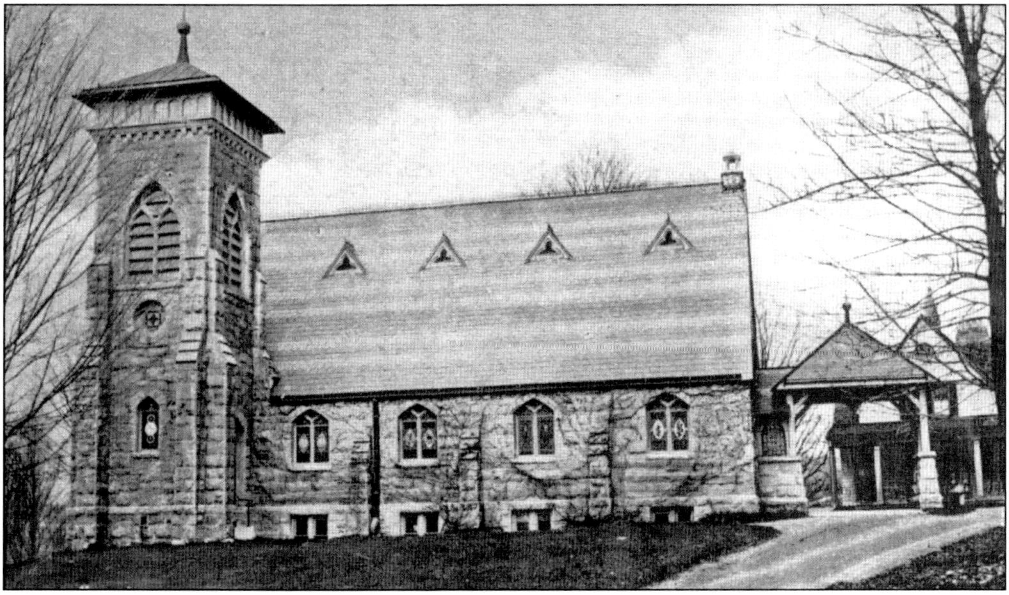

The South Highlands Methodist Episcopal Church (1887) in Garrison stands on Snake Hill Road. The Victorian Gothic church with porte cochere was the third building constructed by its congregation on that site. Earlier wooden church buildings were erected in 1829 and 1866. The Victorian Gothic style was popular between 1860 and 1890. (Courtesy of Mark Forlow.)

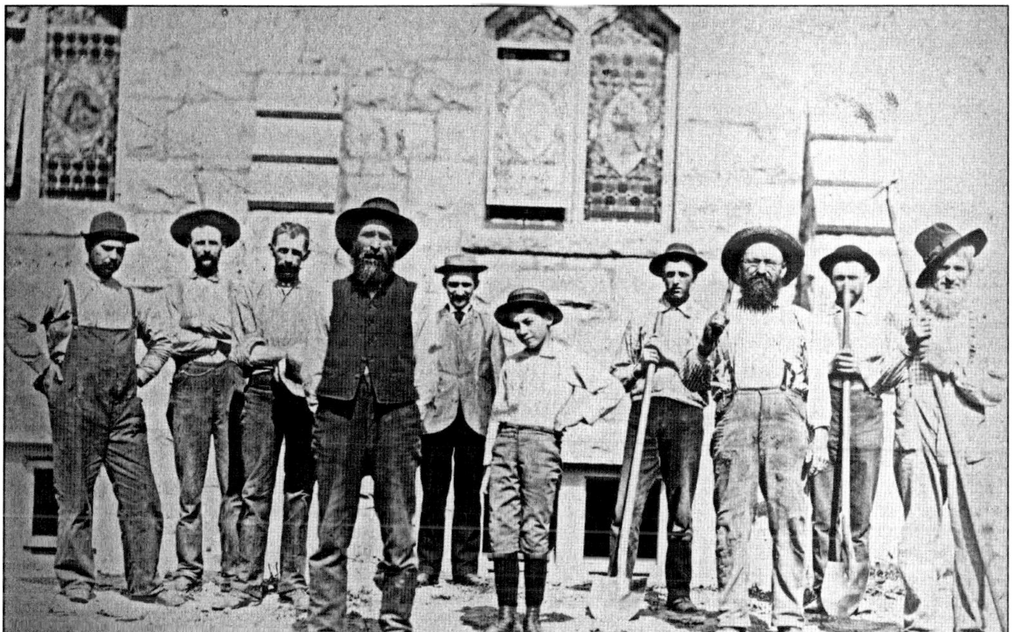

About 1887, a group of construction workers and a boy pose beside the third South Highlands Methodist Episcopal Church in Garrison. There are stained-glass windows behind them. While the church was being built, services were held for nearly three years in the dining room of a boardinghouse owned by Allen Newman, a silversmith and prominent Garrison resident. (Courtesy of PCHS.)

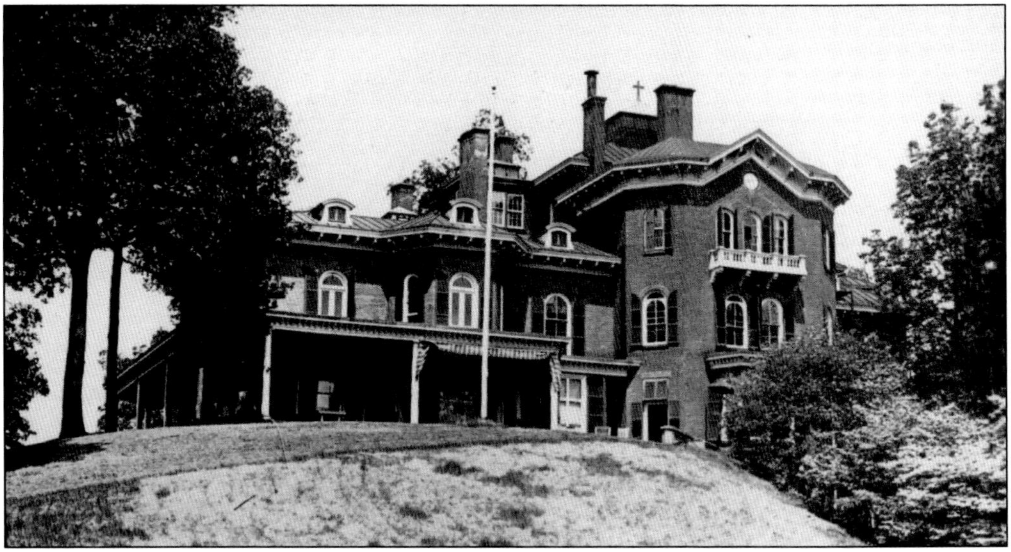

In 1923, the Capuchin Franciscan Province of St. Joseph purchased Glenclyffe, the home of Hamilton Fish. The order altered the building and established a headquarters there, the Glenclyffe Seraphicate. The brick structure shows Italianate influences and has multiple rooflines with heavy bracketing. It stands on property owned by the Open Space Institute. (Courtesy of Janet Selleck Rust.)

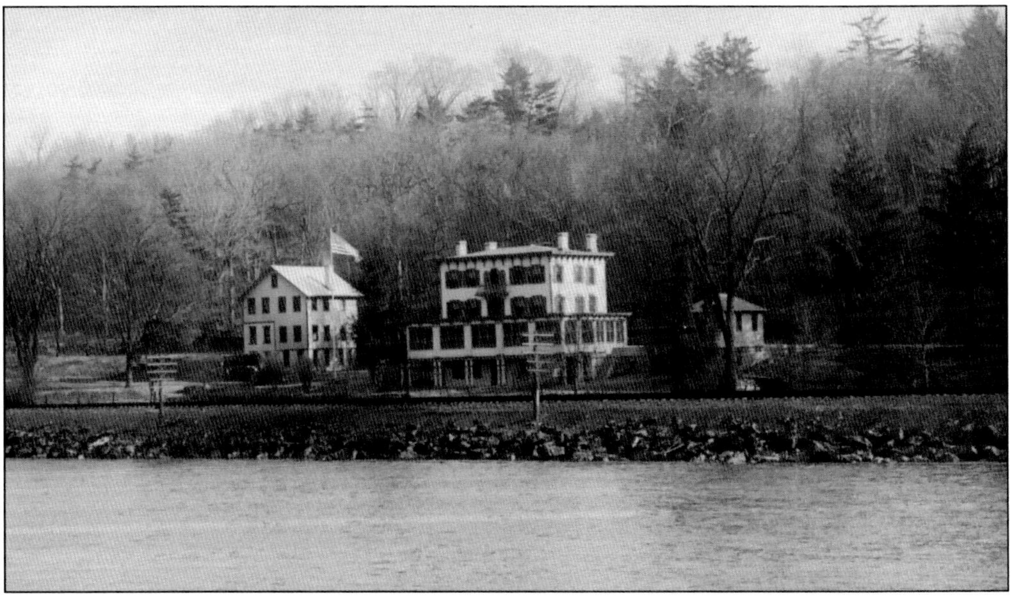

The Third Order Villa, with covered wraparound porch, stands on the Hudson River in Garrison. It was purchased or built about 1924. Associated with the Capuchin Order, it was used by secular Franciscans for retreats. In 1931, the order constructed another building closer to Route 9D, where it conducts a youth and family ministry. (Courtesy of Janet Selleck Rust.)

Seven

On and Off Country Roads

Views, Farming, and Enjoying the Land

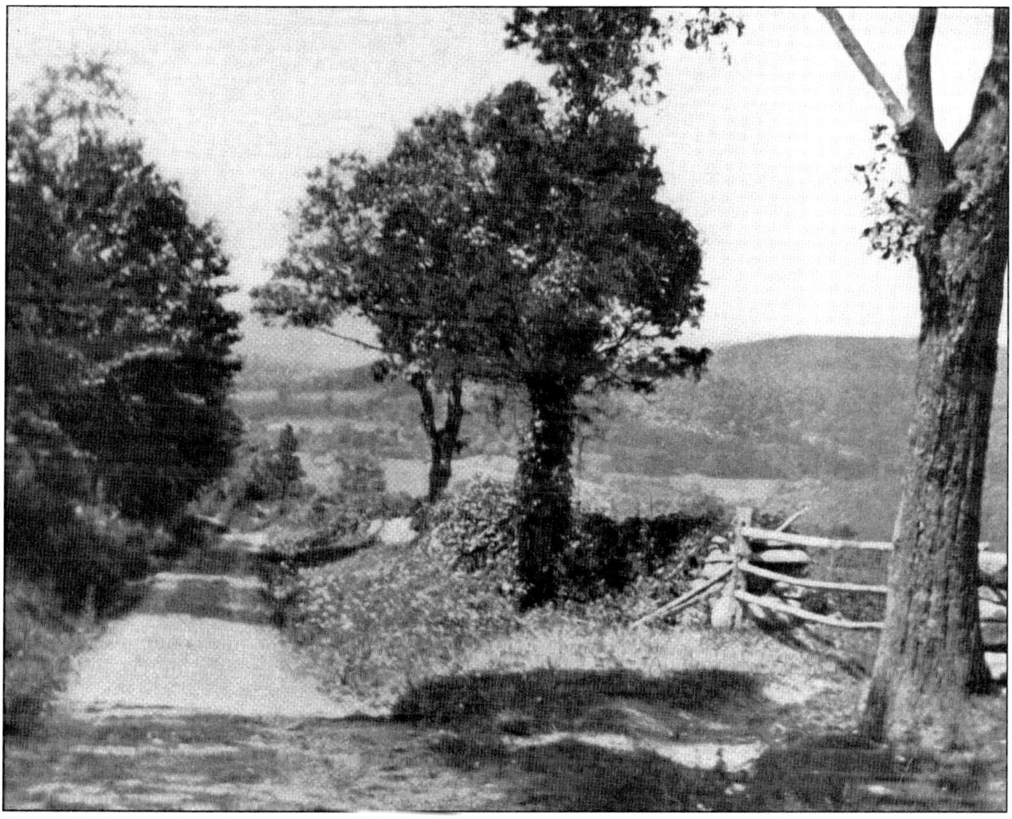

The Old Albany Post Road, one of the oldest unpaved roads still in use in the United States, runs about 6.5 miles, mostly north to south, through southeastern Philipstown. It dates to the mid-17th century and follows Native American trails. The road was used for mail delivery, stagecoach travel, and troop movements during the American Revolution. Some of its 18th-century milestones are still present. (Courtesy of PCHS.)

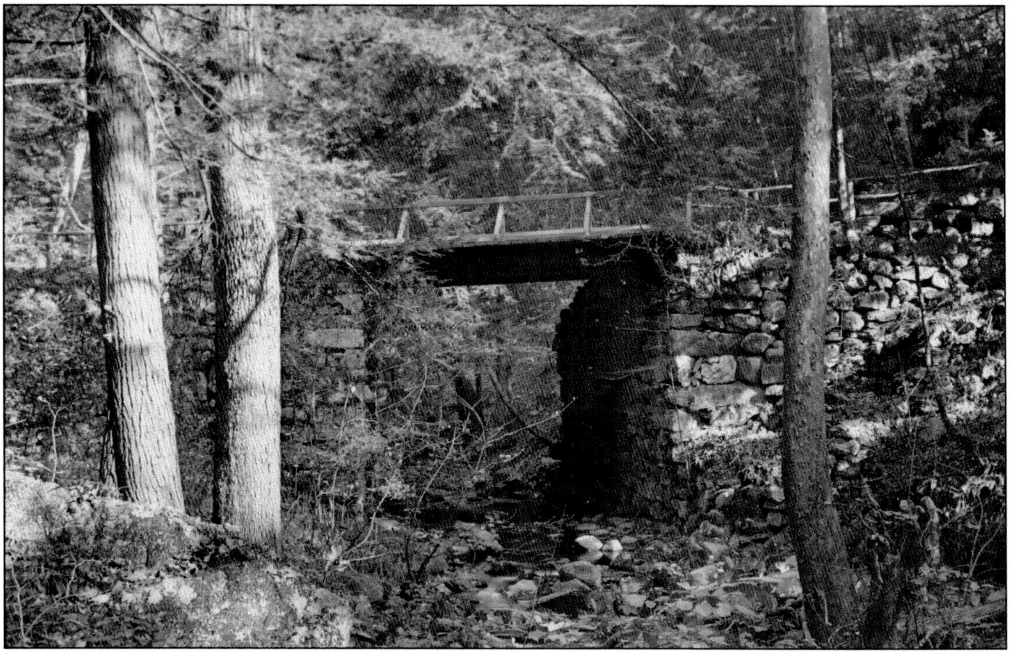

Indian Brook Bridge, which spans a gorge west of Indian Brook Falls (below), was part of an old route between Cold Spring and Garrison. The brook meets the Hudson River at a spot where a Native American people known as Wappingers had a landing site. The old bridge is almost directly under a newer bridge on Route 9D. (Courtesy of PCHS.)

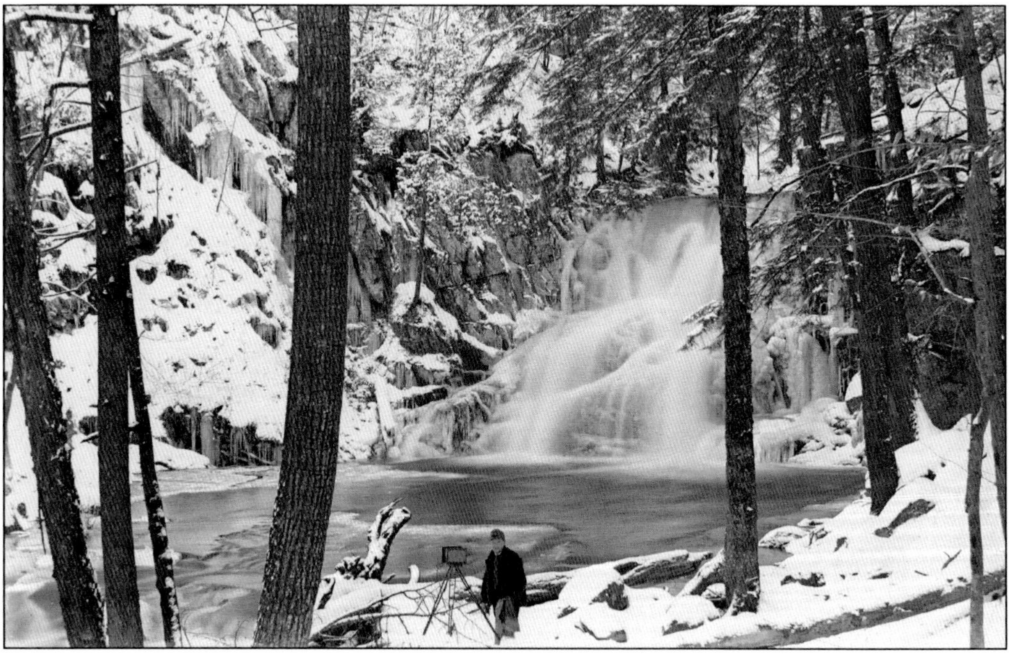

Indian Brook Falls is pictured in 1892 with a photographer near the water. About 200 yards east of Indian Brook Bridge, the falls have inspired photographers, printmakers (including engravers and lithographers), painters, and nature lovers during all seasons since the 19th century. This photograph is probably by Albert Terwilliger. (Courtesy of PCHS.)

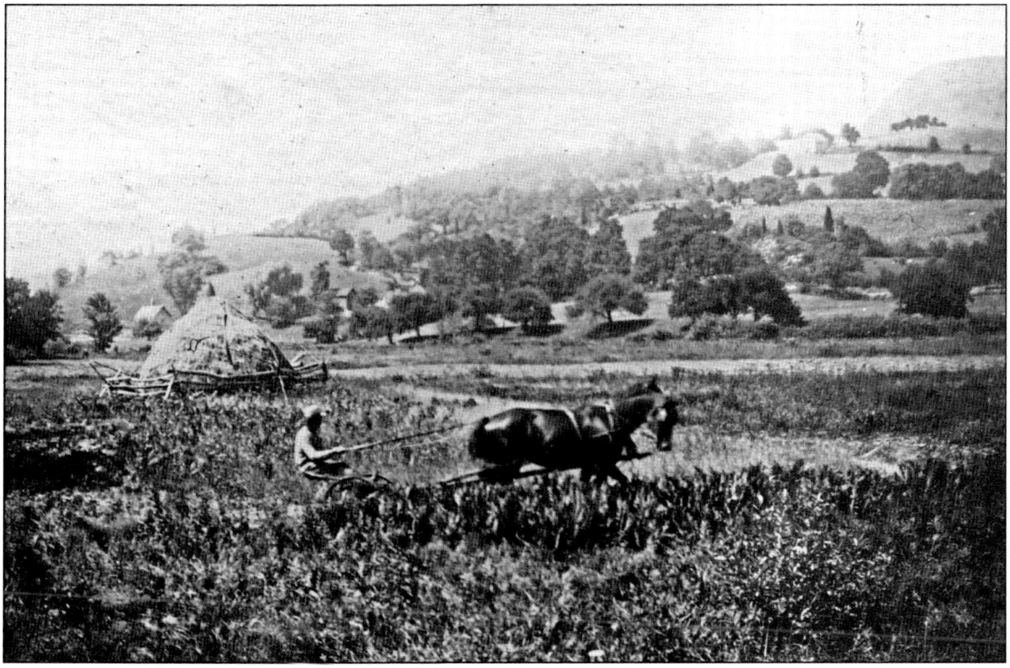

This lovely 1892 photograph shows typical Philipstown farmland, i.e., hilly with a scattering of trees and a sweeping vista. A farmer on a mower drives his fine team past an enclosed haystack not far from a road. Many Philipstown farms produced dairy products because of the limited tillable cropland. (Courtesy of PCHS.)

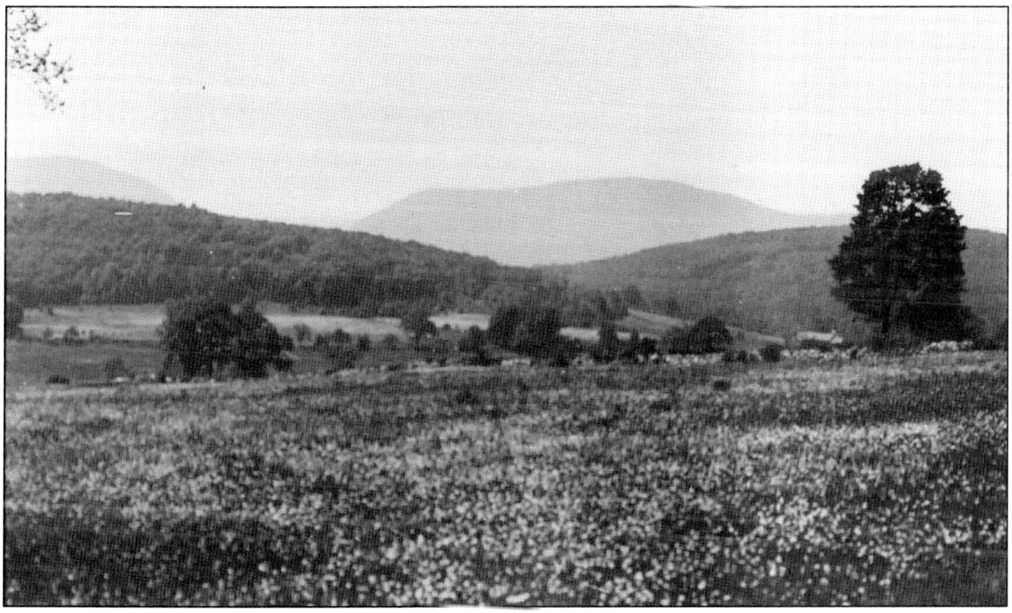

In 1902, William M. Benjamin bought approximately 128.5 acres of land on Avery Road, off Route 9D, and called the property Hayfields Farm. The view here looks north to northwest, with Breakneck and Storm King in the far distance. The route of the Catskill Aqueduct, bringing water from the Catskill Mountains to New York City, went through the property in 1913, cutting it in half. (Courtesy of John Benjamin.)

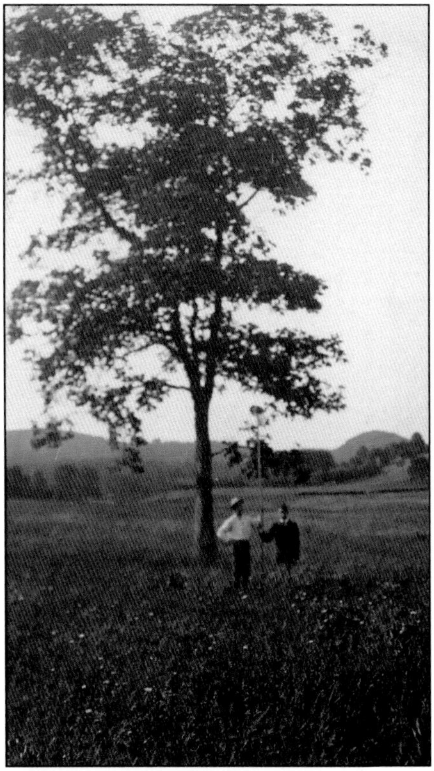

Two men on the Benjamin property hold a pole to indicate the height of the sod that would cover the partially sunken tunnel system to be constructed for the Catskill Aqueduct. Begun in 1907, the system was completed in two stages in 1913 and 1924. It consisted of a complex system of dams, reservoirs, and tunnels. (Courtesy of John Benjamin.)

In 1922, the Indian Brook siphon on the Benjamin property was retrofitted because of hydraulic pressure problems at this site. Such problems occurred elsewhere in the aqueduct system as well. The cut-granite siphon house is one of a pair in view along Avery Road. (Courtesy of Antipodean Books, Maps & Prints.)

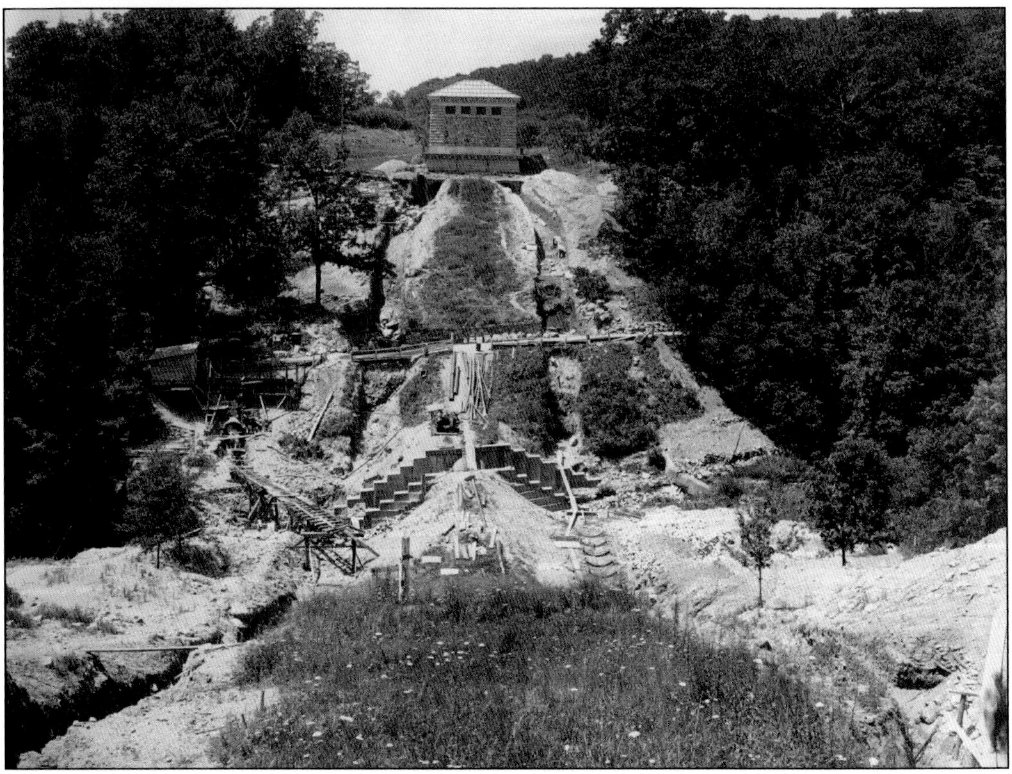

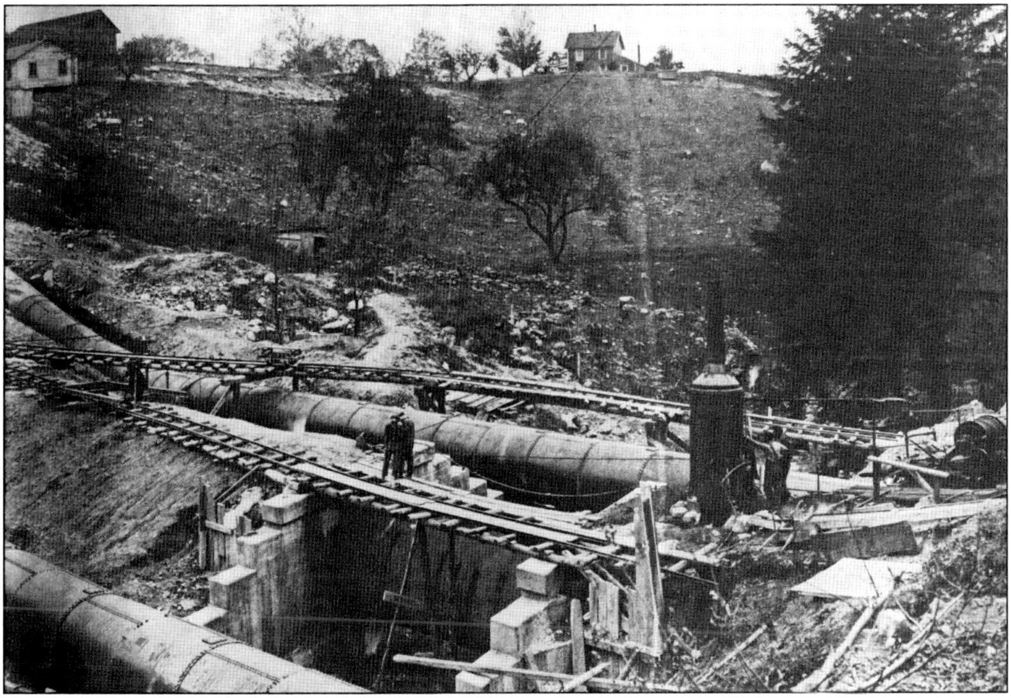

Related to the previous photograph, this shows two additional pipes that were laid parallel to the aqueduct's original tunnel in the center. A Benjamin family house and barn are in the distance. The building at the far left was a workmen's barracks that remains on the Benjamin property. (Courtesy of Antipodean Books, Maps & Prints.)

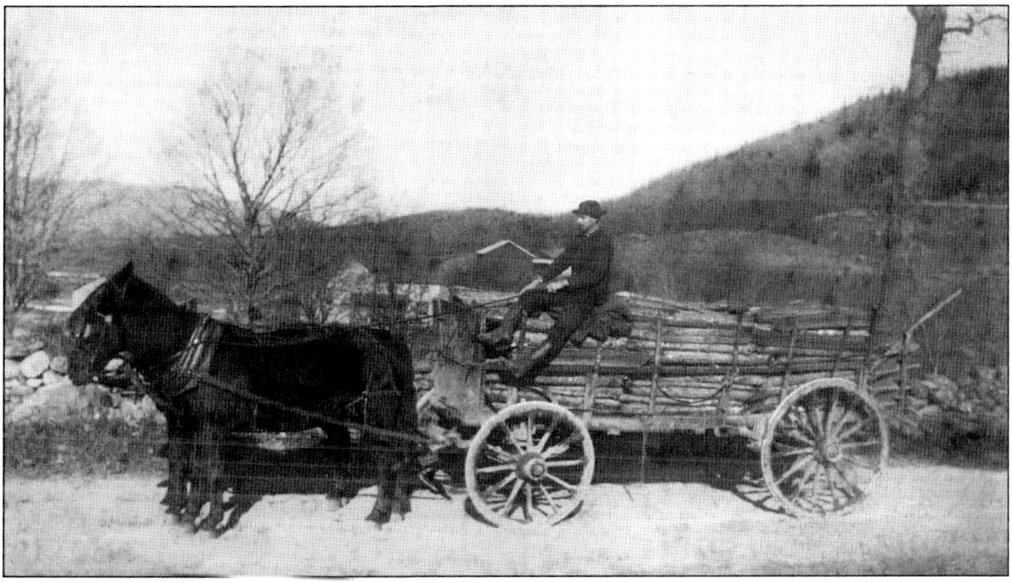

Folded blankets form the driver's seat on this open timber wagon, pulled by a team of mules. The lumber, in roughly five-foot lengths, would have been used as fuel, either burned outright or in the production of charcoal for local blacksmiths. By mid-century, roughly half of Philipstown's forests had been cut down. The driver may be a member of the area's Jaycox family. (Courtesy of Mark Forlow.)

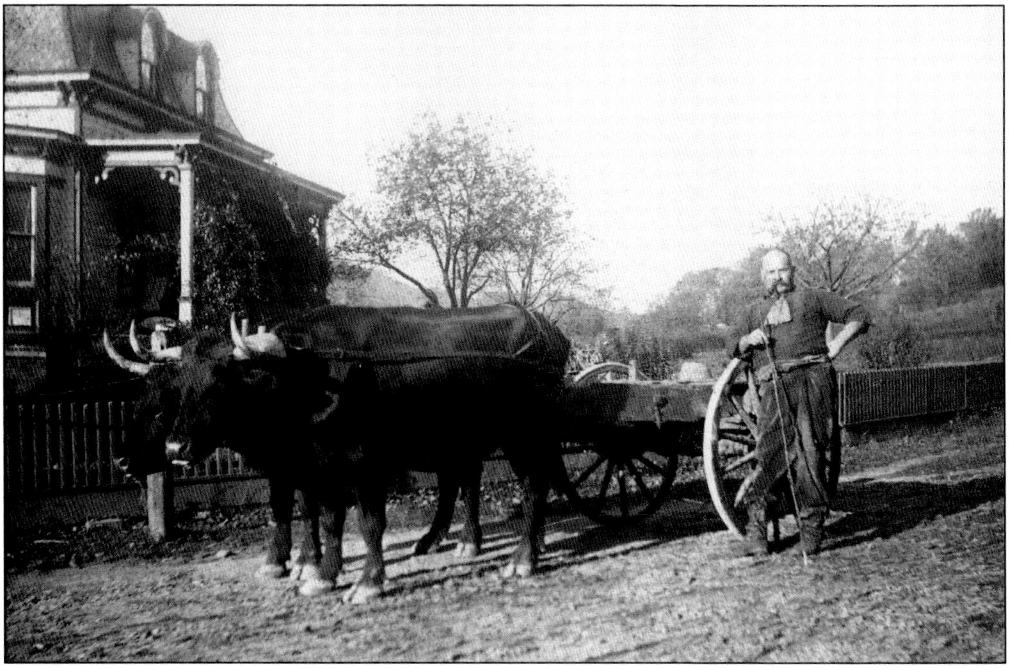

Leaning against the wheel of his cart and holding a switch, a farmer poses with his oxen along a level, well-traveled road about 1880. The oxen are yoked together and harnessed to a heavy farm cart. The house on the left with its half-story, Second Empire mansard roof, as well as dormer and bay windows, has a decorative porch. (Courtesy of PCHS.)

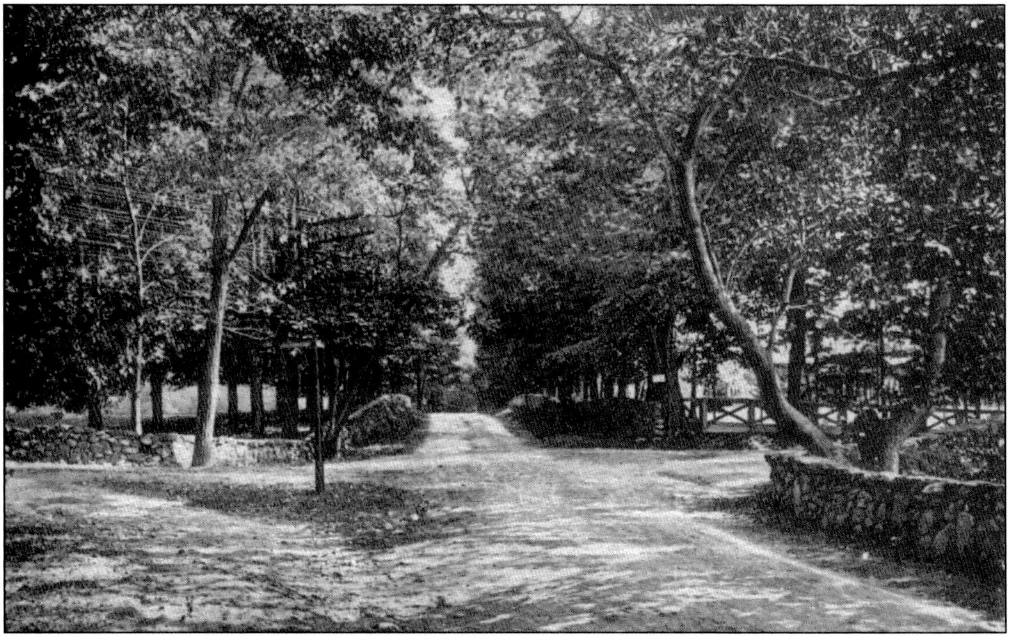

These roads have had different names over the years, and the "Four Corners" is today the intersection of Routes 9D and 403 in Garrison. The Mandeville House remains out of sight to the right, with the Highlands Country Club beyond it. Land to the left has been the site of the Desmond-Fish Library since 1980. (Courtesy of Mark Forlow.)

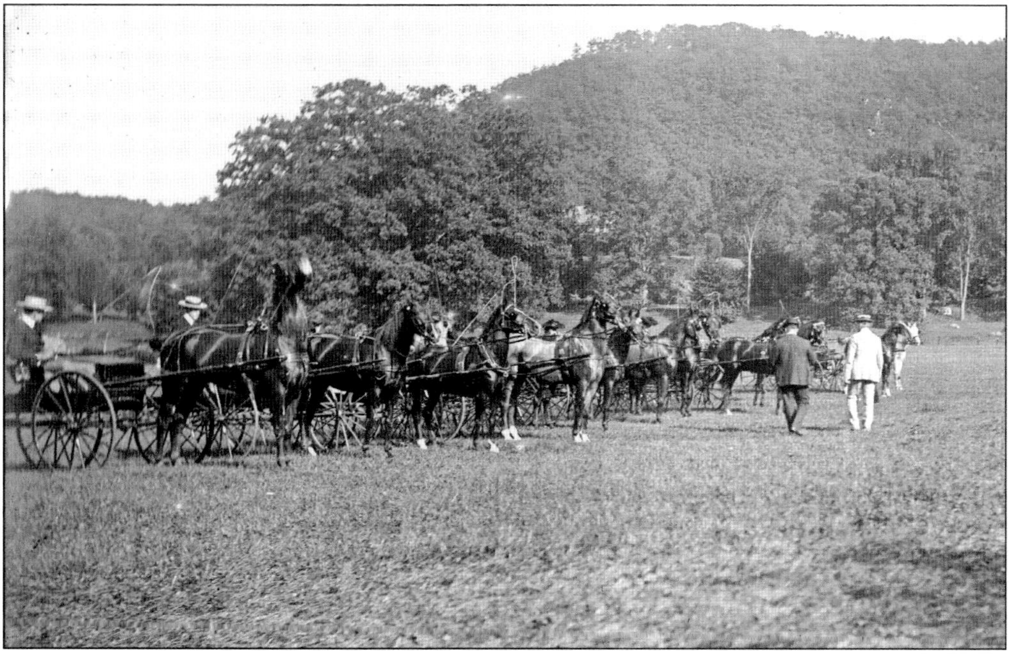

Men and women drivers, about a dozen of them, have lined up their teams in a field on the Samuel Sloan estate and are holding them back preparatory to a buckboard race, probably during the 1890s. Sloan's house can be glimpsed at center through the trees behind them. The field is at the left-hand corner of the Four Corners intersection (see opposite), where the Desmond-Fish Library is now located. (Courtesy of PCHS.)

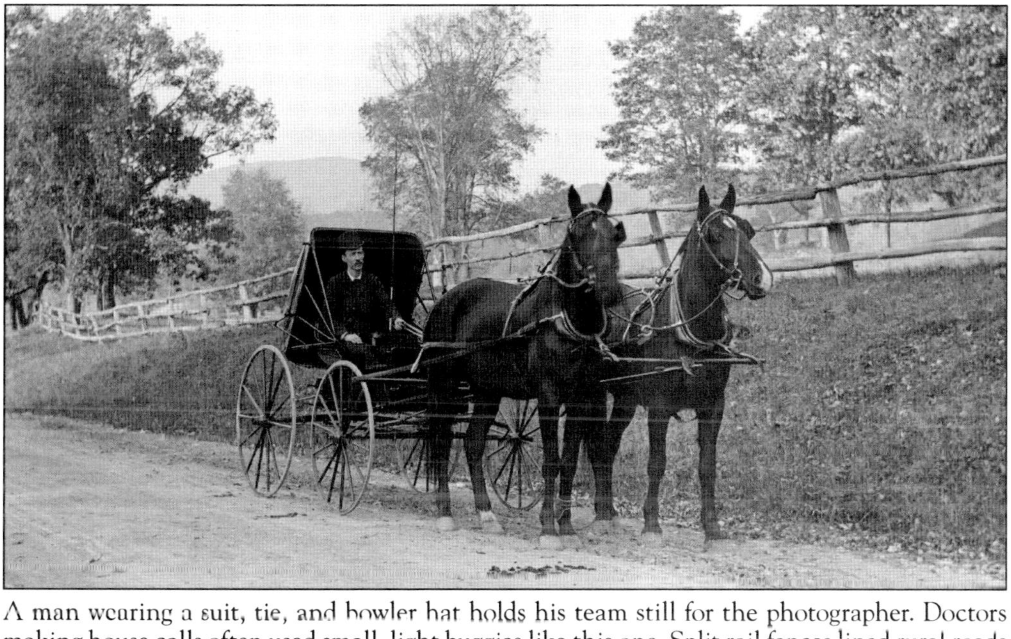

A man wearing a suit, tie, and bowler hat holds his team still for the photographer. Doctors making house calls often used small, light buggies like this one. Split-rail fences lined rural roads where stone had become scarce. Bull Hill, north of Cold Spring, is in the distance. (Photograph by S.B. Hadley, courtesy of PCHS.)

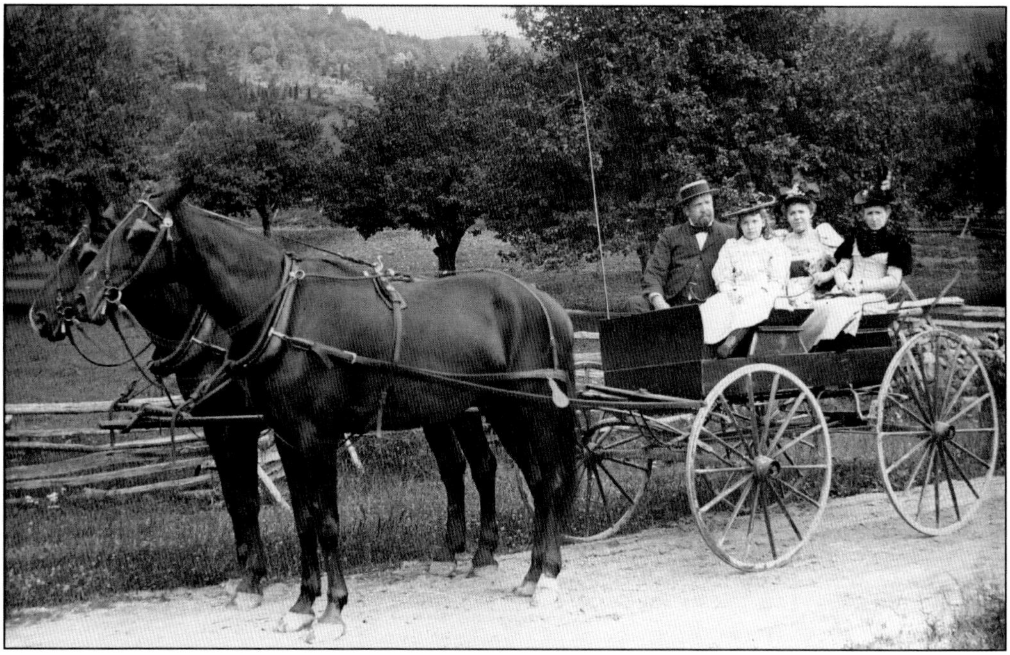

A family poses for the photographer on a summer day about 1895. The father wears a fashionable boater and bow tie. The two women wear summer dresses with corseted bodices and puffed sleeves, the older woman's partly of heavy velvet. Flowers ornament the women's and girl's hats. Buckboards were common because they were relatively inexpensive. (Courtesy of PCHS.)

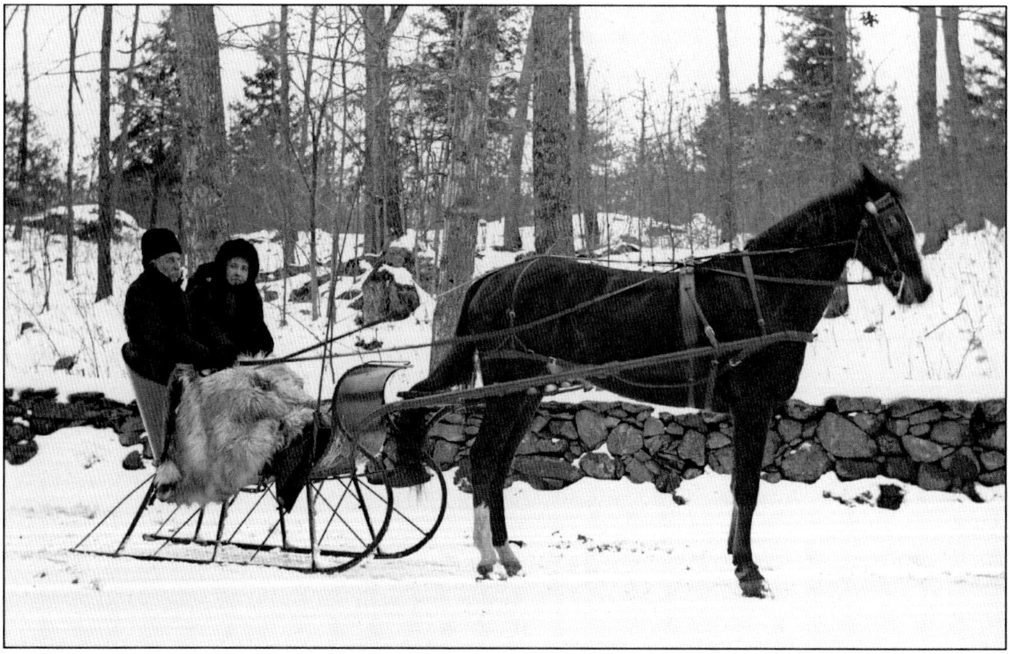

In the early 1890s, a man and woman brave the cold, wearing fur hats and a fur lap robe, as they head out in their lightweight Albany cutter, a two-person sleigh. Sleighs were a necessity for travel in the winter, especially outside of the villages. The stone wall and stony landscape behind them are typical of the Garrison landscape. (Courtesy of PCHS.)

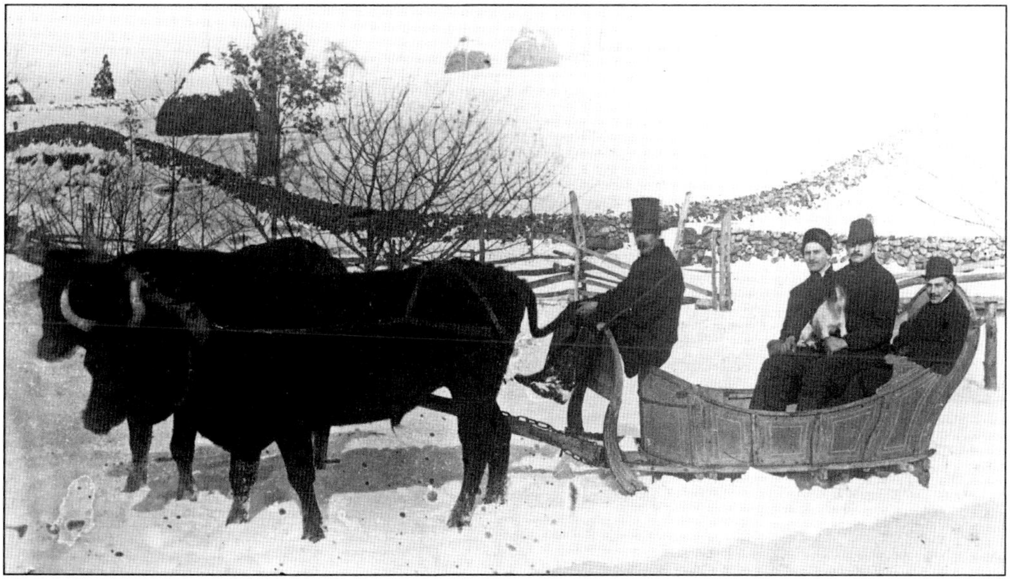

Three passengers from the 1890s and a dog sit in a wide, high-backed, curved wooden sleigh drawn by a team of oxen. The driver, his legs slung over the front, has stuck his switch into his boot. Snowcapped haystacks dot the field, and stone walls beautifully delineate the contours of the land. (Courtesy of PCHS.)

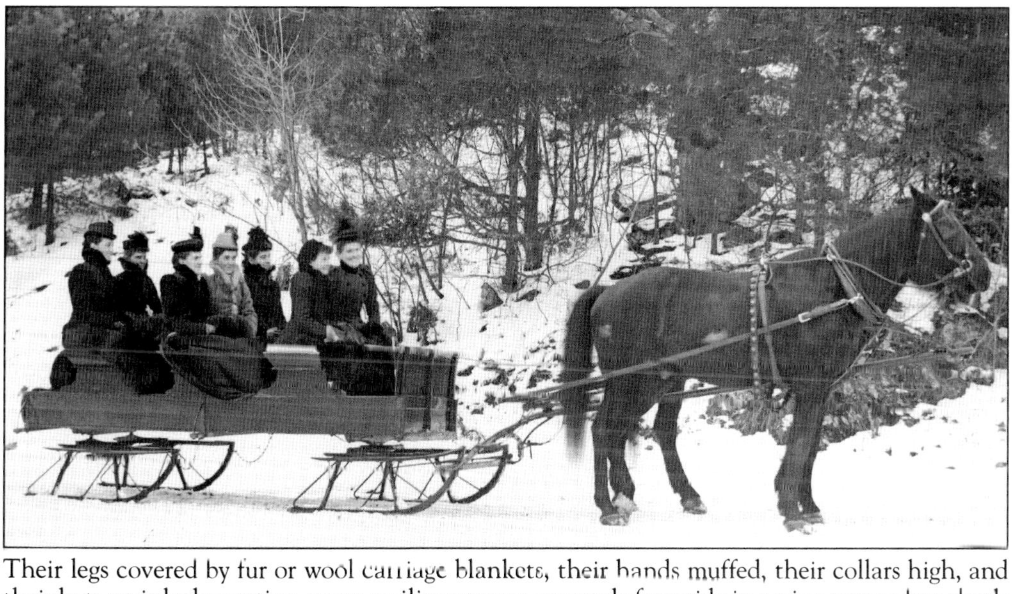

Their legs covered by fur or wool carriage blankets, their hands muffed, their collars high, and their hats mainly decorative, seven smiling women are ready for a ride in a nine-person box sleigh around 1892. Their fitted jackets and coats have puffed sleeves. The third woman from the left wears a matched fur capelet and muff. (Photograph by J.F. Juley, courtesy of PCHS.)

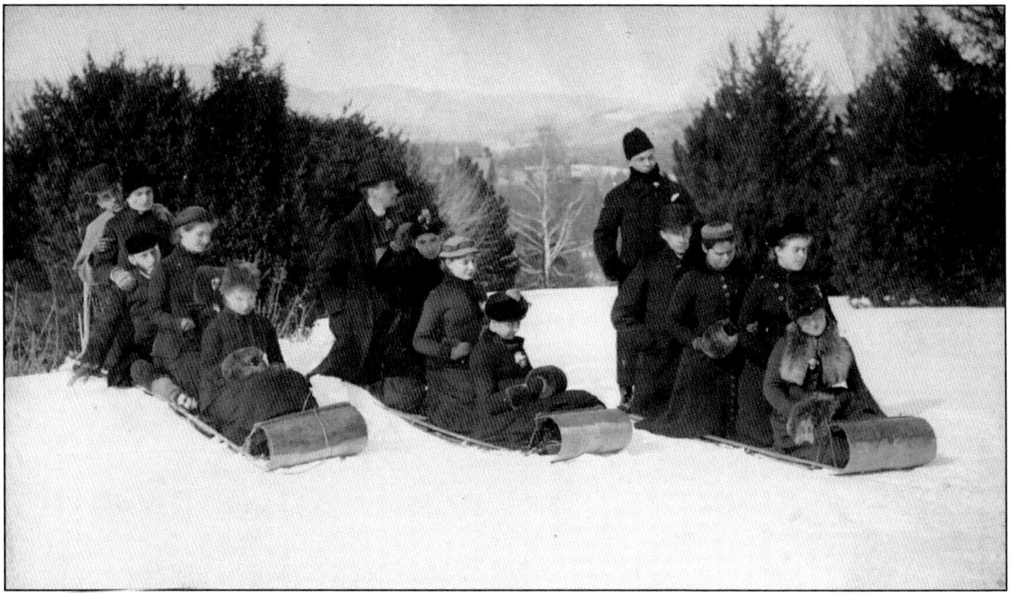

These large toboggans easily accommodate four people. The high view is toward the west-northwest, with the contours of Crow's Nest and Storm King across the river from Cold Spring in the far distance. Aspects of the outfits, such as the sleeves and fit, date this photograph to no later than 1884. (Courtesy of PCHS.)

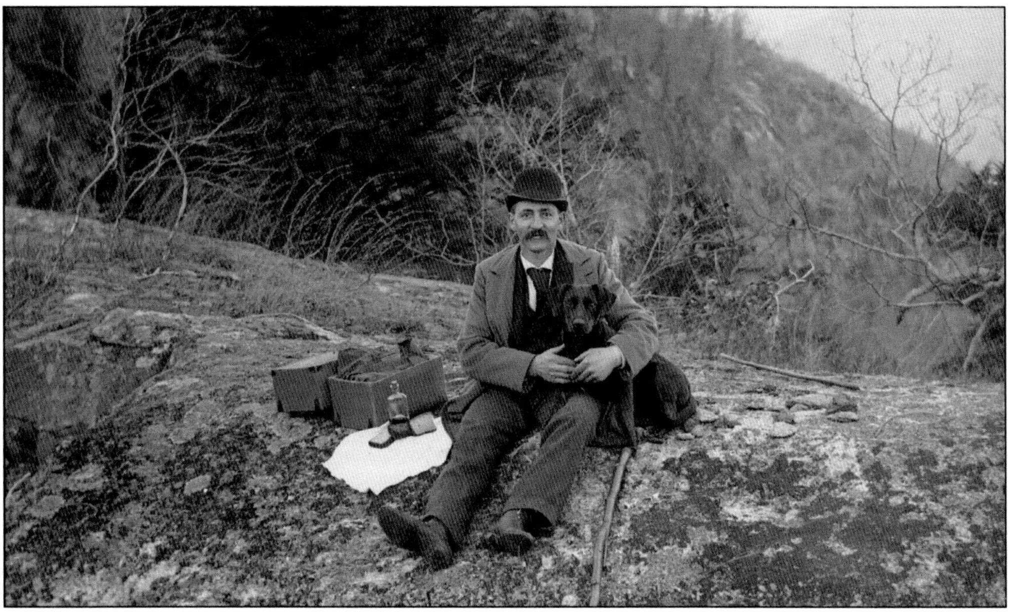

In 1892, the photographer John Riggs pauses during his hike, with his dog, lunch, and a walking stick. Today in Philipstown, hikers still explore the mountains and enjoy the streams and dirt roads as well. Perhaps they feel, as environmentalist John Muir wrote when visiting the Highlands, "Coming to the mountains is like coming home." (Photograph by Albert Terwilliger, courtesy of PCHS.)

Bibliography

Beers, F.W., ed. *Atlas of New York and Vicinity, from Actual Surveys, by and under the Direction of F.W. Beers, Assisted by Geo. E. Warner & Others*. New York: Beers, Ellis, & Soule, 1867.

Centennial Anniversary of Nelsonville: Origin and Development, The. Nelsonville, New York: Village of Nelsonville, 1955.

Cold Spring Architectural and Historic District Review Board. *Design Standards for the Architectural and Historic District, Village of Cold Spring, New York*. Cold Spring, NY: 1999.

DeLanoy, Nelson. Complete articles on the history of Philipstown. *Putnam County News and Recorder*. Cold Spring, NY: Archives of the Putnam County Historical Society & Foundry School Museum, 1975–1985.

Dunwell, Frances F. *The Hudson River Highlands*. New York: Columbia University Press, 1991.

Font, Lourdes M., and Trudie A. Grace. *The Gilded Age: High Fashion and Society in the Hudson Highlands, 1865–1914*. Cold Spring, NY: Putnam County Historical Society & Foundry School Museum, 2006.

Grace, Trudie A., ed. *A Ramble through the Hudson Highlands: A History in Pictures and the Writings of Donald H. MacDonald*. Cold Spring, NY: Putnam County Historical Society & Foundry School Museum, 2007.

———. *"This Perfect River-View": The Hudson River School and Contemporaries in Private Collections in the Highlands*. Cold Spring, NY: Putnam County Historical Society & Foundry School Museum, 2007.

———. "Up and Down the Hudson River in the Life and Work of George Pope Morris." In *George Pope Morris: Defining American Culture*, by Trudie A. Grace and David B. Dearinger. Cold Spring, NY: Putnam County Historical Society & Foundry School Museum, 2009.

Larson Fisher Associates Inc. *Cold Spring Historic District Update Survey 2009–2010: Final Report*. Cold Spring, NY: 2010.

MacDonald, Donald H. Complete articles on the history of Philipstown. *Putnam County News and Recorder*. Cold Spring, NY: Archives of the Putnam County Historical Society & Foundry School Museum, 1998–2011.

The Origin and Development of Cold Spring-on-Hudson, 1846–1946, A Centennial History. Cold Spring, NY: Village of Cold Spring, 1946.

Pelletreau, William S. "Town of Philipstown." *History of Putnam County, New York, with Biographical Sketches of its Prominent Men*. Philadelphia: W.W. Preston, parts 1 and 2, 1886.

Saunders, Jean. *Garrison's Landing*. Garrison, NY: 1966. Offset reproduction. Cold Spring, NY: Putnam County Historical Society & Foundry School Museum, 2010.

Walton, Steven A., ed. Articles by Patrick E. Martin, Steven A. Walton, and others. West Point Foundry special issue, *IA, The Journal of the Society for Industrial Archeology* 35, 1 and 2 (forthcoming).